GOD
VS.
CHANCE

Which Is the Most Probable Explanation for Our Existence?

Marshall "Rusty" Entrekin

Cover Art: The stylistic representation of God is from The Creation of Adam by Michelangelo, which adorns the ceiling of the Sistine Chapel. The starfield in the background is from a portion of the ESO photo entitled *The Milky Way Looms over the Residencia at the Paranal Observatory in Chile's Atacama Desert* by John Colosimo (colosimophotography.com). Used by permission of the ESO. Both of these were digitally manipulated by the author to create the cover design.

PeaceBrooke Publishing Company
Kennesaw, GA

CONTENTS

DEDICATION

- To the Holy Spirit, whom I dearly love and am grateful for, my Comforter, Helper and Counselor, who morning by morning would infuse my mind with ideas for this book as I lay awake enjoying fellowship with Him. His inspiring influence is throughout this book, while any mistakes are of course mine alone.
- To my loving wife and help-meet Julie. "Who can find a virtuous woman? For her price is far above rubies." Thanks for all of the things you do that made it possible for me to write this book, and for your insightful input as well. And thanks for your patience as I constantly discussed the contents of the book with you.
- To my children, whom I deeply love, who patiently endured me excitedly talking about the contents of this book during the years it was being written.
- To Mom (who is now in heaven), and to Dad, thanks for loving Jesus. Mom, thanks for your love of reading and learning. Dad, thanks for teaching me the value of hard work. Had you not modeled those three valuable character traits for me, this book would never have been written.

ACKNOWLEDGMENTS

Immense appreciation and thanks go first of all to the Lord, who proclaims to his children, "Call to me and I will answer you, and will tell you great and hidden things that you have not known." (Jeremiah 33:3)

If you come across any insights or solutions that sound new to you within these pages, this is a testimony to God's faithfulness to keep that promise, for I earnestly called to Him over and over again for answers and understanding during the years that I was writing this book.

This book builds on the solid foundation stones laid by others, especially the Christian apologetics authors I have read and listened to over the years. These include Henry M. Morris, John C. Whitcomb, Josh McDowell, Lee Strobel, Dr. William Lane Craig, Dr. Russell Humphries, Dr. John Hartnett, Dr. Jonathan Sarfati, Dr. Robert Carter and Dr. Jason Lyle to name a few, but also many others. It also builds on the teachings of the ministries of CRS, CMI, and AIG, which have been an immense blessing to me. Their influence has greatly affected this book, though they are likely unaware of it.

Tremendous gratitude is expressed to the following people:

- Ed Caouette, Lee Saar, Ronald May, Dr. Robert Newman, my wife Julie, and Dr. Larry Mellen, who read the entire manuscript and provided valuable guidance, corrections, advice and/or confirmation.
- Dr. John Hartnett, Dr. Robert Carter, Dr. John McCuan, his daughter Sarah McCuan, Dr. Michael Razzanno, Dr. Royal Truman, my son Joshua Entrekin, Ben Jackson, Adam Nisbett, and Kyle Harris, who read portions of the manuscript, or portions of earlier drafts of it and provided excellent advice, corrections and confirmations. Though they deserve thanks, their generous assistance should not at all be considered an endorsement, since some of them only read very small portions of the

book, and none of them read the entire final manuscript. Any mistakes are mine alone.

- The men in my prayer group who consistently prayed for this endeavor - Dr. Michael Razzanno, Lee Saar, Phil Metzger, and Ed Christopher.
- My Christian brethren and friends who helped, encouraged, and prayed for me as I wrote this book.

COMMENTS

Like an investigative reporter, during the years that I was writing this book I endeavored to research, accurately understand, and evaluate the information contained in this book, and then to communicate it effectively to you. If you come across any errors, please let me know by sending an email to comments@peacebrook.org. Your comments and suggestions for improvement are desired and appreciated. Please understand that I may not always have time to reply right away or at length. If you are an avowed atheist, I will read and consider your comments, but will probably abstain from being drawn into lengthy argumentation or debate.

PREFACE

This book asks the question, "Do we owe our existence to God, some other form of intelligence, or chance?" In it, I weigh the relevant evidence mathematically, logically, and philosophically, and find an answer that the evidence points overwhelmingly to.

However, many people believe or disbelieve in God for reasons other than evidence (or the lack thereof). Some people disbelieve because of a bad experience with a *person* who professed to believe in God. It could have been an overbearing, abusive, or absent parent, spouse, or family member. It may have been an immoral or greedy church leader, or the domineering leader of a cult-like group. Others are angry and bitter with God over something such as the death or illness of a loved one. And many others stopped believing because of shattered dreams.

Others disbelieve—or believe—not because they are on a true quest for the truth, but because of what it will get them: social acceptance, a nice job, the approval of colleagues, etc. And many are just having too much fun to think about serious questions like that.

On the other hand, I have met people who believe that there is a God, but who are not yet ready to serve Him, because there is something else that they want more. Their belief is an intellectual assent, but it is not actually a *trust* that extends deeply enough to result in obedience, which is a sign of true faith.

If any of those things have been motivating you, then you know what you need to do. Forgive the people who have hurt you. Forgive God, and trust Him again, if the universe has unfolded in a way that has deeply disappointed you. Stop blaming God for the actions of other human beings and for the consequences of your own unwise choices.

Find the courage to risk the disapproval of others, in order to live by what you believe in. Begin a *sincere* quest for the truth. Trust what you believe to be true deeply enough to *act* on it. Why put it off any longer? You will not find peace until you do.

On the other hand, there are people who have *sincere* reasons for not believing in God. Perhaps you are one of them. Perhaps you have heard persuasive arguments that there is no God. If so, please keep in mind that during a legal trial, the first to present his case seems right, until the cross-examination begins and new evidence for the other side is presented. For this reason, I encourage you to give the other side a fair hearing before arriving at a final conclusion. I say this, because I think there is a very good chance that you will encounter evidence and reasoning within these pages that you have not yet come across.

Let me prepare you before you read this book, however. It will challenge you to think deeply. If you don't care for books like that, then this is probably not the right book for you.

Of course, if God exists, then entering into a relationship with Him requires more than mere evidence. It must even go beyond being persuaded that He exists. Such an encounter must be a spiritual one.

However, the evidences that God has left of Himself in the natural world, including those I present here, can play a part in that, when combined with logic and reason. They can serve as low-lying branches, enabling us to climb just high enough to get glimpses, when the wind sways the trees, of what lies beyond the canopy of this material existence.

At that point, it will be up to you. You can climb back down, or seek a transformative spiritual encounter with God. Should that happen, then like a fresh new butterfly emerging from a cocoon, you can spread your new-found wings and launch into a life that the caterpillars below do not know—into the infinite God—where there are light-filled skies of truth, and the sweet nectars of fellowship, forgiveness, reconciliation, peace, joy and love.

SCRIPTURE TRANSLATIONS USED

1 THE QUESTION THAT WILL DETERMINE THE DIRECTION OF YOUR LIFE

o we owe our existence to God, some other form of intelligence, or chance?

This is not a question to be taken lightly, because your response to it will be one of the most pivotal decisions of your life. Nor is it wise to postpone consideration of this question, because your life will be missing meaningful direction if it is possible to determine the answer to this. What if God exists, but you did not even bother to find out until years from now? Our lives are short, and you could have spent those years living for Him. That opportunity would be lost *forever*.

If there is no God, then common things such as praying for a loved one who is sick, feeling gratitude to God at the sight of a beautiful sunset, and even kind little gestures like saying "God bless you!" would all be misguided. Those who believe that God has called them to sacrificially devote themselves to the service of the poor would all be partly motivated by a delusion. And perhaps most tragically, the martyrs that we have read about in newspapers and historical books such as *Foxes Book of Martyrs*, who chose to be killed rather than deny God, would have all died in vain.

As the Apostle Paul, who died a martyr himself, said about Christians, "If we have set our hopes on the Messiah in this life only, we deserve more pity than any other people." Paul then went on to say, "If the dead are not raised, 'Let's eat and drink, for tomorrow we die.' " - I Corinthians 15:19, 32 ISV

In short, the answer to this question is *far* too important to get it wrong. How then should you go about looking for an answer to it? One of the best ways to approach it is to try to determine which explanation is the most probable in light of the evidence. That's the approach that we will take in this book.

Another approach is to rely upon the most popular hypotheses of modern science. In other words, rather than take the time and trouble to sincerely seek an answer to this question yourself, rely upon the majority opinion of the scientists of our age. But there are risks involved with this approach. To begin with, if you have been blessed with the capacity to evaluate claims and to discern truth from error, your eternal destiny is far too important to naively entrust it into the hands of others to determine for you. Secondly, tremendous upheavals in the most popular scientific explanations have taken place over the centuries, and even over the last few decades. And yet, each generation has been so *confident* that its scientific perspective was correct! Not only that, but in our generation, there is another compelling reason not to place a blind faith in the most popular scientific ideas concerning our origins.

THE RISE OF METHODOLOGICAL NATURALISM

Have you ever wondered why, when confronted with what plainly appears to be a miraculous recovery, some medical doctors will seek a naturalistic explanation, and if they cannot find one, will simply say, "Medical science cannot explain what has happened"?

This is because most of mainstream modern science now adheres to a philosophy called *methodological naturalism (MN)*. MN is simply the philosophy that in science, we should *act* as if there is no supernatural, *whether there is or not.*[1]

Often, methodological naturalism is confused with the *scientific method*, but it's not the same thing. The scientific method is the *process* by which science is conducted, but methodological naturalism is a *philosophical approach to science.*

---

[1] Michael Martin, "Justifying Methodological Naturalism." 2002. http://infidels.org/library/modern/michael_martin/naturalism.html (Last accessed 3/11/2019)

Some people also confuse methodological naturalism with *metaphysical naturalism*, but there's a difference between the two. Metaphysical naturalism is the belief that there is no supernatural. But methodological naturalism does not go so far as to *declare* that there is no God, only that for purposes of conducting science, we ought to *act* as if there is no God.

"Regardless of one's views on materialism as a philosophy," Eugenie Scott of the NCSE argues, "in science, it [MN] is a *methodological* necessity."[2]

That's true, to the extent that we can only observe and perform repeatable experiments on material things. If God exists, then as a transcendent, immaterial being, he cannot be empirically observed or detected unless He chooses to reveal himself, and He is under no obligation to work a miracle upon our demand. It's to be expected, after all, that an all-knowing being would choose to do things we do not understand or anticipate, since His reasoning processes would be far higher than ours, He would see the future, and He would have the lives of billions to people to take into account.

And so we can agree with Ms. Scott that operationally or methodologically, science is confined to performing repeatable experiments only on natural things. That sounds very reasonable, but just as in practice, there was much more to the political philosophy of communism than oppressed factory workers were led to believe, there is also much more to MN as a philosophy than first meets the eye.

To begin with, Ms. Scott is not taking into account the fact that nature can exhibit evidence of things that cannot be empirically observed. For instance, we cannot observe a universe outside of our own. But cosmologists and astronomers have been looking for signs of other

---

[2] Eugenie C. Scott, "Review of Darwin On Trial." Creation Evolution Journal, Volume 13 #2, Winter 1993, pp. 36–47.
http://ncse.com/cej/13/2/darwin-prosecuted-review-johnsons-darwin-trial (Last accessed 3/11/2019)

universes, such as Hawking points,[3] a "dark flow" of galaxies,[4] or "bruises" in the cosmic microwave background radiation.[5] Similarly, proponents of intelligent design point to what they believe is evidence that our universe was intelligently designed. However, because of methodological naturalism, their theories are censored from mainstream science.

Interestingly, the term "methodological naturalism" was coined only in 1986 – by philosopher Paul DeVries, as he argued against scientific creationism.[6] Philosopher Robert T. Pennock later popularized the term as he crusaded against creationism and intelligent design. Like Pennock, who received a "Friend of Darwin " award from the NCSE,[7] those who champion MN most loudly tend to be opposed to the intelligent design and creationist movements.

Perhaps it is for this reason that in practice, MN goes *far* beyond the mere operational methodology Ms. Eugenie Scott was talking about, extending *even into the realm of explanations and hypotheses*. Its

---

[3] Daniel An, Krzysztof A. Meissner, Pawel Nurowski, Roger Penrose, "Apparent Evidence for Hawking Points in the CMB Sky." 17 Dec 2018, arXiv:1808.01740 [astro-ph.CO]

[4] Maggie McKee, "Blow for 'dark flow' in Planck's new view of the cosmos." New Scientist, issue 2911, April 6 2013 https://www.newscientist.com/article/dn23340-blow-for-dark-flow-in-plancks-new-view-of-the-cosmos/ (Last accessed 4/3/2018)

[5] Ivan Baldry, "Could cold spot in the sky be a bruise from a collision with a parallel universe?" Scientific American, The Conversation US on June 2, 2017.
https://www.scientificamerican.com/article/could-cold-spot-in-the-sky-be-a-bruise-from-a-collision-with-a-parallel-universe/ (Last accessed 3/21/2019)

[6] Harry L. Poe and Chelsea R. Mytyk, *"From Scientific Method to Methodological Naturalism: The Evolution of an Idea."* PSCF Academic Journal, Volume 59, Number 3, September 2007 pp. 214-218.
http://www.asa3.org/ASA/PSCF/2007/PSCF9-07Poe.pdf (Last accessed 3/11/2019)

[7] Pennock's name appears in the NCSE's list of "Friend of Darwin" recipients at http://ncse.com/about/friend-of-darwin. (Last accessed 3/11/2019)

enforcers completely *outlaw* any explanations involving God from science! When strictly adhered to (and in most mainstream science periodicals and institutions of science it is), methodological naturalism doesn't just restrict science to investigating the natural cosmos empirically; it prevents science from seriously even *contemplating* God as an explanation for *anything at all.*

By definition, a miracle is an instance in which God creates, reorganizes, or influences nature, altering its natural course and setting it upon a new trajectory. What if such events sometimes actually occur? What if the origin of the universe, the beginning of life, some of the recorded miracles in historical documents, along with some apparent miracles in modern times, *are* actions of God?

Methodological naturalism condemns science to adopting blinders and *completely ignoring* the possibility of this. Consider, for instance, the account in the Bible in which Jesus healed a man with a shriveled hand. According to Mark 3:5, Jesus said to the man, "Stretch out your hand." He stretched it out, and according to the account, his hand was completely restored.

If a scientist restrained by MN were to witness and then document such a miracle in a peer-reviewed mainstream scientific periodical, although it would be as plain as the nose on your face that this was an act of God, the scientist could not acknowledge this (though he could record the new condition of the hand). If compelled to explain how it happened, he'd have to come up with some unreasonable naturalistic explanation!

John Rennie, the former Editor in Chief of *Scientific American*, expressed the prevailing mindset in science regarding methodological naturalism quite well:

> 'Creation science' is a contradiction in terms. A central tenet of modern science is methodological naturalism—it seeks to explain

the universe purely in terms of observed or testable natural mechanisms.[8]

Rennie's statement may be short, but it is *incredibly* sweeping in its intended effect. Because of this, let's consider it more closely.

First of all, notice that MN calls for *censorship* in science of any hypotheses that include God. Whenever someone proposes censorship, we must carefully weigh whether or not the benefit gained by the censorship is worth the cost. Usually, the societal benefits of censoring a free interchange of ideas are not worth the cost, although there are exceptions such as the outlawing of slander, or inciting others to crime or immorality. If there is an alternative way to achieve the desired benefit without censorship, the alternative should usually be adopted instead. And there *is* an alternative that works just as well as MN.

Great scientists of the past such as Sir Francis Bacon, Johannes Kepler, Blaise Pascal, Isaac Newton, Louis Pasteur, Galileo, George Washington Carver, Carl Linnaeus, Gregor Mendel, and Robert Boyle were able to conduct excellent science although they believed in the miraculous interventions of God. Many modern scientists believe that God sometimes works miracles, and also conduct excellent science.[9] How are they able to do this? Because they combine their faith with the recognition that *ordinarily*, the universe follows natural laws that God Himself has set in place. Somehow, science managed to get along just fine before the articulation of MN as a philosophy in 1986!

And so, the claim that one cannot conduct good science without MN *simply isn't true.* A theistic or agnostic philosophical methodological approach that leaves room for the possibility of God's intervention, but

---

[8] John Rennie, "15 Answers to Creationist Nonsense." Scientific American 287, 1, (July 2002), doi:10.1038/scientificamerican0702-78 (https://www.scientificamerican.com/article/15-answers-to-creationist/, Accessed 3/11/2019)

[9] https://creation.com/creation-scientists contains a list of great scientists of the past (and present) who not only believed in God, but also the Biblical account of creation. (Last accessed 3/11/2019)

assumes that the universe ordinarily follows natural laws can work just as well as MN.

Secondly, notice that Rennie calls MN a "central tenet" of modern science. MN is indeed becoming a central tenet of modern science. But *should* this be happening? We ought to carefully consider that question, because a tenet is a *belief* associated with a religion or a philosophy. It is fine for modern science to have a philosophical tenet that makes it function well operationally. We can all agree with a tenet that accomplished only that. But when a proposed tenet prevents a free exchange of ideas, this means that its promoters are trying, in an Orwellian sort of way, to control us by *exclusively* binding their own beliefs together with science.

Of course, we are all free – and ought to remain free - to adopt whatever philosophy of science we choose, including one that combines religion *or* atheism together with science. We are also free to try to convert others to our philosophical or religious tenets. But let's be honest about it when we are doing so, and not try to forcefully impose our beliefs on everyone else by censoring all philosophical approaches but our own. And let's not claim that others cannot conduct good science unless they adopt *our* particular philosophical approach when there are other approaches that work well, too.

Thirdly, notice just how *strictly and broadly* Rennie interprets methodological naturalism (and no doubt, enforced it while he was the editor-in-chief of Scientific American). He believes that science should attempt to explain *even the origin of the universe itself* only by natural mechanisms! Let's take just a moment to contemplate the implications of that. It would condemn science to being forever antithetical to religion, wouldn't it? It would bind science to a *naturalistic religion or philosophy* that is at odds with theism. Is that what we want science to become? Tragically, thanks to increasing adherence to this kind of strict methodological naturalism, that is *exactly* what prevailing modern science is becoming!

Fourthly, notice how Rennie's association of science with methodological naturalism leads him to conclude that "creation science is a contradiction in terms." In effect, Rennie is saying, "Sorry theists, but we define the word 'science' in a way that does not include you. So if you dare to advance any theories that include the idea of God being responsible for creating or doing *anything at all* in the universe, then you are not engaging in true science."

What a convenient way for atheists who control scientific periodicals to advance their worldview! It reminds me of the US Supreme court's infamous 1857 Dred Scott decision, which in effect said to blacks, "Sorry, but we define the word "citizen" in a way that excludes you. Since you can't be a citizen, you are not entitled to the protection of the US Constitution."

A final observation we can make about Rennie's comment, is that the enforcement of methodological naturalism at his magazine is not that consistent– *except* when it comes to the matter of a *divine* intelligence as an explanation of the universe. As you can easily see by perusing past issues of *Scientific American*, there are popular explanations in modern science, especially regarding the hypothetical multiverse, that are neither observable nor testable, that have appeared within the magazine. In short, explanations that are not testable are often permitted and even appealed to in mainstream science journals, *provided they are exclusively naturalistic.*

Contrast this with the original intent of the founders of Scientific American, who stated "We shall advocate the pure Christian religion, without favoring any particular sect" in their very first 1845 issue![10]

---

[10] Rufus Porter (Editor) "*To the American Public,*" Scientific American, Series 1, Volume 1, Issue 01, (August 1845): p. 2. Porter also wrote in the first issue, "First, then, let us, as rational creatures, be ever ready to acknowledge God as our Creator and daily Preserver; and that we are each of us individually dependent on his special care and good will towards us, in supporting the wonderful action of nature which constitutes our existence; and in preserving us from the casualties, to which our complicated and delicate structure is liable."

Strict MN has become so widely accepted now, that saying there's a tendency for modern science to be anti-theistic would be an under-statement. Jerry Bergmann's book *Slaughter of the Dissidents* docu-ments what has happened to the careers of many scientists who have dared to inject any serious consideration of the notion of God as the architect of our universe or life into science. [11] How many scientists and academics, for the sake of their careers and livelihoods, have caved in to this pressure and kept their faith in God as Creator to them-selves?

This strict adherence to methodological naturalism in mainstream modern science when it comes to the matter of God is a practice that we will examine more closely later. But for now, suffice it to say that *any hypothesis which gives recognition to the possibility of the exist-ence of God is typically excluded from mainstream science.*

Because of this, you need to be aware that when it comes to the origin of life and our universe, *you have not been getting an unbiased answer* from mainstream science! You have been getting *only* naturalistic ex-planations for our universe and life from it. But are they more proba-ble, or more sensible than theistic ones? How could science *possibly* make that determination when it *censors* theistic explanations and does not even permit them a hearing? That's like presuming a man to be guilty and throwing him into jail without a trial!

Since mainstream science *refuses* to give God a fair hearing, you'd be a fool to rely upon it alone to answer the question that this book is all about!

In light of the constantly changing opinions of science, and *the very real pressure* that exists to exclude God from it, do you *really* want to en-trust your eternal destiny to the opinion of modern scientists who adopt MN as their credo? Aren't they human beings who are just as susceptible to error and the effects of peer pressure and intimidation as anyone else? A science degree certainly does not make a man or a woman an infallible oracle of truth when it comes to the matter of

---

[11] Jerry Bergmann, *Slaughter of the Dissidents*. Leafcutter Press, 2011

origins, and since great pressure and indoctrination exists in many modern institutions of science to conform to naturalism, adopting MN as your mantra would *surely* hinder your quest for ultimate truth.

In his book *The Everlasting Man*, G.K. Chesterson wrote,

> "A dead thing can go with the stream, but only a living thing can go against it."

A live trout is quite capable and willing to swim against the current whenever he needs to. A dead fish, however, is carried along by the current. Unless you prefer to be a dead fish who flows along with the most popular opinions in mainstream science, it falls upon *you* to be brave enough to consider the evidence for both sides and come to a conclusion! In order to do so, you will need to adopt a philosophical approach that is different from MN, one that is open to considering possible evidence for the existence of God, which does not reject hypotheses before even investigating them.

And so, although in this book we will take into account *observational evidence* from science, we will refuse to be chained by methodological naturalism as we explore this question of whether the universe was formed by God, some other form of intelligence, or chance. After all, if we *sincerely* want to know the answer to this question, why would we *not* be open to following the evidence wherever it may lead?

We will also take into account information theory, mathematical probabilities, philosophy, and ethics. Lastly, any serious consideration of the existence and nature of God must of course include some comparative religion and theology.

WHAT IS YOUR METAPHYSICAL PHILOSOPHY?

Let's begin by considering the broader contemplative discipline known as *metaphysics*, of which theology is a branch. Metaphysics is the quest to describe ultimate reality and being in ways that include things that go beyond what we can observe, detect, or measure. It can address vitally important questions such as:

10

- What caused our universe to begin?
- Why is our universe finely tuned for life?
- Does God exist?
- Does man have an eternal spirit?
- How did complex life arise?
- Do we have an ultimate purpose?

The answer that you choose to these questions and others like them is (or will be) your own personal metaphysical philosophy.

THE SPECTRUM OF BELIEF

Adherents of the different metaphysical philosophies are categorized in the following ways:

- Those who have concluded that there is no supernatural at all, and that all which exists came about by chance, are called *metaphysical naturalists*.
- Those who do not believe that there is a God or gods are called *atheists*. Most atheists are metaphysical naturalists, but it is possible to be an atheist and still believe in some supernatural things such as ghosts. Atheists like to divide themselves into two camps: *strong atheists* and *weak atheists*. Strong atheists assert that there is no God, or that there is probably no God. Weak atheists are very close in the spectrum to agnostics. They include those who do not believe because they have never heard about God, and "doubting Thomas's who insist upon seeing God or a miracle with their own eyes before they will believe.
- Those who are undecided whether or not God or gods exist are called *agnostics*.
- Those who believe in multiple gods are called *polytheists*.
- Those who have decided that there is a Creator who set the universe in motion, but who has had no involvement with it since, are called *deists*.
- And lastly, those who believe that there is a Creator who actively cares about the universe, sometimes alters the natural

course of it, and sometimes even reveals himself, are called *monotheists,* or *theists* for short.

Of course, the actual metaphysical reality may not be what a person thinks it is. This is because there is very good reason to believe that reality is an objective, not a subjective thing. In fact, the very idea that all of reality is subjective is self-refuting. This is easily illustrated by the old joke about the college professor who said, "Everything is relative. There is no absolute truth!" To this, a student raised his hand and asked, "Professor, are you absolutely certain about that?" "Yes, absolutely!" the professor replied.

If all of reality were subjective, of what use would the scientific method be to us? We could not rely upon the concept of repeatable experiment!

In my lifetime, I have had some very interesting conversations with two different men who believed that they were Jesus. That delusion may have made them feel quite good about themselves, and very special, but it did not change their true identity. The truth exists independently of whether we accurately perceive it or not. Whatever the metaphysical reality is, it is under no obligation to conform to our wishes or perceptions!

If you *honestly* want to know the truth, then your metaphysical philosophy therefore ought not to be custom designed according to desire, like a wealthy woman choosing one of many dresses, shoes, belts, and earrings to wear. If you are a *sincere* seeker after truth, you will not choose your metaphysical philosophy based on what will make you the most happy, or what will be the most pleasing to your parents, friends, or colleagues. Nor will you choose it because it will enable you to satisfy your desires with the least amount of guilt. Instead, you will choose it based on what you genuinely believe the truth actually is, or probably is. And of course, it will be difficult for you to discern the truth if you do not take the time to seek for it, and especially if you do not really care to know it.

In short, one's personal metaphysical philosophy *should* be the result of an earnest thirst and quest to know what the truth really is. If you live with people who seek to shape your views for reasons other than a love of truth, it will require courage for you to break free from this pressure to conform and earnestly seek the truth. If you live in that kind of an environment, your quest for truth may come at a cost. Perhaps even at a great cost. Even so, I encourage you to buy the truth no matter what the cost, and do not *ever* sell it out. Why? *Because the truth is priceless.* Only a greedy fool or a coward would knowingly trade it away!

2   IS THERE A METAPHYSICAL REALITY?

"Beware lest you fight a rearguard retreat against the evidence, grudgingly conceding each foot of ground only when forced, feeling cheated. Surrender to the truth as quickly as you can." — *Eliezer Yudkowsky*

s there a metaphysical reality that is beyond the reach of our current powers of observation and detection? There is very good reason to think so.

First of all, the very fact that our universe appears to be expanding tells us that it had a beginning. And *something* must have caused it to begin. The idea of our universe being part of a chain of *infinite causal regress* – cause and effect going back forever – does not appear to be logically possible, for reasons which we will discuss later in this book. Therefore, if some form of cyclic universe theory were true, with repeating cycles of a big bang or bounce followed by a big crunch, what originally got the cycles started?

Modern discoveries regarding the fine-tuning of the universe and the complexity of the cell now point both theists *and* most atheists to a metaphysical reality, for reasons which we will look at in more detail.

Geometry and modern physics also suggest to us the possibility of a metaphysical reality. String theorists envision ten or more dimensions. Quantum-field theorists and cosmologists also speculate that there are higher dimensions.

The concept of higher dimensions has made us aware of some intriguing possibilities. In 1884, Edwin Abbot wrote a short novel about a two-dimensional world entitled *Flatland: A Romance of Many Dimensions.*[12] In that book, three-dimensional beings were able to watch the intelligent inhabitants of a two dimensional world without being

---

[12]Edwin A. Abbott, *Flatland: A Romance of Many Dimensions,* 1884. You may read Flatland in its entirety at http://www.geom.uiuc.edu/~banchoff/Flatland/. (Last accessed 03/11/2019)

seen. Abbot's book raised some interesting questions. If you were to poke your finger into a two dimensional world like Flatland to do a good deed, your finger would seem to appear out of nowhere to its inhabitants! That would likely be regarded as a miracle by those who witnessed it, unless they refused to believe their own two-dimensional eyes!

Abbot's book intentionally provoked another question, too. Just as we could hypothetically look at beings in a two dimensional world and not be seen by them, could higher dimensional beings similarly observe us? For instance (although Abbot did not raise this specific question) could the angels of biblical literature, called "Watchers" in the book of Daniel,[13] be beings who live in a higher dimensional realm, who are able to observe our own space-time universe without being seen, and can interact with it when instructed to do so?

Basing their assumptions upon the most popular form of Big Bang cosmology called the ΛCDM *(Lambda Cold Dark Matter)* model, scientists analyzing data from the Planck Satellite came up with the following "recipe" of the constituent ingredients that make up our universe:

- 4.9% ordinary matter
- 26.6% dark matter
- 68.5 % dark energy [14]

Scientists are not yet certain exactly what dark matter and dark energy are, but most of them believe that we are detecting the effects of both. Dark matter is employed to explain the spiral motions of the galaxies and gravitational lensing, and dark energy is utilized to explain the accelerating expansion of the universe. (Colliding galactic clusters,

---

[13] Daniel 4:13, 17, 23

[14] ESA, "Citing the Legacy of ESA's Plank Mission." Esa.int http://www.esa.int/Our_Activities/Space_Science/Planck/Celebrating_the_legacy_of_ESA_s_Planck_mission (Last accessed 3/11/2019)

however, have been observed behaving in ways that may be at variance with the dark matter hypothesis.) [15]

The hypothesis of dark matter is becoming so popular, that some scientists have begun to speculate that dark matter could be a shadow universe right on top of ours that exists in other dimensions. [16] In fact, an article at Space.Com was entitled "A New Form of Dark Matter Could Form Dark Atoms." [17] Reflecting on this possibility, Neal Weiner, associate professor in the Center for Cosmology and Particle Physics at New York University, has been reported to amusingly…

> "…spin stories about Professor Dark Matter, a researcher from the other side who has formulated a far-out theory about a missing ingredient in the universe called 'visible matter.' The professor accurately describes all the details of our world to her incredulous colleagues — with the end result that she fails to get tenure." [18]

Of course, if the ΛCDM model is correct and dark matter does turn out to exist, it could be incapable of supporting any form of life. But if it can, here is another thought-provoking possibility to consider: could this other-dimensional universe of dark matter be a part of the spiritual realm? Even if it is not, and even if dark matter turns out not to exist, or to be incapable of supporting life, the idea of a shadow universe of dark matter *does* serve to open our minds to the possibility of a co-existent spiritual reality.

---

[15] Hubblesite, "Dark Matter Core Defies Explanation in Hubble Image." Mar. 2012, Hubblesite.org. http://hubblesite.org/news_release/news/2012-10 (Last accessed 03/11/2019)

[16] Corey S. Powell, "The Possible Parallel Universe of Dark Matter." Discover, July 11,2013. http://discovermagazine.com/2013/julyaug/21-the-possible-parallel-universe-of-dark-matter (Last accessed Mar. 11, 2019)

[17] Charles Q. Choi, "New Kind of Dark Matter Could Form 'Dark Atoms.'" Space.com. http://www.space.com/21508-dark-matter-atoms-disks.html (Last accessed Mar. 11, 2019)

[18] ibid.

Not only does the concept of higher dimensions and dark matter suggest to us the possibility of a metaphysical reality, but computer technology does, too. Suppose that one day, a programmer were to create the first conscious artificial intelligences living in a simulated computer universe. Unless their programmer chose to make himself known to them, those intelligences would be totally unaware of their creator watching them. To them, hearing of the very concept of a programmer would be an occasion for faith or doubt. If they were told of the real world that exists outside of the computer, how many of them would believe it? To them, their virtual world would appear to be the real world!

Interestingly, in recent years some scientists have been exploring the possibility that we live in a computer simulated universe. Think of it. If a computer generated universe inhabited by conscious artificial intelligences were created that was perfect down to the very last detail of every one of its most fundamental subatomic particles, this would be reality to its conscious inhabitants. In effect, *a new reality would have been created.* In a July 2013 article entitled *Do We Live in the Matrix?* Discovery magazine reported the following:

> Seth Lloyd, a quantum-mechanical engineer at MIT, estimated the number of "computer operations" our universe has performed since the Big Bang — basically, every event that has ever happened. To repeat them, and generate a perfect facsimile of reality down to the last atom, would take more energy than the universe has. "The computer would have to be bigger than the universe, and time would tick more slowly in the program than in reality," says Lloyd. "So why even bother building it?" [19]

Given the fine detail of our universe, that makes it highly unlikely that we live in a computer program that is detailed to the last particle, unless the host computer exists in a reality that is incredibly vaster,

---

[19] Zeeya Merali, "Do We Live In The Matrix?" Discover, Nov. 15, 2013 http://discovermagazine.com/2013/dec/09-do-we-live-in-the-matrix (Last accessed 3/11/2019)

exceedingly more complex, and faster than our own. A simulation that renders detailed reality only when conscious life examines it would be more likely, and some researchers have attempted to determine if that is the case also, but with inconclusive results. [20]

Taking into consideration the billions of conscious intelligences in our world, and the fact that the human brain far exceeds the sum of the abilities of any man-made computer, even a simulation like that would be far beyond the computational capability of any computer that man can currently make. The computer coding required would also far, far exceed the current depth of our understanding and programming skills.

But this does suggest another possibility to us. Neither of these alternatives would be beyond the capability of the mind of the omniscient, omnipotent, omnipresent God of Judeo-Christian theology, especially if He exists outside of time, as many theologians believe. Although God is described in the Bible as a *personal being*, not a computer or a machine, one result of dwelling outside of time would be that He would have instantaneous cognitive and computational abilities far exceeding that of any human mind or man-made computer. Isaiah 55:9 essentially tells us that very thing:

> "As the heavens are higher than the earth, so are My ways higher than your ways and My thoughts than your thoughts."

Though human minds are immaterial, they are dependent upon matter to exist. But as a transcendent Spirit, the mind of God would not be dependent upon material things to exist, and therefore His mind would be qualitatively different from ours and material computers in many respects. Just as some humans astound us with their ability to perform math calculations in their heads, we can expect that God would be capable not only of much higher level reasoning than we are,

---

[20] Justin Mullins, "The idea we live in a simulation isn't science fiction." Scientist 2895, Dec 2012. http://www.newscientist.com/article/mg21628950.300-the-idea-we-live-in-a-simulation-isnt-science-fiction.html#.U1VVE3lOXRY (Last accessed 3/19/2019)

but also of computing abilities far beyond the reach of any supercomputer man could conceivably build. Many Judeo-Christian theologians believe that the knowledge of all possible universes is instantly available to the mind of God. Since matter behaves in predictable aggregate patterns, it seems reasonable that God could run symbolic simulations of universes which are simpler than reality, and yet completely accurate.

Recently, cosmologists have begun to run computer simulations of various cosmological models to see if they produce universes that resemble our own. Since God dwells outside of time, entire simulations like this (though much more complex and detailed) of all possible universes, from their birth to death, could be run instantaneously inside His mind. Since the simulations would be symbolic, there would be no actual pain or suffering in these imagined universes, and there could be entire categories of universes, such as those that are lifeless, or those in which too much evil would predominate, that God would not need to run as simulations at all, although they would be instantly available for Him to access at will.

This is not to imply that God needs to experiment to learn, but rather that just as the best chess players are able to foresee possible moves far in advance of the average player, God is able to reason, plan, and see all possible contingencies. This would include the ability to foresee all possible universes. In short, if these theologians are correct, there is a symbolic *multiverse* consisting of *all* possible universes instantly available to the mind of God!

God could choose from the most meaningful of these universes to create "programs" (and I say that *figuratively*) of them which are not symbolic and are complete down to every one of their very most basic constituent particles. Let's call such a hypothetical universe a *theistically sustained reality,* or TSR. We can consider it to be a reality rather than a virtual reality because it will be completely detailed, and every particle within it will consistently follow behavioral laws. A TSR is an answer to the question of how an immaterial mind could create, sustain and have power over the material universe.

And so, although it seems highly unlikely that we live inside of a computer simulation, the concept serves as a useful *analogy* of how a highly detailed reality might be sustained within the mind of God. I say *analogy* for several reasons:

1. The computations God performs are most likely very different from the binary electronic calculations that take place in our computers. They may not be binary at all.

2. God's computations may take place independently of time, or at least of time as we know it. If they take place independently of any form of time, causality within God's mind could be logic-based rather than time-based (more on this in a later chapter). Or if they take place within some sort of time, He may control the speed of the flow of thoughts relative to us, so that He can perform what for us would be thousands of years of thoughts within a second of our time. Or He might simply perform multitudes of parallel processing tasks within His infinite mind.

3. As an infinite immaterial mind (spirit), God has infinite computational resources available. He is not limited by RAM or storage space.

4. God may not be limited to thinking within three dimensions of space, which would add interesting dynamics to thought processes within His mind.

5. God is distinct from His creation and His creatures. It is not Him, and He is not it, though He fills and sustains all things. Also, He is not us, and we are not Him.

6. God is a personal being, not a machine, though He may have set aside personal resources to perform automatic computations.

7. Unlike simulations, human beings appear to have the freedom to choose how to respond to stimuli.

8. It appears that God sustains the universe in such a way that it is self-computing. If so, then if He sustains it by computation, His computations probably normally (but not always) take place at the sustaining level. This would explain why our universe consistently follows physical laws unless God intervenes.

However, please keep in mind that a TSR is not the only conceivable way that an immaterial God could have created the universe, and be actively sustaining it. More on this in a later chapter.

As a matter of fact, the New Testament teaches that the cosmos *is* sustained within God, for in Acts 17:28 the Apostle Paul told the Athenians regarding God,

> "For in him we live and move and have our being."

And in Colossians 1:17 Paul wrote,

> "He is before all things, and in Him all things hold together."

Lastly, in Hebrews 1:3 in we read,

> "The Son [Jesus, the 3rd person of the Christian Trinity] is the radiance of God's glory and the exact expression of his nature, sustaining all things by his powerful word." (Christian Standard Bible)

However, as the title of this book suggests, the idea of a wonderfully powerful transcendent Intelligence is not the only popular explanation for our origin. *Chance* must also be considered. Most of the explanations that involve chance suppose that our universe is much larger than can be observed or is infinite, and that it is part of a multiverse – a realm in which there are a vast or infinite number of universes. We will carefully consider these ideas in this book. And so, when it comes down to it, there are only two *basic* possible explanations of our origin:

    A. *Our Universe formed naturalistically.*
       —OR—
    B. *It was Intelligently designed and created.*

But if it was intelligently designed and created, why must our creator have been the God of monotheism? Couldn't it have been a team of aliens working together, one or more of the gods of polytheism such as Athena or Zeus, or "The Flying Spaghetti Monster," as many modern atheists are so fond of saying?[21]

The vastness of interstellar distances combined with the speed limitations imposed by the special theory of relativity, and the disappointment of the SETI project make the prospect of us having been genetically engineered by aliens seem unlikely. Besides, if we had been engineered by an alien race, that would not at all answer the question of the ultimate origin of life, for we would then need to ask, "How did *they* get here?"

Most civilized westerners find the gods of polytheism to be too capricious and fanciful. (They are often quite promiscuous, too!) In short, the polytheistic gods seem to have been created in the image of man, not vice versa.

In addition, the preexistence of one God having a simple underlying nature seems much more probable than multiple preexistent gods. Furthermore, polytheism violates a guideline for choosing between competing explanations called *Ockham's razor.* A common way of stating Ockham's razor is, "Don't multiply entities beyond necessity." Most polytheistic religions tend towards monotheism anyway, in that they hold one god as sovereign or supreme over the rest. If there were multiple creators of the universe who were co-equal in authority, then unless they all co-operated and worked in harmony, the universe would probably be non-uniform, like a painting that is the work of multiple artists. The fact that our universe is expanding in all directions indicates that it came from one central place of origin rather than many, which also likely points to one God. Lastly, only *one* God could be the *first* cause of all other things.

And I hardly need to go into the merits of monotheism over that god so often rhetorically mentioned by atheists, The Flying Spaghetti Monster! Suffice it to say that unlike the Judeo-Christian God, there is no history of revelation from the Flying Spaghetti Monster going back to

---

[21] Dan Verganao, "'Spaghetti Monster' is noodling around with faith." *USA Today*, 3/26/2006. http://usatoday30.usatoday.com/tech/science/2006-03-26-spaghetti-monster_x.htm. (Last accessed 3/11/2019)

ancient times, nor do we have the testimony of multitudes of honest people who testify that they spiritually commune with him on a daily basis!

But why couldn't our universe have been created by an intelligence that was not divine? Why could it not have been created, as Seth Shostak, senior astronomer at the Search for Extraterrestrial Intelligence (SETI) Institute suggested, by "the science fair project of a kid in another universe?"

> "Quantum mechanical fluctuations can produce the cosmos," Shostak said. "If you would just, in this room, just twist time and space the right way, you might create an entirely new universe. It's not clear you could get into that universe, but you would create it."[22]

Although Shostak deserves credit for fun and colorful imagery, a vacuum field—which is what quantum mechanical fluctuations are thought to occur in—is a notoriously slippery thing for humans to grab hold of and twist. And we don't *really* know if a quantum mechanical fluctuation can create a universe. It seems much more likely that it would create a simple particle and antiparticle. Despite the popularity and widespread acceptance of this idea, we have so far been unable to test it or observe it happening.

But let's suppose that the idea is correct. Let's also imagine that a team of scientists in another universe figured out how to make quantum mechanical fluctuation guns, commercialized the technology, and made them so affordable that some kid in a science fair project was able, after mowing blue alien lawns all summer long, to purchase one to create experimental universes.

---

[22] Eddie Wrenn, *"With physics, you can get universes: There is no need for a God to cause the Big Bang, says scientist."* Daily Mail, 26 June 2012. http://usatoday30.usatoday.com/tech/science/2006-03-26-spaghetti-monster_x.htm. (Last accessed 3/11/2019)

Astronomer Hugh Ross has identified 140 fine tuning parameters of our universe, without which life as we know it would be impossible.[23] That's akin to 140 radio tuning dials that have to be simultaneously tuned to precisely the right frequency. A divine Being with precise control over time and space, and multiple methods of creation at his disposal, would be able to easily adjust all of those dials. But the problem that our science fair kid is facing, is that a quantum mechanical fluctuation is the only means of creating a universe that he has available. And so, to create a universe like ours, the poor kid has to spin all 140 tuning dials to exactly the right spot with just one shot – one big bang!

How accurately would he have to aim? When a marksman takes aim at something, we can describe his target by imagining a sphere around him, with his eye at the center of that sphere, and the outer edge of the sphere at the end of his gun. His target can be designated by a spot on that sphere. If his target is very far away, the spot will be very small, and his aim will have to be more accurate.

Just how accurately would a fluctuation have to be aimed to create an orderly (low entropy) universe like ours? Cosmologist and mathematician Roger Penrose has calculated this. He applied his calculations to God creating the universe in one big bang, but they would apply to our much less capable science fair kid, too. Our young marksman would have to aim at a spot so tiny, that it took up only $1/10^{10^{123}}$ of the surface area of the sphere![24]

(Just in case you were wondering, that number is typed correctly - the second exponent *does* belong!) That fraction is so diminutive, that it has *more zeros in it than there are atoms in our observable universe*! The problem with a spot *that* little, is that it is smaller than the Planck

---

[23] Hugh Ross, *Why the Universe is the Way it Is. Appendix C:* Fine-Tuning for Life in the Universe, 2008. You may read his list of 140 fine tuning parameters of the universe at https://d4bge0zxg5qba.cloudfront.net/files/compendium/compendium_part1.pdf

[24] Penrose, *The Emperor's New Mind,* Oxford University Press, 2002, p. 445.

length![25] The Planck length is $1/10^{20}$ the diameter of a proton. It's considered impossible to determine the difference between two locations that are less than one Planck length apart.

And so, not only would it be impossible for our science fair kid to aim a fluctuation accurately enough, but it would be impossible for a team of the very best scientists in his entire universe to do it, no matter how sophisticated the instruments they had were. So even if we *did* figure out a way to create tiny universes from quantum fluctuations, we could create them until our own universe ends, and the odds are that we would not get any life-bearing ones.

Generating complex order from an explosion or a rapid expansion is a very difficult thing to do, because typically, explosions produce disorder and chaos. Perhaps that is why when a modern missionary explained the big bang theory to a primitive tribe, they found the idea to be funny! How could *a bang* produce all of this order? That would be like a lightning bolt striking a tree, and after all of the debris falls to the ground, finding a fully assembled hut, perfectly cut to measure!

But what if the laws in our science fair kid's universe were different from our own? Even if they were, the underlying quantum mechanical laws of his universe would be the same as ours, and those laws would need to be used by him to create a universe like ours.

And so, it seems quite unlikely that a non-divine intelligence living in another universe created our own universe. Even if one could create a universe, the odds of it being hospitable to life are astronomically low, and as Shostak himself pointed out, getting inside it to do anything or even observe what is happening there might be impossible.

---

[25] The average rifle barrel is about 24 inches long, giving us a radius of 0.6096 m. That gives us an aiming sphere with an area of 4.66982 m². We must divide this by the square of the Planck length, which is 1.6 x 10-35 m², to get the number of square Planck lengths our young marksman can aim at, which turns out to be 2.91 x 10^{46}. A 1/2.91 x 10^{46} fraction of his aiming sphere is far, far larger than our young alien's tiny $1/10^{10^{123}}$ target, which he would have to hit in order to produce a universe like ours.

Instead, the sheer size and finely-tuned-for-life order of our universe, the dependable physical laws that it obeys, and the staggering order and complexity of the life forms within it causes us to think that if it were created, this transcendent Creator was not only vastly powerful and intelligent, but had the ability to plan, create, control and organize the very molecular, subatomic, and quantum components of our universe. And of course, the Planck length would not be a limitation for a Being whose existence is not dependent upon the dimensions of space which define quantum vacuum fields.

And so, out of all of the different metaphysical philosophies, most educated people in the civilized West appear to be reasoning soundly when they reject ideas such as polytheism, tribal creation tales, and creation by non-divine intelligences, narrowing their choices down to what they consider to be the two most reasonable alternatives.

The first of these is *monotheism*, the belief that there is one omniscient and omnipotent God who created the universe.

The second is *metaphysical naturalism*. This is the belief that there is no God and that the entire universe, including the life within it, was formed by natural processes.

We will therefore restrict our consideration in this book to these two explanations, and leave debate regarding the merits of explanations that seem much less likely to others. If like most Westerners, you have narrowed down your choices to either theism or naturalism, then here is a logical axiom that will help you to choose between the two:

> *If either A or B is true, then if A is not true, B must be true.*

Therefore, as we carefully consider these two alternatives that most of us have narrowed our choices down to, if reason and probability dictate beyond a reasonable doubt that one of them is *not* true, this means that the other one *must be* true, *whether you can empirically observe and measure it or not.*

Even if you are someone who holds to an explanation other than the-ism or naturalism, I hope you will find what follows to be interest-ing. Although it will also be obvious that I favor and present reasons why I hold to the Judeo-Christian concept of God, many of my argu-ments will apply to theism in general, so even if you are a polytheist, or a monotheist who is not a Jew or orthodox Christian, you might find the contents of this book to be of interest to you as well.

3 WHAT MY MATH PROFESSOR WAS AFRAID TO SAY

"We cannot improve the world if we are conformed to the world." — Neal A. Maxwell

f metaphysical naturalists are correct, and there is no God who created life, the first cell had to come into existence through chemical processes. This idea is called *abiogenesis*: life arising from non-life. If we want to determine if life actually came into existence by chance, then we need to explore just how probable abiogenesis would have been.

Abiogenesis, if it ever actually happened, would have been an extremely rare exception – likely (as you are about to see) the *only* exception ever to have occurred in the observable universe to the *law of biogenesis* made famous by Louis Pasteur. It is commonly expressed by the Latin phrase *Omni vivum ex vivo*, which means "all that is alive came from something living."[26]

According to Webster's dictionary, a law is "a statement of an order or relation of phenomena that so far as is known is invariable under the given conditions." Biogenesis has been recognized as a law of biology because life has only been observed coming from previously existing life. Only in recent years is it being called into question as a law. But the reasons for challenging it have nothing to do anyone having observed life forming naturalistically. That has never happened. So the law still holds, even though some atheistically-inclined scientists perceive it as running counter to their worldview and are advocating against it being recognized as a law.

---

[26] *Aristotle to Zoos: A Philosophical Dictionary of Biology* By PB Medawar, JS Medawar, Harvard University Press, p. 245.

In short, abiogenesis has *never* been observed happening. It is an unproven hypothesis, as is acknowledged by all honest and informed metaphysical naturalists.

One of my college math professors was a brilliant man whose chalk danced across the blackboard so quickly, that his students often had to ask him to slow down. After he taught us the basics of how to determine probability, I privately inquired of him after class to learn what he thought the odds of abiogenesis might have been, since the subject was of interest to me and seemed relevant to what he had just taught.

He thought abiogenesis to be highly improbable, but said that if he were to ever publish such a conclusion, he would be subject to ostracism by his colleagues. That was over 25 years ago, and believe it or not, he taught at a Christian college!

The academic environment is even less tolerant of dissent from metaphysical naturalism today, even in the science departments of most (but not all) Christian universities. In recent years, some public high school biology teachers who have dared to call it into question have been dismissed from their jobs, and some college professors who have challenged it have had their careers derailed as a result. (Again, for extensive documentation of this, see Jerry Bergmann's formerly mentioned book, *Slaughter of the Dissidents*.) [27] It is no wonder that my professor was afraid to voice his mind on this important issue! As a result, very few students have ever heard the other side of the story in school.

But when an issue is *this* important, shouldn't students have the chance to hear the things my math professor was afraid to say? If abiogenesis really *is* highly improbable, is it right to withhold this information from them?

Let's examine whether or not that is the case, by using the very same method of calculating probability that my professor taught us in that class. If the idea of doing that sounds daunting to you, it is not as hard to do as you might think.

---

[27] Jerry Bergmann, *Slaughter of the Dissidents*. Leafcutter Press, 2011.

How to Calculate Probability

Flipping a coin and rolling dice can both serve as excellent examples of the basics of how to calculate probability.

Let's look at flipping a coin first. Each time you flip a coin, the probability of getting heads is one in two, which may be written as $\frac{1}{2}$. So to have 100% *theoretical* probability of getting heads, you must flip the coin twice. This is because $\frac{1}{2} + \frac{1}{2} = \frac{2}{2}$, which equals 100% probability.

You might be thinking right now, *theoretical probability does not always match experimental probability.* If you are thinking that, you are correct. You might have to flip a coin several times before you get heads. But if you flip a coin twice enough times, you will find that *typically*, you will get heads within two flips. So even though theoretical probability and experimental probability do not always match up exactly, theoretical probability is *still* a very good guide for making decisions or (if you are a gambler) placing bets.

Next, let's consider, what are the odds of getting heads twice in a row in only two flips? The probability of getting heads twice in a row is one in four, because $\frac{1}{2} \cdot \frac{1}{2} = \frac{1}{4}$. So, you must make four attempts at flipping a coin twice to obtain 100% theoretical probability of getting heads twice in a row. This is because $\frac{1}{4} + \frac{1}{4} + \frac{1}{4} + \frac{1}{4} = \frac{4}{4}$.

Likewise, the probability of getting a one if you roll a single dice is one in six. So you must make six attempts at rolling a dice to obtain 100% theoretical probability of getting a one.

The probability of getting "snake eyes" (a pair of ones) when you roll two dice is much lower, however, because $\frac{1}{6} \cdot \frac{1}{6} = \frac{1}{36}$. That means you must make 36 attempts at rolling a pair of dice, or 36 attempts at rolling a single dice twice, to get 100% theoretical probability. That is something to keep in mind the next time you are playing a game that involves dice, and especially if you are gambling with dice!

Now suppose that you flip a coin, and then roll a dice. What is the probability of getting a heads and a six? They are one in twelve, because $\frac{1}{2} \cdot \frac{1}{6} = \frac{1}{12}$.

Now that you are armed with this handy knowledge, please keep it in mind, because we will soon apply it to the matter at hand:

What is the probability of life forming by chance?

WHY THE DNA CODE IS A FORM OF LANGUAGE

"Language is the dress of thought." - Samuel Johnson

n order for life to have formed naturalistically, somehow all of the components of the cell, including its genetic information, must have formed and become arranged in functioning order without any intelligent guidance. In order to better appreciate what would have been required for this to happen, let's take a very quick look at DNA, RNA, and the process of protein synthesis.

If you are thinking, "I could have purchased a biology textbook for this," please bear with me. This is only a summary of the processes involved, like an executive brief. And it contains ideas which are very relevant to the question that this book is all about, that you simply won't find in a standard biology textbook. Please trust me, you will find it worth just a little mental effort to learn some of the basics of protein synthesis. I have worked hard to make it easy to understand. As icing on the cake, I've included plenty of illustrations, too!

DNA stands for *deoxyribonucleic acid*. It's called this simply because it contains a sugar called *deoxyribose*, and consists of a long chain of *nucleotides* which overall are acid in PH. The *deoxy* prefix comes from the fact that this sugar is just like the sugar ribose, except that it is missing one oxygen atom. (See **Figure 1**).

That's why RNA is called *ribonucleic acid*. Another difference is that RNA is single stranded, having only one sugar backbone. By contrast, DNA is double-stranded, with two sugar backbones. (See **Figure 3).**

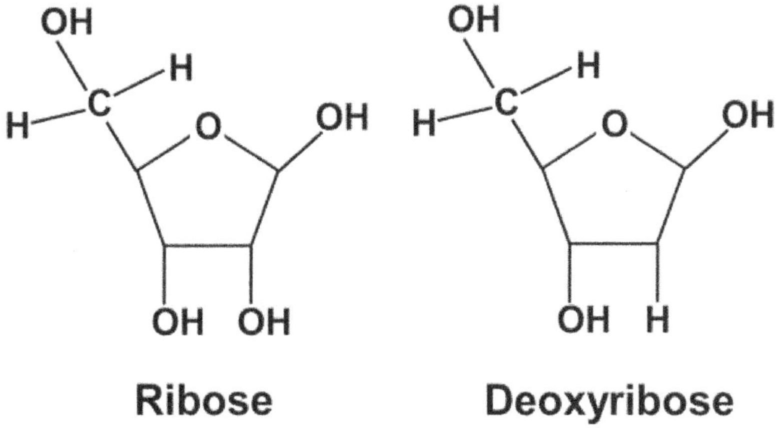

Figure 1. Note the bottom right-hand corner of each sugar molecule. Ribose has an extra oxygen atom, but deoxyribose does not.

A *helix* is a shape that looks like a wire spiraling up a pole. Because DNA has a shape resembling a twisted ladder, it is often called a *double helix*. The "sides" or "handrails" of this ladder are the backbones of the DNA molecule, and are made up of alternating phosphate and sugar groups. (In chemistry, a functional *group* consists of the chemically reactive atoms in a molecule.)

The two helices in DNA have an angle or tilt to their spirals, and tilt in opposite directions in relation to each other. For this reason, the two helices are said to be *antiparallel*. (See **Figure 3).**

Like kids with a sweet tooth, the "steps" of the DNA ladder attach *only* to the *sugar* groups in the "rails" or helices. Each of these steps in the ladder is made up of a pair of nitrogen *bases* bound together by a hydrogen bond.

A base is the opposite of an acid, because when in solution, it will accept rather than release a hydrogen ion. Since acids release hydrogen ions when in solution, and bases accept them, bases are often used to neutralize acids. Bases tend to feel slippery and taste bitter. Since the bases are on the *inside* of the DNA molecule, and the acidic phosphate groups are on the *outside*, the overall pH of DNA is acidic, and that is why it is referred to as deoxyribonucleic *acid*.

There are four different kinds of bases in a DNA molecule. These are adenine (A), thymine (T), cytosine (C) and guanine (G).

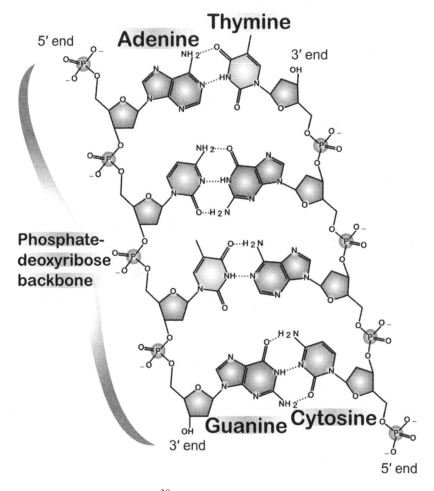

Figure 2. Credit: Madprime[28]

---

[28] "DNA chemical structure" by Madprime (talk · contribs) - Own work. The source code of this SVG is valid. This vector image was created with Inkscape. Licensed under CC BY-SA 3.0 via Commons -

This means that the DNA code is not binary (with only two characters), but digital (with more than two digits).

Like choosy best friends who hang out only with each other, adenine and thymine only bond with each other, and cytosine and guanine only bond with each other. This is called *complementary base pairing*. The steps in the DNA spiral ladder are called *base pairs*. Since they might pair up from either the left or the right, there are four different kinds of base pairs: AT, TA, CG, and GC.

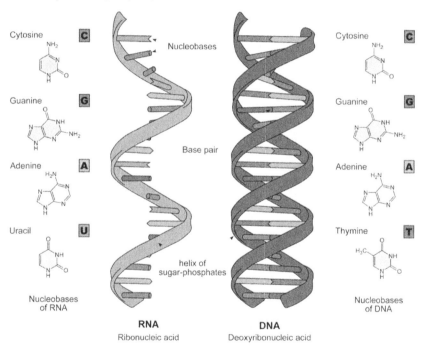

Figure 3. DNA and RNA. Credit: Roland1952 [29]

The bases which attach to the sugar backbone of RNA are the same as those of DNA, but with just one exception: uracil (U) replaces thymine (T). (See **Figure 3).**

Because adenine only pairs with thymine in the DNA molecule, and cytosine only pairs with guanine, this is what makes it possible for DNA to replicate during cell division. If a chemical engineer came up with that idea, we would complement him on having come up with an amazingly brilliant design, wouldn't we?

As DNA splits into two separate helices during replication, each of these bases bonds only to its base partner, and voila! A new DNA molecule is formed, as seen in **Figure 4.**

THE LANGUAGE-LIKE CHARACTERISTICS OF DNA

One day I was invited to see a small system board being assembled by a machine. The process was amazing to watch. Each of the electronic components was on a roll of tape. A robotic arm quickly grabbed each component off the tape, inserted it into the precise location on a printed circuit board where it belonged, and the part was automatically soldered to the board from below. This robotic machine was following a set of programmed instructions written in computer code.

The code in DNA is similar to the code that robotic machine was following, for it is instructional code describing how an organism is to be made. *This means that DNA, like any instructional machine language, carries information.*

DNA also has many characteristics in common with written human language. In fact, the human genome may be likened to a book composed of strokes, letters, words, sentences, notes and chapters.

Just as all hand written letters are made up of straight and curved lines of varying lengths and curvature, the four different possible base pairs comprise the **strokes** of the DNA alphabet. The human genome

https://commons.wikimedia.org/wiki/File:Difference_DNA_RNA-EN.svg#/media/File:Difference_DNA_RNA-EN.svg (Last accessed 3/12/2019)

consists of a staggering *3 billion* base pairs. Just think about it. That is a *lot* of coded information!

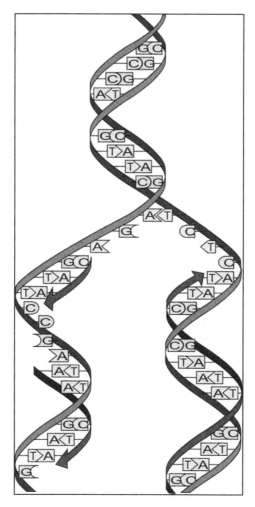

Figure 4. DNA replication, also known as DNA synthesis, is the duplication of a double-stranded DNA molecule. This process is made possible because each base will only bond to one other particular base partner. (Please note that this stylized picture does not illustrate the entire process by which the replication occurs.) Credit: Madeleine Price Ball

Three base pairs in a row form a *codon*. These are the **letters** of the DNA alphabet. Codons "code" for a single amino acid. Proteins are made up of folded chains of amino acids. Since there are four different kinds of bases or "strokes" in the DNA alphabet, and three make up a codon, the entire codon "alphabet" of DNA consists of 64 letters! (This is because $4 \cdot 4 \cdot 4 = 64$.)

Of the 64 different possible codons, three of these are stop signals which trigger the end of protein synthesis. So only 61 codons code for amino acids. Since there are only 22 different amino acids, most of them can be created by *more than one* codon. Amazingly, the frequency of an amino acid's occurrence in the genome corresponds roughly to the number of codons that code for it. In other words, the more often an amino acid occurs in the genome, the more ways there are to code for it.[30] This redundancy is also brilliant, because *it makes it less likely that a mutation will be harmful.* The human genome contains about a *billion* codons. By contrast, the last print edition of the *Encyclopedia Britannica* contained only 248 million characters![31]

Next are the **words** of the book, known as *exons* . Exons code for proteins.

The words of the book are interrupted by what we might call **editor's notes**, called *introns*. Introns vary in length, and are portions of DNA that do not code for proteins.

A group of codons consisting of exons or a combination of exons and introns forms a *gene.* (On average, there are about eight introns in

---

[30] M. Beals, L. Gross, and S. Harrell, "Amino Acid Frequency," tiem.utk.edu, 1999. http://www.tiem.utk.edu/~gross/bioed/webmodules/aminoacid.htm (Last accessed 3/22/2019)

[31] John Markoff, "44 Million Words Strong, Britannica to Join Internet." New York Times, Feb 8, 1984. http://www.nytimes.com/1994/02/08/business/44-million-words-strong-britannica-to-join-internet.html (Last accessed 03/11/2019). 248 million characters is based on an average of 5.6345 letters, spaces and punctuation marks per word (See http://www.viviancook.uk/Punctuation/PunctFigs.htm)

each gene. [32]) Each gene contains the information to create a single protein. You might compare genes to the **sentences** contained within a chapter.

A collection of genes comprises a *chromosome* . Each chromosome is one complete DNA molecule, and may be likened to a **chapter** in the book that describes how you are to be constructed. There are 23 pairs of chromosomes – 46 in all - within the nucleus of the human cell. 22 of these pairs of chromosomes look superficially similar in all healthy humans, and are called *autosomes*. But one pair – composed of the *sex chromosomes* – looks different in males and females. Just as some books have more chapters than others, different species have different numbers of chromosomes.

All 46 chromosomes collectively contain the information that is known as *the human genome,* the complete **book** describing how you are to be made. Please keep in mind that the genome is the *message* contained within that book. Just as different books have different messages, different genomes code for different organisms. This means that a genome is the *information* contained within DNA. By contrast, the *genetic code* is the *system* which specifies which of the 64 letters in the DNA alphabet corresponds to the 22 amino acids during protein synthesis.

Despite these commonalities, the DNA code is *not* a written or spoken *human* language. Nor is its purpose (at least as far as we currently know) to convey a message from one sentient being to another. As such, we need not expect it to have *all* of the characteristics of human languages. However, it shares many of them including Zipf's Law. Zipf's Law is a word frequency usage pattern found in semantic

---

[32] M.K. Sakharkar, V.T Chow, and P. Kangueane, "Distributions of exons and introns in the human genome." In Silico Biology, vol. 4, no. 4, pp. 387-393, 2004.

languages. Introns, which constitute 97 percent of human DNA, follow Zipf's law! Exons do not. [33]

The DNA code shares the following characteristics with all languages:

- It is a system for storing information.
- It carries meaningful messages (in this case, instructions for building functional proteins and intracellular molecular machinery).
- It uses a limited set of characters, each of which has meaning (the 64 codons).
- These characters are organized into discrete units containing sets of increasing information (exons, introns, genes, chromosomes, and genomes).
- It contains signals which occasion the start and stop of the reading of those discrete sets of information.
- The stored information is not random noise, like a scrambled set of letters. Rather, it is organized in a functional way. Just as human language carries functional information organized by an intelligence, the DNA of a cell carries instructions organized in such a way as to construct a living organism.
- Most of eukaryotic DNA - that which is contained in introns - follows Zipf's law, an empirical word usage pattern found in all human languages.
- The process of protein synthesis follows an important model of communication, as described below.

HOW PROTEIN SYNTHESIS PARALLELS THE PROCESS OF COMMUNICATION

Amazingly, the process of protein synthesis closely follows the Shannon-Weaver model of communication! The diagram below illustrates

---

[33] R. N. Mantegna, S. V. Buldyrev, A. L. Goldberger, S. Havlin, C.-K. Peng, M. Simons, and H. E. Stanley. "Linguistic Features of Noncoding DNA Sequences." Physical Review Letters, Vol. 73, #23, 5 Dec 1994 http://polymer.bu.edu/hes/articles/mbghpss94.pdf (Last accessed 03/19/2019)

the steps in the model, and how the process of protein synthesis parallels it.

The Information Source

The information source is of course the chromosome, which within its exons contains all of the code needed to produce proteins, and introns containing regulatory information. This is the *message* contained within the chromosomes. Though we are emphasizing the process of protein synthesis, let's not forget the importance of the message itself, which is most of the blueprint and instructions for the design of a living organism.

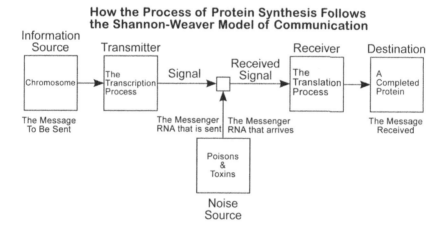

How the Process of Protein Synthesis Follows the Shannon-Weaver Model of Communication

The Encoding Transmitter

In the first step in the process of protein synthesis, called *transcription*, RNA polymerase attaches to a DNA nucleotide and travels down it, temporarily "unzipping it". One side of the DNA strand is used as a template to create a string of pre-messenger RNA (pre-mRNA). Next spliceosomes cut introns from the pre-mRNA, and the exons are spliced together and capped to create a completed string of mature messenger (mRNA). (Refer to **Figure 5** for more details.)

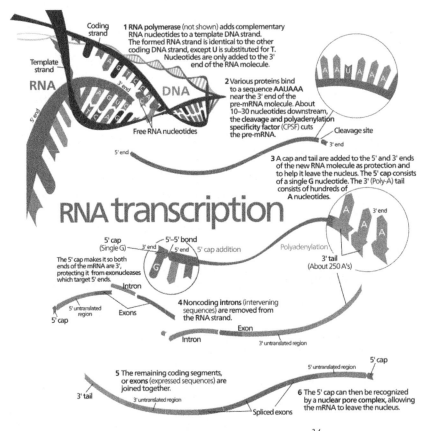

Figure 5. The Transcription Process. Credit: Kelvinsong.[34]

But what, you may be wondering, happens to the Introns? After the RNA coded for by the introns is released into the cell, it plays very important roles in the regulation of gene expression.[35] Introns used to be referred to as "junk DNA," and were often referred to by atheists as evidence of evolution, because they assumed them to be leftovers from it. However, the fact that introns follow Zipf's law is an important

---

[34] "MRNA" by Kelvinsong - Own work. Licensed under CC BY 3.0 via Commons, https://commons.wikimedia.org/wiki/File:MRNA.svg#/media/File:MRNA.svg

[35] Chorev M, Carmel L. "The function of introns." Front Genet. 2012 Apr 13;3:55. doi: 10.3389/fgene.2012.00055. eCollection 2012.

clue that they contain useful information, and sure enough, biologists have since discovered that introns are not junk – they play important roles, including regulating splicing, enhancing gene expression, controlling mRNA transport or chromatin assembly, and affecting nonsense-mediated decay. [36]

Interestingly, only the more complex organisms whose DNA is enclosed in a nuclear membrane, called *eukaryotes,* have introns. *Prokaryotes*, which have no nuclear membrane, have only exons. And of course, it makes sense that a more complex organism would require more components.

Signal Transmission

Once the spliceosome has done its work, the completed messenger RNA (mRNA) passes out of the nuclear membrane through a pore and into the cytoplasm.

The mature mRNA is the *signal* that is being transmitted. Just as background noise can interfere with a radio or an audio signal, poisons can degrade the mRNA signal. This includes the amatoxins contained in some mushrooms, and certain antibiotics in the case of bacteria.

Reception & Decoding

After the it passes through the pore in the nuclear membrane, a ribosome attaches to the messenger RNA to begin the decoding process. As the ribosome travels down the messenger RNA, *transfer RNA* (tRNA) molecules attach to the mRNA. They attach because each tRNA molecule has three complementary bases called *anticodons*. On the other end of each tRNA molecule is an amino acid.

In this manner, all of the original DNA is decoded into a polypeptide, which is a string of amino acids. This process is called *translation.*

---

[36] Jo, B. S., & Choi, S. S. (2015). Introns: The Functional Benefits of Introns in Genomes. Genomics & informatics, 13(4), pp. 112–118. doi:10.5808/GI.2015.13.4.112

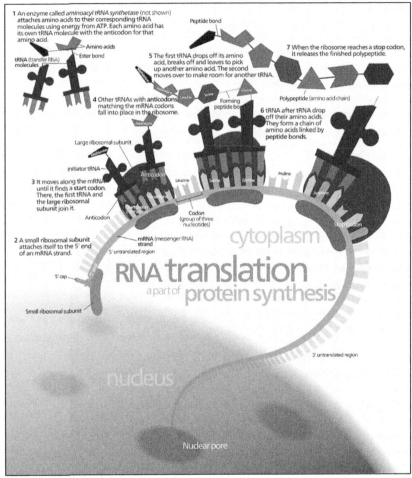

Figure 6. The RNA Translation Process. Credit: "Protein Synthesis" by Kelvinsong [37]

After the newly synthesized polypeptide string is released, it folds into a protein. You may refer to **Figure 6** for a more detailed explanation. And so, like all semantic languages, DNA is part of a system of storing, coding, transmitting, receiving and decoding complex information.

WHY DNA IS A LANGUAGE

If we define language in the broadest sense, as a method of storing or conveying meaningful, descriptive, or functional information by means of code, DNA definitely qualifies as a kind of language.

But if it is not a human spoken language, what kind of language is it? DNA is a *molecular machine language* that stores instructions for constructing a living organism.

But is DNA a *semantic* language that carries *meaning* like human languages do?

In his excellent article in the *Stanford Encyclopedia of Philosophy* entitled, "Semantic Conceptions of Information," Luciano Floridi writes:

> "Instructional information is a type of semantic content." [38]

Floridi may not have had DNA in mind when he wrote this, and so the question naturally arises, since the meaning of DNA is not being consciously interpreted by the cell, does this mean that DNA is not a semantic language?

The meaning of DNA *must* be correctly interpreted, albeit unconsciously, by the molecular machinery of the cell in order to synthesize the proteins it codes for. That is why we use the word *"translation"* to describe the step in which a molecule of messenger RNA is decoded by a ribosome and tRNA to produce a polypeptide (amino acid chain). Indeed, if something goes wrong in the transmission process (such as when an antibiotic interferes with the translation process in bacteria) and the polypeptide is not accurately synthesized, then the molecular machinery has not properly interpreted the meaning of the code.

Although cells and assembly line robots make use of semantic instructional information, they do not comprehend it consciously. Only a

---

[38] Floridi, Luciano, "Semantic Conceptions of Information." *The Stanford Encyclopedia of Philosophy* (Spring 2015 Edition), Edward N. Zalta (ed.), http://plato.stanford.edu/archives/spr2015/entries/information-semantic/.

conscious intelligence can do that. So does that mean that the DNA code is not a semantic language? No, and here's why:

A *chatbot* is a computer application programmed to converse with humans. A Russian chatbot named "Eugene Goostman" recently barely passed the Turing Test, meaning that human judges conversing with Eugene by text thought they were speaking with a human more than 30 percent of the time.[39] Obviously, a chatbot is not conscious. And yet at least 30 percent of the time, Eugene was able to carry on a sensible conversation that fooled humans into thinking he was a human using the English language! Eugene had to be able to unconsciously "interpret" what humans said in order to be able to generate an appropriate response. This means that consciousness is *not* a requirement for utilizing *or* interpreting a semantic language! Therefore the DNA code, like other forms of instructional information, *is* a form of semantic language that carries meaning! That meaning, among other things, is how to synthesize proteins and regulate cellular functions.

Richard Dawkins himself, that champion of naturalism, acknowledged the striking commonalities between computer language and DNA when in his book *The Blind Watchmaker* he wrote,

> It is raining DNA outside. On the bank of the Oxford canal at the bottom of my garden is a large willow tree, and it is pumping downy seeds into the air...Those fluffy specks are, literally, spreading instructions for making themselves. They are there because their ancestors succeeded in doing the same. It's raining instructions out there; it's raining programs; it's raining tree growing, fluff-spreading, algorithms. *This is not a metaphor; it is the plain truth.* It

---

[39] Chris Green, "Turing tested: an interview with Eugene Goostman, the first computer program to pass for human" Independent, Indy/Life p. 13, June 2014. http://www.independent.co.uk/life-style/gadgets-and-tech/news/turing-tested-an-interview-with-eugene-goostman-the-first-computer-programme-to-pass-for-human-9535740.html

couldn't be any plainer if it were raining floppy disks. [emphasis mine] [40]

And so the question is, *how did all of that complex semantic instructional information get into those willow seeds that were floating about Dawkins' garden?*

Saying "through natural selection" is a hypothesis that (if correct) does not completely answer the question. There had to *originally* be a functioning cell containing instructional information, in order for it to hypothetically evolve into willow seeds! So where did that information come from to begin with?

An article that appeared in the peer-reviewed planetary science journal *Icarus* sheds some light on this. Experts in planetary science sometimes speak of the idea of *directed panspermia*, which is intentionally seeding planets with genetically engineered organisms. This is often discussed as a strategy for terraforming planets (making them more earth-like). But it is also considered possible that earth was seeded with life by directed panspermia. Two scientists in Kazakhstan, Vladimir shCherbak of the Department of Mathematics at al-Farabi National University, and Maxim Makukov of the Fesenkov Astrophysical Institute, decided to investigate this possibility.

Using the same principles utilized by the SETI project to examine radio signals from outer space for signs of intelligent origin, they analyzed the genetic code found here on Earth. The results of their analysis were published in the peer-reviewed journal *Icarus* under the title, The "Wow! Signal" of the Terrestrial Genetic Code."[41]

In their article abstract they conclude that "the terrestrial code displays a thorough precision-type orderliness matching the criteria to be considered an informational signal." They also wrote, "The signal displays readily recognizable hallmarks of artificiality, among which are

---

[40] Dawkins, Richard. *The Blind Watchmaker*, p. 111

[41]Vladimir shCherbak and Maxim Makukov, *The "Wow! Signal" of the Terrestrial Genetic Code*, Icarus Volume 224, Issue 1, May 2013, P.s 228-242.

the symbol of zero, the privileged decimal syntax and semantical symmetries."

This means that the genetic code exhibits strong signs of being of intelligent origin. Keep in mind that the code is the "language" itself, not the message conveyed by the language. So that does not even take into account the message information content that is contained within the genome!

Lingua is the Latin word for language, so it seems appropriate for us to call the creation of a new language *linguagenesis.*

We have only observed new languages being invented by intelligent minds. Like the related law of biogenesis, this observation has been so invariable and consistent, that we are also justified in concluding that it is a law.

The Law of Linguagenesis:
Languages are invented only by intelligences.

There's a very good reason for this observed law, as we are about to see in the next few chapters. And so to conclude this chapter, the answer to the question is a definite "Yes! The DNA code *is* a semantic language that carries meaning, and the instructional message contained within the genome is that meaning."

4 HOW SIMPLE CAN AN EVOLVABLE SELF-REPLICATOR BE?

"Biology is the most powerful technology ever created. DNA is software, proteins are hardware, cells are factories." -*Arvind Gupta*

COULD A CELL HAVE BEEN SPONTANEOUSLY GENERATED IN THE PREBIOTIC SOUP?

n the DNA primer in the previous chapter, we only *scratched the surface* of the complexity of the details of protein synthesis.

DNA is so complex that it appears to have been intelligently engineered and organized, doesn't it? Because of its complexity, naturalistic scientists acknowledge it is highly unlikely that the *components* of the DNA alphabet formed by chance all at once. But even if all of the components *had* formed all at once, that would have been only a small part of the battle. Next they would need to become *organized* in such a way as to code for a living organism.

The more meaningful or functionally organized complexity something has, the less likely it is to have formed by chance. Just as it would be next to impossible to find neatly lined wooden letters arranged to form a mystery novel in the aftermath of a Scrabble® factory explosion, it's also virtually impossible that the base pair arrangement needed to code for an entire living cell formed in one unbroken sequence of chemical events.

Humans are remarkably functionally complex, but even the *simplest* form of free-living life that we know of, *Pelagibacter ubique,* is also *incredibly* functionally complex. Although this single-celled organism has the smallest known genome of any free-living organism, it nevertheless has *1,308,759* base pairs of DNA! [42]

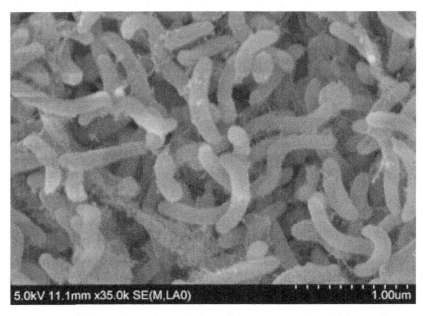

5.0kV 11.1mm x35.0k SE(M,LA0)   1.00um

Figure 2. *Pelagibacter ubique.* It is the simplest known free-living cell, but is incredibly complex, having 1,308,759 base pairs. Credit: Kehau Manoi; C-MORE University of Hawai'i. Under guidance of Megan Huggett and Michael Rappé.

A *eukaryote* is an organism in which the DNA is contained within a nuclear membrane. By contrast, a *prokaryote* such as Pelagibacter ubique has no nuclear membrane. One very interesting thing about Pelagibacter ubique is that it is a *heterotrophic alphaproteobacteria,* meaning that it feeds upon dead organic matter. This means that it depends upon existing life to survive. This dependence upon existing life partly explains why it's genome is so simple. It's genome is also highly streamlined, in that it is almost completely encoded. It has no introns, duplicate entries, or viral genes!

---

[42] Stephen J. Giovannoni, H. James Tripp. et al. "Genome Streamlining in a Cosmopolitan Oceanic Bacterium". Science 19 Aug 2005: Vol. 309, Issue 5738, pp. 1242-1245, DOI: 10.1126/science.1114057

This means that you can't take that much of Pelagibacter ubique's genome away and still have a functioning organism. However, even if we could take 99.9% of its genome away and still have a functioning organism, leaving only *1/1000th* of it, the probability of its base pair sequences arranging by chance would still be only $1/4^{1,309}$. That is astronomically small odds! But its genome is only *one* of its many components! And so the odds of an even much simpler version of this organism forming spontaneously in a single, unbroken succession of chemical events are so low as to be virtually impossible.

Unlike Pelagibacter ubique, it seems reasonable that the first cell would need to have been *autotrophic* (able to synthesize its own food from inorganic substances using light, electrical or chemical energy). The simplest autotroph known to man is *aquifex aeolicus*, which has 1,551,335 base pairs. [43]

Experiments with *Mycoplasma genitalium*, which as far as we know has the smallest genome of any organism that can be grown in pure culture, indicated that 382 out of its 482 protein encoding genes (79%) were essential.[44] (It has a genome that is about 60% the size of Pelagibacter ubique's. It causes a sexually transmitted disease, so it is also dependent on existing life to live.)

The organism with the smallest genome discovered so far (as of April 2019) is *Carsonella ruddii*. It is a symbiotic bacterium that lives inside of psyllid insects. According to Science News,

[43] Gerard Deckert et al. "The complete genome of the hyperthermophilic bacterium Aquifex aeolicus." Naturevolume 392, pages353–358, 26 March 1998. https://doi.org/10.1038/32831 (Last accessed 04/22/2019)

[44] John I Glass et al. "Essential genes of a minimal bacterium." *Proceedings of the National Academy of Sciences of the United States of America* vol. 103, 2 (2006): 425-30. doi:10.1073/pnas.0510013103. https://www.ncbi.nlm.nih.gov/pmc/articles/PMC1324956/ (Last accessed 04/07/2019)

It's the smallest genome -- not by a bit but by a long way," said co-author Nancy A. Moran, UA Regents' Professor of ecology and evolutionary biology and a member of the National Academy of Sciences. "It's very surprising. It's unbelievable, really. We would not have predicted such a small size. It's believed that more genes are required for a cell to work."

Carsonella ruddii has only 159,662 base-pairs of DNA, which translates to only 182 protein-coding genes, reports a team of scientists from The University of Arizona in Tucson and from Japan.[45]

Since *Carsonella ruddii*, which has the smallest genome known to man, is a symbiote that lives inside of insects, it is highly unlikely that the hypothetical first living ancestor of all life could have had fewer base pairs than it does (159,662).

Because we now know that a living cell is *extremely* complex, it is often compared to a *city infrastructure* when the functions of the cell are being taught to biology students.[46] Recently, as I discussed the complexity of DNA with a physician's assistant at the doctor's office, she remarked "I hope you don't mind me interjecting my personal opinion, but when I think about the complexity of DNA, it is difficult for me to believe that there is no God."

---

[45] University of Arizona. "Researchers Find Smallest Cellular Genome." ScienceDaily, 14 October 2006. http://www.sciencedaily.com/releases/2006/10/061012184647.htm (Last accessed 04/7/2019)

[46] See the video "Eukaryopolis - The city of animal cells" for an example of this at https://www.khanacademy.org/partner-content/crash-course1/crash-course-biology/v/crash-course-biology-10. (Last accessed 03/11/2019)

She is not the only one who has come to this conclusion. What he called the "integrated complexity" of the cell led prominent and long-time atheist Antony Flew to believe in a deistic Creator.[47]

In a widely popularized statement regarding the complexity of the cell, astronomer and mathematician Sir Fred Hoyle noted that the odds of the "random formation of whole chains of amino acids like enzymes" in a primordial soup of the primitive earth would be comparable to the following:

> A junkyard contains all the bits and pieces of a Boeing 747, dismembered and in disarray. A whirlwind happens to blow through the yard. What is the chance that after its passage a fully assembled 747, ready to fly, will be found standing there? So small as to be negligible, even if a tornado were to blow through enough junkyards to fill the whole Universe.[48]

So, *could* a cell have spontaneously generated in the prebiotic soup? To say that the odds are very much against it would be a gross understatement!

WHAT ABOUT THE RNA WORLD HYPOTHESIS?

Because DNA-based life is so complex, and carries so much instructional information, a popular speculation is that self-replicating RNA molecules formed first and evolved into more complex DNA

---

[47] Some atheists have suggested that the dementia from which Flew died might have led to his change of heart, but well before that, Flew gave sound explanations of his reasoning in an interview with Lee Stroebel. I therefore suggest that we respectfully permit this tree to lie where it chose to fall. Watch Lee Stroebels' interview of Flew at https://www.youtube.com/watch?v=VHUtMEru4pQ (Last accessed 03/11/2019)

[48] *The Intelligent Universe: A New View of Creation and Evolution* (1983), p.19. You may read Hoyle's quote in context at http://www.charliewagner.net/hoyle.htm.

replicators. But even the hypothetical replicators of what is called the "RNA World" hypothesis are so complex, and the odds so small that all of the conditions needed for their formation would happen at just the right times, that it is virtually impossible that they arose in a single sequence of chemical events.[49] Furthermore, even if all of the components formed, how would they become arranged in the proper order?[50]

Information theorist Herbert Yockey studied the application of information theory to the origin of life. In *The Journal of Theoretical Biology* he wrote,

> Taking into account only the effect of the racemic mixture the longest genome which could be expected with 95 % confidence in 10^9 years corresponds to **only 49 amino acid residues.** This is **much too short to code a living system** so evolution to higher forms could not get started. Geological evidence for the "warm little pond" is missing. It is concluded that belief in currently accepted scenarios of spontaneous abiogenesis is based on faith, contrary to conventional wisdom.[51]

It is therefore thought that RNA self-replicators themselves must have arisen from simpler self-replicators, but exactly what kind of replicator is not certain.[52]

---

[49] http://creation.com/origin-of-life-the-chirality-problem

[50] http://www.evolutionnews.org/2009/07/scientists_say_intelligent_des022621.html#more

[51] Hubert P.Yockey, *"A calculation of the probability of spontaneous biogenesis by information theory,"* Journal of Theoretical Biology, Volume 67, Issue 3, 7 August 1977, pp. 377-398

[52] News Staff, "New Evidence For 'RNA World' Hypothesis." science20.com, February 21st 2010. http://www.science20.com/news_articles/new_evidence_rna_world_hypothesis (Last Accessed 3/25/2019)

WHAT MUST THE FIRST MOLECULAR REPLICATOR HAVE BEEN LIKE?

And so, because of the complexity of even the simplest symbiotic and parasitical organisms, as well as the *hypothetical* RNA World forerunners of the first living cell, scientists who are metaphysical naturalists have been forced to speculate that abiogenesis must have happened by means of a simple non-living replicator gradually evolving into life. This idea is known as *biopoesis* (From *bio*, meaning "life," and *poieo*, meaning "to make").

What qualities must this hypothetical replicator have had?

- **First of all**, it must have been evolvable. That means it must have had some means of mutation, and some means of "remembering" beneficial mutations to pass them on to its offspring. That requires a certain degree of complexity, ruling out the simplest replicator designs.
- **Secondly**, it must have been of a design which was flexible enough to survive mutating into many intermediate forms of increasing complexity as it evolved into a single-celled form of life. In other words, it could not have had only vital parts which were of a design so critical that any change in them would render it incapable of functioning. That *also* rules out many or all of the simplest possible designs.
- **Thirdly**, it must have been of a design which was able to utilize the "parts" available in its environment, and distinguish them from parts that do not belong in order to assemble those parts in the proper order.
- **Fourthly, it must have lived in an environment in which all of the parts it needed were available.** These parts would also contain information in their structure, so the prebiotic soup would need to be just right to make the formation of those parts likely. This means that many replicator designs which could work in other environments would not have the parts that they would need to form on the primitive earth. That rules out a lot of possible designs.

- **Fifthly,** it must have been composed of simple parts. In order for formation of the parts to be likely in the prebiotic soup, the parts could not be too complex.
- **Sixthly,** it must have had a means of replication. This requires functional design of some complexity.
- **Seventhly,** it must have been able to survive "in the wild." A molecular replicator which will work in the protective environment of a cell likely would not in the wild. This means that the replicator must have been in a protective "niche" environment providing not only ample parts, but also protection from harmful elements, or that it must have had protective structures such as a cell wall.
- **Eighthly,** it must have had some method of utilizing energy to construct a copy of itself.

And so, the hypothetical replicator that led to life must have had a certain degree of complexity. But how much complexity?

Clues As To How Complex the First Replicator Would Need to Have Been

In lectures delivered in 1948 and 1949, as a "thought experiment," the mathematician John Von Neumann developed a conceptual model of a "kinematic self-replicating machine" that was amazingly predictive of the molecular machinery later to be found in cells.[53] Since *kinematics* is the study of motion without regard to the cause of that motion, and *kinetics* is the study of both motion and its causes, this name was probably chosen because Von Neumann did not take into account the sources of energy that his self-replicating machine would have required, or the mechanisms needed to convert that energy into useful work. This would have added a lot of additional complexity to his thought experiment, making it much more difficult to conceptualize.

---

[53] John Von Neumann, *Theory of Self-Reproducing Automata*, edited and completed By Arthur W. Burks, University of Illinois Press, Urbana and London, 1966.

To simply summarize Von Neumann's ideas, he hypothesized that such a self-replicator must have the following large basic components (which in turn are composed of many smaller ones):

- A memory "tape" that stores instructions for assembling a copy of itself.
- A manipulator or "constructor" that follows the instructions on the tape to assemble a copy of itself, and then copies its contents onto the duplicate's tape.
- Structural framework components. At least four logic elements to send and receive stimuli.
- Lastly, it would need to float in a reservoir or "sea" of readily available parts.

It is thought that the number of small parts a self-replicator like this might have could run into the *hundreds of thousands or millions*.[54] Amazingly, it was later discovered that the cell is a Von Neumann-type replicator.

The Von-Neumann-style replicator is the *only* kind of free-living self-replicator known to man, and is so complex that it is highly unlikely to have formed spontaneously. Scientists have been attempting to create simpler evolvable self-replicators that replicate in a different fashion in the lab, but so far without success.

Once he got into it, the enormity of the task of developing a complete 3D replicator model must have been daunting even to the brilliant mind of Von Neumann. To make his idea of a self-replicator easier to develop and analyze than a three dimensional machine, his fellow mathematician Stan Ulam suggested the idea of a two dimensional model, which is called a *cellular automaton*. This consisted of two-dimensional squares called "cells" that could exist in different

---

[54] Walter R. Stahl, "Self-reproducing automata," Perspect. Biol. Med. 8, Spring 1965, pp. 373-393.

states. Each cell would behave differently depending on its current state and the state of the cells next to it. Von Neumann's work on this was completed and published after his death by Arthur Burke in the book *Theory of Self Reproducing Automata*.[55]

Even a self-replicating 2D Von Neumann cellular automaton turned out to be not so simple. When a computer model of one (with three more states than Von Neumann had envisioned) was finally successfully implemented by Nobili and Pesavento in 1995, it also turned out to be very complex: the tape was 145,315 cells long, and replication required 63 billion time steps![56, 57]

In 1970, what became a very popular solitaire game based on the idea of cellular automata was invented, John Conway's *Game of Life*. Initially it was played on an Othello game board, but then on computer. Michael Hogg has compiled a database of Game of Life patterns. Here is Hogg's summary of the simple rules:

> The *Game of Life* (also known as *Life*, or *GoL*) is played on an infinite grid of square cells, each of which can be "alive" or "dead". Each cell interacts with the eight neighboring cells surrounding it, using the following simple rules:
>
> - A live cell stays alive if it has 2 or 3 live neighbors, otherwise it dies.

[55] Neumann, *Theory of Self-Reproducing Automata*.

[56] Umberto Pesavento, "An Implementation of von Neumann's Self-Reproducing Machine." Artificial Life 2, 1995, pp. 337–354. http://web.archive.org/web/20070621164824/http://dragonfly.tam.cornell.edu/~pesavent/pesavento_self_reproducing_machine.pdf (Last accessed 03/19/2019)

[57] Tim Hutton, "Von Neumann's Self-Reproducing Universal Constructor." Sq3.org.uk, March 21, 2010. http://www.sq3.org.uk/wiki.pl?Von_Neumann%27s_Self-Reproducing_Universal_Constructor (Last accessed 03/11/2019)

- A dead cell comes to life if it has 3 live neighbors, otherwise it stays dead. [58]

The game board, cell states and rules in the Game of Life constitute what is called a *mathematical universe*. Mathematical universes like this are useful as simplified models of the kinds of universes that could arise if certain multiverse theories are true. Please keep this in mind, as it is an important concept that we will return to later in this book.

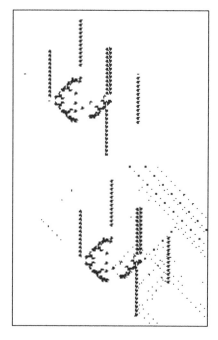

Gemini in the process of self-replication. You may watch a video of Gemini self-replicating at https://youtu.be/A8B5MbHPlH0.

The Game of Life is also what is called a *zero player game*. Enthusiasts set up starting patterns of dead and alive cells, let the program run, and then watch what happens. For fans of this game, it was a day for celebration when in 2010 Andrew Wade invented *Gemini*, a Von-Neumann-style self-replicator that duplicates in 34 million time-steps. Since this may have implications for the formation of life, Wade's achievement was even reported in the science journal *New Scientist*.[59]

Just as cellular life in our universe does with DNA, Gemini uses a very long "instruction tape." To give you an idea of how complex life must be even in a simple two dimensional mathematical universe such as the Game of Life, it will be

[58] http://www.michael-hogg.co.uk/game_of_life.php#g

[59] Jacob Aron, "First replicating creature spawned in life simulator." New Scientist, Magazine issue 2765 , published 19 June 2010. http://www.newscientist.com/article/mg20627653.800-first-replicating-creature-spawned-in-life-simulator.html?p.=2#.U-1pb3l0y9l (Last accessed 03/11/2019)

helpful to read the following quote. After Wade first announced his creation, One Game of Life enthusiast congratulated Wade by writing,

> "And it replicates in only 34 million generations [time steps]?! The best estimate so far for a typical UCC-based Life replicator was 10^{18} generations. I see that you have removed all but the bare minimum - *that is probably the simplest possible self-replicator, and very elegant, too.* I thought that we might see these things appearing by about 2020, but you are a decade ahead of your time! Well, congratulations—you have single-handedly beaten the collaborative effort between myself, Dave Greene and Paul Chapman to realize a Life replicator."[60] [emphasis added]

The Game of Life is *Turing Complete*, meaning that we can create one or more objects within it that are capable of universal computation. Besides the Game of Life, there are other mathematical universes capable of supporting cellular automatons that are Turing Complete. Some with simpler cellular automatons that are self-replicators have been created. Of particular note is a very simple cellular universe called *Rule 110* that is Turing Complete. It is a one-dimensional form of cellular universe with all of the cells existing on a single line rather than an infinite grid. It is significant because it indicates to us that a mathematical universe of very simple natural laws can be used to create objects that exhibit complex behavior.

Since that time, cellular automata have been invented on triangular and hexagonal grids of one, two, three, four or more dimensions, with multiple states represented by colors! They even have been introduced into the popular computer game known as Minecraft! The realm of mathematical universes is indeed an interesting one!

Summary

To summarize this chapter, so far the Von-Neuman-style replicator is the *only* evolvable real-life, free-living self-replicator known to man.

---

[60] Calcyman's post on ConwayLife.com forum, http://conwaylife.com/forums/viewtopic.php?f=2&t=399&start=0, at May 19th, 2010, 2:23 AM.

Since *Carsonella ruddii*, which has the smallest genome known to man, is a symbiote that lives inside of insects, it is highly unlikely that the hypothetical first living ancestor of all life could have had fewer base pairs than it does (159,662). However, that's *far* too complex to have been likely to form spontaneously.

So right now origin-of-life researchers are operating on faith, hoping to somehow surmount the probabilistic odds to create in the lab a simple form of self-replicator that could have formed and survived on the primitive earth.

In an award speech, the information scientist Marcel Golay shared what he thought to be the minimum amount of structure or information that a self-replicator in our *real* universe must have. For reasons which I will later explain, it is highly unlikely that a free-living self-replicator could be simpler than that. It is hoped that somehow, perhaps something simple like that could have formed and survived in an isolated, nurturing niche environment on the primitive earth—such as in a hydrothermal vent.

But before I share Golay's figure with you, in order for you to be able to fully appreciate it, it will be very helpful for you to understand exactly what information is, and how it is quantified. That's what the next chapter is all about.

5 WHAT EXACTLY IS INFORMATION, AND HOW DOES IT APPLY TO THE ORIGIN OF LIFE?

"I'm fascinated by the idea that genetics is digital. A gene is a long sequence of coded letters, like computer information. Modern biology is becoming very much a branch of information technology." — *Richard Dawkins*

Information theory began back in 1948 when Claude E. Shannon wrote his landmark paper, "A Mathematical Theory of Communication." The study of information has many branches, and different methods have been used to define and classify information depending on the needs at hand. In this chapter we are only going to look at the most important aspects of it that relate to the formation of life. In the process, we will take an approach to classifying information that is unique in some respects, which I hope you will find to be useful, accurate and meaningful.

Information, at its most basic level, is simply orderly *arrangement.* This sentence, for instance, contains letters that have been *arranged* to convey a meaningful message. But orderly arrangements do not just convey messages. They can also result in beautiful structures such as the Taj Mahal or a queen's tiara, recognizable patterns, or they can create things that perform work, such as a farm tractor or an air conditioner.

TWO CATEGORIES OF ARRANGEMENTS

If you think about it, we can divide arrangements into two primary **categories**:

1. **Chaotic Arrangements:** *These are arrangements that have little discernable order*. They are also the most probable kinds of arrangements. When an arrangement has little discernable order,

we say that it has *high entropy.* Since chaotic arrangements are the most probable, in our universe all orderly arrangements have the statistical tendency to move back to a disordered, chaotic state. For this reason, entropy is known as *the arrow of time.* In Claude Shannon's theory of information, any arrangement can be viewed as containing information, *even if it has no meaning, orderly structure, or functionality.* The Shannon theory of information is used primarily for statistical and quantitative purposes. It is not used to measure the meaning, structural intricacy, or functionality of information, so for our purposes here, we will not use Shannon's definition. We will not regard chaotic arrangements as containing information.

2. **Ordered Arrangements:** *These are arrangements in which we can discern structural, functional, or meaningful order.* Orderly arrangements, rather than disorderly ones, are what most of us regard as information, so for our purposes here we will adopt the following very simple definition of information:

> *Information is orderly arrangement.*

THE FOUR KINDS OF INFORMATION

There are four basic *kinds* of information:

1. **Structural information:** This is the design, architecture, shape or pattern of an arrangement. Examples include language symbols, seashells, crystals, sidewalks, homes, and the 3D shape of a synthesized and folded protein. Structural order goes up as the *complexity* of the structure increases. A simple mud wall would have less structural information than a modern wall with 2x4 studs, insulation, wiring and sheetrock, which is more intricate.

2. **Operational Information:** This is an arrangement that results in a task or work being performed. This kind of information is the way that structures interact with each other

or their environment to perform tasks. Machines, operating system code, a computer application, electric cars, living cells, the DNA code, language systems, and numerical systems all contain operational information. Operational order goes up as *operational complexity* increases. A Ford truck, for instance, has much more operational order than a toy replica of it. *Operational order differs from structural order in that it is 4-dimensional, involving not just 3D space but time.* Quantifying it requires envisioning time steps: what happens at each step in time. This means that a lot of 4D planning may need to go into creating a functional system.

3. **Semantic Information:** This is coded information that contains meaning. Examples include speech, descriptive information, numbers, books, songs, and art that is not merely decorative, but intended to convey a message. Semantic Information also includes directions for constructing something, such as blueprints, how-to instructions, recipes, and the genomes of living cells (which contain most of the instructions for how to make a living organism). The quality of semantic order goes up as *depth of meaning* increases, and can range from shallow to deep meaning. A bird song, though it may have simple meaning to other birds, usually contains much less semantic information than human conversational speech.

4. **Platonic Information:** When higher forms of order are created by an intelligence, they are often planned and exist in the mind first, in the realm of ideas. *Semantic information is simply a coded representation of platonic information.* High order structural and functional information, on the other hand, is the *material* implementation of platonic ideas.

Platonic information also enables us to conceptualize structural and functional order that already exists. The concepts of math are an example of this. Though platonic mathematical information does not exist outside of the mind, it is used to model and plan the creation of things in the material world. The fact that our universe can be mathematically modeled causes us to suspect that it may have a platonic (intelligent) origin. As you will see later in this chapter, there is an experimentally and mathematically verifiable principle called *The Principle of Information Origin* which confirms this suspicion to be correct.

Since we often think using coded information, why draw a distinction between semantic and platonic information? First of all, not all thought is coded or symbolic. Secondly, high-order structural, operational, and semantic information created by intelligences often has a platonic counterpart that contains more information than its material expression.

For instance, a hammer has a function, but the information that describes that function is not in the hammer itself. It is in the mind of the designer of the hammer, and in the minds of the people who use the hammer. Or consider the word *human*. The platonic information represented by that small amount of semantic information is vast.

Since ideas are immaterial, you may be wondering, how can platonic information be measured? By converting it into semantic information first.

FIVE MEASUREMENTS OF INFORMATION

There are five primary **measurements** that we can make of information.

- The first is the **quantity** of information. This is the amount of orderly information something contains. Information is usually quantified by the *bit*. I will explain what a bit is shortly.

- The second is the **quality** of the information. This is the simply how accurate the information is, and how efficiently and well the information accomplishes the task it is intented for. Two engines may weigh the same and take up the same amount of space. But if one lasts longer, costs less to make and has more horsepower than the other does, it contains higher quality information (is of a better design).
- The third is the **density** of the information. This is simply the average quality of the information per unit of quantity.
- The fourth measurement is the **probability** of the information forming naturalistically, without an intelligence arranging it. This can be very useful in certain situations, such as when a SETI researcher needs to determine if a signal from space originates from an intelligence, or if a government needs to know if a radio signal is static or an encoded messages from an enemy during time of war. We will discuss how the probability of information forming naturalistically is calculated later in this chapter.

A MEASUREMENT OF ENTROPY

- **Entropy** is the disorder that an arrangement contains. Since highly ordered things tend to move to a more probable state, they tend to degrade. Noise or static in a radio signal, faded letters in a paper copy of a document, and scratches on an LP record as it is playing are all examples of entropy. Though entropy is also measured in bits, we are *not* defining entropy as information for our purposes here. *Entropy can reduce the quantity, quality, and/or density of information.*

TWO RANKS OF INFORMATION

Information (orderly arrangement) may be divided into two *ranks* by probability:

I. **Low-order information:** Low-order information is naturalistically probable information, so it is the most common. It may be very high in quantity, but *on average* it is lower in density. It also can include *very short* sequential quantities or strings of dense information. These are the kind of orderly arrangements most likely to arise from non-living natural processes. They include crystals, snow-flakes, undulating desert sands, pulsar radio signals, rocks, the color and brightness of light frequencies, the water cycle, hurricanes, etc. *These arise from the functional structure of the natural elements.*

II. **High-order information:** These are naturalistically improbable, orderly arrangements that have structural complexity, operational complexity, or semantic meaning. As we will soon see, as information increases, high-order arrangements quickly become *extremely* improbable.

WHAT IS A BIT?

A *bit of information* is a convenient and useful way of quantifying (counting how much) information there is in something.

A *bit* is simply a choice that has been made between two equally likely alternatives, in order to accurately construct, describe, or accomplish something, including constructing a message.

The table on the following page contains some examples of choices that can be quantified as a bit of information.

We represent bits with the fraction $\frac{1}{2}$. This signifies that a bit of information was one out of two equally likely choices or alternatives. Just in case you have gotten a little out of practice with fractions since school, you may recall that we can convert a fraction to another one with a different denominator. This means we can convert the selections needed to create something into bits. For instance:

$$\frac{8}{16} = \frac{4}{16} = \frac{2}{4} = \frac{1}{2} = 1 \text{ bit.}$$

So, let's say that a child chooses one out of eight different-looking logs when making a toy log house. Since there are 8 possible pieces to choose from, he has made 1 selection out of 8 choices. We represent that with the fraction $^1/_8$. Then we can convert that to bits by solving the following problem:.

$$\frac{1}{8} = \left(\frac{1}{2}\right)^b$$

Since $\frac{1}{2} \cdot \frac{1}{2} \cdot \frac{1}{2} = \frac{1}{8}$, we know that $b = 3$. So, the choice that child made may be quantified as 3 bits of information.

Examples of Selections that May be Quantified as One Bit of Information:

Choice	Equally Likely Alternative 1	Equally Likely Alternative 2
A binary programmer selecting the number "0" while coding.	0	1
A football player selecting "heads" during the toss of a fair coin.	Heads	Tails
A driver turning when the road dead-ends into another street.	Right	Left
A distraught young woman deciding which of two equally desirable suitors to marry.	She loves me.	She loves me not.

Now let's look at some examples that are just a little harder, but still easy to understand.

WHAT'S THE WAY OUT OF THE CORN MAZE?

Suppose that an entrepreneurial farmer made a corn maze. In this particular maze, there were many left turns available, and many right turns available, but no places, except at the end of hallways, where you could turn either left or right. Because of this, each time you came to a turn in his maze, you had some choices to make. Those choices were left or right, left or straight, and right or straight. A simpler way to say this, is that the choices at each possible turn were leftmost and rightmost. To help a friend of his get through the maze as quickly as possible and thereby impress a beautiful date with his supposed brilliance, the farmer gave his friend a tiny cheat sheet. The cheat sheet contained the code: "LLRLRRRL". This code told the farmer's friend what to do each time he came to a turn, by using the following two symbols:

L= Take the leftmost choice.
R=Take the rightmost choice.

How much information is in this code? Exactly eight bits of information, because the correct choice between two equal alternatives must be made eight times. This can be written out as $(\frac{1}{2})^8$. Interestingly, this number also is the odds of someone randomly guessing his way out of the maze on the first try. On average, only one out of 256 visitors to the corn maze will make it out on the first try, because $(\frac{1}{2})^8 = \frac{1}{256}$.

This means that the bit is not only useful as a way to measure information content, but also for determining the probability of correct information being randomly selected or assembled.

This is a key concept that we will take into consideration in this book.

SHOULD YOU TRY TO GUESS THE OFFICE SUITE?

Likewise, suppose that you are a newly hired salesperson whose manager gave you directions to a potential customer's office. There are eight buildings in the customer's office park, numbered 1 - 8, and eight suites in each building, labeled A-H. He tells you to go to suite 3C. How many bits of information has he given you? He has given you the correct choice out of 64 possible office suites. That equals exactly six bits of information, because $(\frac{1}{2})^6 = \frac{1}{64}$. If you were to forget the suite number, you would be better off calling your sales manager to ask for it (even though this would be somewhat embarrassing), because your chances of finding the office on the first try are only 1 in 64.

HOW MANY BITS OF INFORMATION ARE IN A TWO DIGIT NUMBER?

Written messages and numbers can often easily be quantified by bits of information, since they involve choices between a only a small number of symbols.

When I type the number 24, how many bits of information have I selected? Here's how to figure it out. Each time I typed a number, I chose one out of 10 possible number symbols. We can represent that with the fraction $1/10$. But since I selected two numbers, we represent that by multiplying the first selection by the second selection:

$$\frac{1}{10} \cdot \frac{1}{10} = \frac{1}{100}$$

This means that I picked one out of 100 different two digit number combinations! (These are 01-99.) However, a bit involves selecting one out of two choices, not one out of ten. So to convert our choices to bits, we must solve for the following:

$$\frac{1}{100} = (\frac{1}{2})^b$$

Here *b* represents the number of bits of information. The answer turns out to be between 6 and 7 bits of information. (Or 6.64385619 bits of information, for those who prefer a more precise figure.)

As Bits Increase, Odds Quickly Decrease

When it comes to quantifying information by bits, the number of possible combinations adds up *exponentially* and that means that the probability of correct chance selection goes quickly down. Most of us instinctively know this, because we can quickly recognize whether or not something is a product of an intelligence or the blind forces of nature.

For instance, we can immediately recognize that an iron nut was arranged by an intelligence, and that a rock of raw iron ore was not. We know this even though the iron nut is very simple and does not have that much complexity. Why? Because the odds of natural forces heating up iron ore and forming it into a hexagonal shape with a hole lined by uniform spirals in the middle are very, very low.

Verifying This Concept by Experiment

Here's a simple little experiment you can perform to empirically verify that as bits go up, the probability of chance formation goes quickly down.

Let's suppose you need a particular word to complete a meaningful sentence. You want to find out what the odds are of forming that word by chance selection. So you place all 26 letters of the alphabet into a paper bag. To get each letter by chance, you draw out a letter (without looking into the bag or feeling the letter's shape) and write it down. Then you put the letter back into the bag, shake it, and draw the next letter. Each time you try, you make the same number of draws as there are letters in the word. If you do not get the correct word, you cross it out and try again.

How many tries will it theoretically take, on average, to get the word you need? Below is a chart of the probabilities. As you can see, as the length of the string of letters goes up, the probability of chance formation quickly goes down.

Word Strings			
Word Needed	**Bits of Information**	**Probability of Correct Chance Selection**	**Number of Attempts Required**
a	4.70043972	$1/26$	26
be	9.40087944	$1/676$	676
car	14.1013192	$1/17,576$	17,576
good	18.8011905	$1/456,976$	456,976
grape	23.5021986	$1/11,881,376$	11,881,376
supposes	37.6035177	$1/208,827,064,576$	208,827,064,576

APPLYING INFORMATION THEORY TO THE FORMATION OF LIFE

Like English words, DNA and RNA are also strings that contain information. They contain *high-order instructional information*, which is a form of semantic (meaningful) information. The meaning contained within them is how to construct the protein components of a functioning cell.

Let's suppose that a string of RNA base pairs is needed to synthesize a protein to complete the first free-living self-replicator, and all of the base pairs needed are conveniently floating around in a prebiotic soup.

As you can see in the table on the next page, as the number of bits goes up, the number of tries required very quickly becomes *more than the number of chemical events that could have taken place on earth.*

The average-size exon would require $2.29 \cdot 10^{105}$ tries to create natu-ralistically. However, in 4.5 billion years, no more than $1.9 \cdot 10^{72}$ chem-ical events could have happened on Earth![61]

DNA AND RNA STRINGS

Let's apply what we have learned to determine what the probability is of short, orderly DNA and RNA strings being selected by blind natural processes. (Assuming all of the base pairs needed are conveniently floating nearby in a prebiotic soup in equal numbers). On average, how many chemical "attempts" are required?

The table on the next page reveals the probability of a base pair se-quence forming. When looking at it, please keep in mind the following:

- Since there are four different base pairs, the odds of one base pair forming are ¼ , which equals two bits of information, since $\frac{1}{2} \cdot \frac{1}{2} = \frac{1}{4}$.
- Three base pairs forms a codon. A codon codes for a single amino acid or a stop code (which is a signal to stop amino acid synthesis.)
- An exon codes for a protein or a shorter peptide sequence.
- Due to redundancy in the DNA code, from one to six codons codes for each amino acid, and three codons code for a stop.[62] Of the twenty amino acids, the probability of the average amino acid being coded for by blind chance is therefore $\frac{2.76}{64}$.

Because of this, the naturalistic formation of an amino acid, peptide or a protein requires fewer chemical attempts than there would be if this

---

[61] Assuming 4.543 billion years times 31,536,000 seconds per year, times a volume on earth of $1.33 \cdot 10^{50}$ atoms, times the unrealistically high rate of 10^6 chemical reactions per second = $1.9 \cdot 10^{72}$ chemical events.

[62] Since the frequency of amino acid occurrence in the genome corresponds roughly to the number of codons that code for an amino acid, this figure should also be roughly accurate.

DNA & RNA Strings

String Needed	Base Pairs	Bits of Information	Number of Chemical Attempts Required to form. (Place a "1/" over this number for the probability of chance formation.)
A Base Pair	1	2	4
A Codon	3	6	64
A Very Small Exon	21	42	4,398,046,511,104
An Average-sized Exon	177	354	36,695,977,855,841,144,185,773,134,324,833,391,052,745,039,826,692,497,979,801,421,430,190,766,017,415,756,929,120,296,849,762,010,984,873,984
An amino acid	3	4.53533173	23
A peptide	21	31.7473221	3,604,925,080
A small protein	177	267.584572	474,284,397,516,047,136,454,946,754,595,585,670,566,993,857,190,463,750,305,618,264,096,412,179,005,177,856
An average-sized protein	900	1360.599519	38,130,067,632,913,195,680,540,855,924,713,218,334,555,827,810,891,346,224,714,900,841,022,966,020,733,765,309,677,910,287,104,525,930,432,932,335,795,796,433,741,497,242,984,493,322,190,762,509,473,564,649,287,795,721,696,702,111,328,756,678,429,193,638,872,484,003,904,933,483,070,928,464,075,009,756,616,165,623,303,269,541,719,711,831,010,297,856,302,166,965,703,562,205,204,040,620,567,537,538,686,102,464,149,458,965,648,816,710,282,587,065,807,713,538,033,582,367,131,474,737,076,341,923,980,442,211,594,455,688,196,088,747,481,127,381,328

redundancy did not exist, and the bits of information are therefore lower. As you can see from the table on the previous page, the probability of the RNA forming naturalistically to encode only *one* small protein is so miniscule that it is virtually zero! Of course, the calculations in this table do not at all take into account the odds of the DNA or RNA backbone forming, the odds of the base pairs forming, or the odds of the molecular machinery required to synthesize a protein forming!

And yet, 175 base pairs is only a *tiny* fraction of what is required to construct even the simplest free-living cell known to man, which has over *a million base pairs!* In fact, even the simplest cell contains the following forms of information:

- **Structural information** (such as in the 3D folding of proteins).
- **Operational information** (in the design of its complex systems).
- **Semantic information** (in the genome).

That causes us to suspect this information has a platonic origin, and as we will soon see, there are very good reasons to believe that hunch is correct.

Biochemist Harold Bernhardt of the University of Otago writes,

> "RNA is an extremely complex molecule, with four different nitrogen-containing heterocycles hanging off a backbone of alternating phosphate and D-ribose groups joined by 3',5' linkages."

The title of the article Bernhardt wrote that this quote is taken from is very telling:

> "The RNA World Hypothesis: the Worst Theory of
> the Early Evolution of Life (Except for All the Others)."[63]

All origin-of-life hypotheses face the same probabilistic challenges. But if a method of creating a self-replicator in the lab *is* ever devised and

---

[63] Harold Bernhard, "The RNA world hypothesis: The worst theory of the early evolution of life (except for all the others)." Biology Direct, 13 July 2012, 7:23. https://doi.org/10.1186/1745-6150-7-23 (Last accessed 3/22/2019)

experimentally demonstrated, would that mean life actually formed that way? No, not unless primitive conditions were just like that, and that's something we could not possibly know for certain. But it *would* mean that a hard-working team of intelligences can design a way to create a self-replicator, which would not be what they are hoping to demonstrate!

PROBABILITY OF FORMATION

Probability is obtained when the likelihood of the naturalistic formation of an orderly arrangement is greater than or equal to one. This occurs when the number of attempts at creating the information is equal to the denominator of the probability of getting it in only one attempt. An "attempt" is one complete try at making *all* of the selections required.

For instance, as we discussed in an earlier chapter, the probability of getting a one when rolling a dice is $\frac{1}{6}$, so I must roll the dice 6 times to obtain 100% theoretical probability. However, the probability of getting a one *twice in a row* is $\frac{1}{6} \cdot \frac{1}{6} = \frac{1}{36}$. So I must make 36 attempts at rolling a dice twice to theoretically get two ones in a row. Or I must roll a *pair* of dice 36 times.

In bits of information we can express it like this:

> *a* = chance **attempts** (number of chance attempts to make all of the selections required to create the information). In the example above, this is the number of times a single dice is rolled twice, or the number of times a pair of dice is rolled.

> *b* = Number of **bits.** In our example above, two snake eyes equals 5.169925 bits of information, because when we solve for *b* in the equation $\frac{1}{36} = (\frac{1}{2})^b$, the answer is 5.169925.

> *p* = **Probability** of formation. This is the when the number of attempts divided by 2^b is equal to or greater than 1. This is written as $a/2^b \geq 1$. In our example, $36/(2^{5.169925})$ equals 1, so we have a

100% theoretical probability of getting snake-eyes if we roll a pair of dice 36 times.

THE THRESHOLD OF IMPROBABILITY

This is when the odds of chance arrangement are so close to zero that it is likely the arrangement did not occur naturalistically.

The threshold of improbability is what separates high-order information created by intelligences from low-order information produced by random chance.

For instance, suppose your spouse has left a Scrabble® game box on the kitchen table and asked you to set it up before leaving the room. When you remove the old, loosely fitting box lid, inside the box you see Scrabble® pieces arranged in the following sequence:

I LOVE YOU

Without doing any math, you would quickly conclude that your spouse had arranged the pieces, because the threshold of improbability had been crossed. So your spouse will likely be rewarded with a hug and a kiss when he or she gets back.

Or, suppose that you are hiking in the woods and see three sticks broken and arranged to form a symmetrical arrow. Though the arrangement is simple, you will conclude that the sticks were likely arranged by an intelligence.

We can discern a statistical principle at work here. Let's call it *The Principle of Information Origin.* It is defined in the graph on the next page, and represented by the overlapping probability and chance formations curves just below it.

As this graph illustrates, once probability of formation goes below 100%, it very quickly crosses a threshold at which chance formation becomes highly unlikely. Once that threshold is passed (at 10 additional bits beyond $f = 1$), formation by an intelligence is very likely and grows exponentially more certain with each bit.

The Principle of Information Origin:

Since every bit halves the odds of the chance formation of information, once formation becomes improbable, with the addition of only eight more bits the probability of chance formation runs next to zero. At that point, origin by an intelligence is very likely and grows exponentially more certain with each additional bit. (Since this principle concerns the *origin* of information, it excludes information resulting from non-intelligent processes previously designed by an intelligence.)

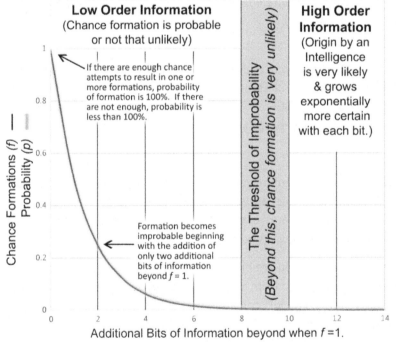

Low Order Information
(Chance formation is probable or not that unlikely)

If there are enough chance attempts to result in one or more formations, probability of formation is 100%. If there are not enough, probability is less than 100%.

Formation becomes improbable beginning with the addition of only two additional bits of information beyond $f = 1$.

The Threshold of Improbability
(Beyond this, chance formation is very unlikely)

High Order Information
(Origin by an Intelligence is very likely & grows exponentially more certain with each bit.)

Chance Formations (f) — Probability (p)

Additional Bits of Information beyond when $f = 1$.

Legend: —— $f(f) = a(1/2^b)$ **Chance Formations**
$f(p) = 1/2^b$ **Probability of Formation** decreasing from when $f = 1$ (indicated by 1 on the vertical axis) as each new bit is added.

How to Read this Graph

Why This Graph? This graph illustrates how once probability of formation becomes less than 100%, it quickly falls to almost zero as each new bit of information is added. The threshold where this begins (at 6-8 bits after the beginning of improbabilty) can serve as a useful tool to help us distinguish when intelligent design is likely.

Why Only Two Axes? Since the horizontal axis reflects *additional* bits of information beyond when $f=1$, the zero additional bits mark floats as the value of a changes, so the graph reflects a consistent pattern that holds true for all values of a. Because of this, three axes are not needed.

Information is defined here as simply orderly arrangement.

b = Number of *bits*. A *bit* is a correct selection that must be made between two equal alternatives in order to produce a specific orderly arrangement. Bits are a useful way of quantifying the selections required to produce an orderly arrangement.

a = The number of chance *attempts* made towards creating an orderly arrangement. Since the probability of choosing a correct bit by chance in one selection is 1/2, the probability of selecting 7 correct bits by chance in a single attempt is $(1/2)^7$. That equals 1/128, so 128 attempts at 7 chance selections must be made to acheive 100% theoretical probability. This means that one attempt equals a single go at making *all* of the selections needed to create the information. The number of selections needed is equal to the number of bits.

Chance Formations (f) are determined by multiplying the number of chance attempts *(a)* made towards forming the arrangement by the probability of achieving the arrangement in a *single* attempt at the number of selections required. Since a bit reflects the probability of a single chance selection, This means the chance formations represented by f equal $a(1/2^b)$, or $f = a/(2^b)$.

Probability of Formation (p) falls below 100% if there have not been enough attempts to attain the first formation.

Improbability of Formation begins when the probability of a single formation is less than .5. [This is when $a/(2^b) < .5$] Each bit beyond that reduces the odds of formation by half, which is why the curve goes to almost zero so quickly.

The Threshold of Improbability is the range beyond which the probability of a single chance formation runs next to zero (6 to 8 bits of information beyond the beginning of improbability.) Beyond this threshold, formation by an intelligence is very likely and grows exponentially more certain with each additional bit. In this case the zero line that the probability curve draws incrementally nearer to, but never touches, is known as its *asymptote*.

Just like the threshold to your home is a board rather than a line, the threshold of improbability is range of values rather than a line because some subjective judgment is used, but it is not a very wide range because the odds get close to zero very quickly with each additional bit of information, beginning at 6 bits after improbability sets in.

As you can see in the graph, at 8 additional bits from f=1, the probability curve is running close to zero, and at 10 bits the probability curve runs so closely to zero that it is virtually indistinguishable from it. This is the domain of high-order information. Once the probability of chance orderly arrangement goes beyond that threshold, formation by an intelligence is likely, and when it goes far beyond it, you can be highly certain (though not beyond a *very* tiny sliver of doubt) that the arrangement was placed in order by an intelligence.

In this case, the zero line is called an *asymptote* because the distance between the curve and the line tends to zero as both head toward infinity.

The ability to subconsciously apply the Principle of Information Origin appears to be instinctively built into humans, or at least operative at an early age, because usually, we can quickly recognize the work of an intelligence—without consciously performing any math calculations! *It is why the majority of the people in the world agree that there is a Creator, though they do not all agree on exactly who the Creator is.*

Let's summarize our argument:

THE INFORMATION ORIGIN ARGUMENT

- Once information content becomes improbable, then when only eight additional bits of information are added, the probability of chance formation becomes almost zero. With each added bit, intelligent origin becomes exponentially more certain.

- The fundamental components of our universe and even the simplest forms of life have so much functional order that they contain far more than eight bits of information beyond improbability.

∴ Therefore, it is almost certain that life and our universe were created by an intelligence.

Many atheists claim that life merely has the *appearance* of design, so they say that you should not trust your gut instincts that life has been designed. They also claim that there is no evidence that we are intelligently designed, and that there is no experiment to verify the existence of an intelligent designer. The principle of information origin, however, can easily be verified mathematically and by repeatable experiment. *It clearly demonstrates that they are wrong on all three counts.*

The Principle of Information Origin is *very* strong evidence that life and our universe were created by an intelligence, and it is why the apostle Paul wrote,

> For since the creation of the world God's invisible qualities--his eternal power and divine nature--have been clearly seen, being understood from what has been made, so that people are without excuse. (Romans 1:10)

WHAT ABOUT PRIONS?

But what about infectious prion proteins? Could they be a low-information precursor to life, as some researchers have suggested? They replicate, can survive in hostile environments outside of the cell, and can even evolve![64]

---

[64] Omar Lupi, Paula Dadalti, Eduardo Cruz, Paul R. Sanberg. The Cryopraxis' Task Force for Prion Research, *"Are prions related to the emergence of early life?"* Medical Hypotheses (2006) 67, pp. 1027–1033.

Prion genes are *thousands* of base pairs in length,[65] so they are definitely not a *low-information* precursor to life! As we can easily tell from the table above, that makes their naturalistic formation *extremely* unlikely.

Not only that, but infectious prions cannot self-replicate like a cell does. They are misfolded proteins that replicate by causing *pre-existing* healthy prion proteins to misfold so that they also become infectious prions. As *Science Daily* explains,

> "Mammalian cells normally produce cellular prion protein or PrP^c. During infection, abnormal or misfolded protein -- known as PrP^{sc}-- converts the normal host prion protein into its toxic form by changing its conformation or shape. The end-stage consists of large sheets (polymers) of these misfolded proteins, which causes massive tissue and cell damage."[66]

This means that prions depend on *pre-existing* cellular components, because RNA and other cellular machinery is needed to synthesize a *healthy* prion protein in the first place! It also means that there are some tough questions for proponents of the prion hypothesis to solve:

- How could a *healthy* prion protein containing so much high-order information have formed in the prebiotic environment in the first place?
- How could there be enough of these extremely improbable, high-order healthy prion proteins around for the infectious prions to spread and evolve, since healthy prions cannot self-replicate? Talk about a chicken and egg problem!
- It's apparent that in order for abiogenesis to have happened, an *extremely* simple form of self-replicator (much simpler than

---

[65] Inyoul Y. Lee, David Westaway, Arian F.A. Smit, Kai Wang, et al. *"Complete Genomic Sequence and Analysis of the Prion Protein Gene Region from Three Mammalian Species,"* Genome Research, 1998, volume 8, pp. 1022-1037.

[66] The Scripps Research Institute. "Prions mutate and adapt to host environment." ScienceDaily. ScienceDaily, 18 December 2010. https://www.sciencedaily.com/releases/2010/12/101217083232.htm (Last accessed 03/12/2019)

prions) must have formed first, and then evolved into a more complex form of life. And if there were already self-replicating proteins around, why would we need prions?

- Lastly, how could a prion have evolved into DNA-based life?

All of these things indicate that prion proteins are unlikely candidates for the first ancestor of life.

Can a molecule complex enough to **self-replicate** and survive in the wild, but simple enough to form by natural processes exist? That is what we will investigate in the next chapter.

APPLYING INFORMATION THEORY TO THE ORIGIN OF OUR UNIVERSE

But before we go on, in light of what we have just discussed about information, we should take just a minute to consider the arrangement of the subatomic components of our universe, such as photons, electrons, neutrons, and protons. They have organized structure, functional order, finely tuned parameters, are able to exist in multiple states, exchange state information with each other and react to it (which is a form of low-level computation), and in the case of light, even convey information across long distances! Each time a photon of light strikes the retina of one of your eyes, information is being communicated.

Why is it that atoms form into remarkable (and sometimes very beautiful) lower-order information patterns and shapes such as snow-flake crystals, and combine to form molecules with unique properties? It is because of the operational and structural information that was placed in them to begin with!

How likely is it that this kind of functionality, which is a form of high-order information, could be generated by chaotic, low-entropy quantum processes?

Physicists, information scientists, mathematicians and cosmologists tell us that the likelihood of a low-entropy universe like ours arising by chance is so low, that it is *next to nothing* unless there is a vast or infinite multiverse.

As Cosmologist Bernard Carr said, "If you don't want God, you'd better have a multiverse!"[67]

But a vast or infinite multiverse is an empirically unverifiable idea. So, as we will see in the following chapters, atheists are now being forced to retreat into metaphysics and faith in things that cannot be scientifically verified to defend naturalism.

Besides, even if there were a multiverse, you can still safely conclude that your spouse arranged those letters in the Scrabble® box. Maybe, if a lot of other universes exist, in one of them that would happen by chance. But that makes it no more likely it will happen in *your* universe, and especially in *your* home!

This is *The Principle of Insufficient Local Tries:*

The Principle of Insufficient Local Tries

Even though 1024 attempts at ten coin flips makes it probable you will get ten heads in a row, that makes it no more probable that you will get it in only one attempt!

Both of these principles—the principle of information origin and the principle of insufficient local tries—point to an intelligence as the source of the orderly arrangement of our universe and life rather than chance. As we are about to see in the next chapter, the bits required

---

[67] Tim Folger, "Science's Alternative to an Intelligent Creator: the Multiverse Theory." Discover Magazine, December 2008. http://discovermagazine.com/2008/dec/10-sciences-alternative-to-an-intelligent-creator (Last accessed 3/11/2019)

to create even the simplest conceivable evolvable self-replicator makes the chance formation of one highly improbable.

"Looking for the origin of life in physics and chemistry is like looking for the origin of literature in the chemistry of ink"

Cynthia Yockey[67]

---

[68] Cynthia Yockey, "Information theory, evolution and the origin of life." Blog post. Feb 20, 2009. http://www.hubertpyockey.com/hpy-blog/2009/02/20/hello-world/#comments (Last accessed 03/11/2013) Cynthia Yockey is the daughter of the late information scientist Hupert Yockey.

6 WHAT IS THE PROBABILITY OF AN EVOLVABLE SELF-REPLICATOR FORMING?

"Many investigators feel uneasy stating in public that the origin of life is a mystery, even though behind closed doors they admit they are baffled." — Paul Davies

MARCEL GOLAY'S ESTIMATE OF THE SIMPLEST POSSIBLE SELF-REPLICATOR

 ith all of the things discussed in the last few chapters in mind, let's read Marcel Golay's estimate of the minimum amount of information that a self-replicator must have:

"Suppose we wanted to build a machine capable of reaching into bins for all its parts, and capable of assembling from these parts a second machine just like itself. What is the minimum amount of structure or information that should be built into the first machine? The answer comes out to be of the order of 1,500 bits - 1,500 choices between [two different] alternatives which the machine should be able to decide. This answer is very suggestive, because 1,500 bits happens to be also of the order of magnitude of the amount of structure contained in the simplest large protein molecule which, immersed in a bath of nutrients, can induce the assembly of those nutrients into another large protein molecule like itself, and then separate itself from it."[69]

Golay never shared how he arrived at this figure, however, or identified what specific protein he was referring to. Clearly, in order to come up with an accurate figure, he would have needed to develop or describe an actual replicator design, which would have been a daunting and complex task. And so this figure must have been an

---

[69] Marcel Golay, *Reflections of a Communications Engineer*, Analytical Chemistry, Volume 33, June 1, 1961, p. 23. Golay was an information theorist, physicist, and mathematician.

estimate. When I wrote to a friend with a PhD in biology to ask him what protein Golay might have been referring to, he skeptically responded,

> "I have no idea what protein he is talking about, and the real proteins that do this type of work are a whole lot more complicated than that and need things like ATP (produced by an entire set of complex proteins arranged like a motor) to function."

Note that the anonymous self-replicating protein Golay referred to came from within a cell, not from the wild. And so Golay clearly was not talking about an evolvable self replicator capable of surviving in the wild, but something much simpler. Given the complexity of Von Neumann machines, and the complexity of actual self-replicating proteins that have the ability to harness energy, it looks as if real evolvable self-replicating molecular machines require considerably more complexity than this. Furthermore, as mentioned in the preceding chapter, prions, which have recently been suggested as candidates for early self-replicators, are much more complex than this. *And so in light of all of new information we now have, Golay's figure is almost certainly an underestimate.*

When we think of the idea of a molecular self-replicator simpler than life evolving into complex DNA based life, a question naturally arises. Where *are* all of the simple self-replicators? No free-living self-replicators simpler than life exist in the wild on the earth. We would expect that myriads of different kinds of them would have evolved, and adapted to environmental niches all over the planet. Because of this, it seems that they ought to be found everywhere.

But there are not any that we have found yet, and there are none that have been preserved in ancient strata that have been identified. This causes us to view the hypothesis of biopoesis with skepticism from the start, but let's not let that discourage us so much that we fail to mathematically investigate the probability of it having happened. Perhaps none these self-replicators lent themselves to self-preservation. And perhaps not a single one of them was able to adapt to survive under the current environmental conditions on the earth. Admittedly this seems unlikely, and it causes us to strongly suspect that no free-living self-replicator simpler than life could exist on the earth.

But let's extend the benefit of the doubt to biopoesis in general, and assume that an evolvable self replicator as simple as Golay envisioned *can* exist. It is highly doubtful, however, that an evolvable self-replicator any simpler than that which is able to survive in the wild could exist. Indeed, this was the *minimum* amount of information that Golay thought possible for a *non-evolvable* self-replicator that lived *inside* the cell.

Furthermore, the simplest evolvable self-replicating 2D cellular automaton created so far that this author is aware of is called *Evoloop.*[70] It consists of about 472 bits of information and is a kinematic simulation, not a kinetic one (a kinetic one takes the causes of motion, and therefore the energy needed to perform work into account). We can therefore expect true evolvable kinetic 3D self-replicators in our universe to be considerably more complex, because our universe contains staggeringly more possible molecular states to choose from than the mere nine states possible in the simple universe of the Evoloop replicator, and a true replicator must be kinematic.

Again, all of these things indicate that a true evolvable self-replicator in our universe needs to be considerably more complex, but let's give biopoesis the benefit of the doubt, and assume it's possible for an evolvable self-replicator with an information content of only 1500 bits to exist in our universe. In order for it to form, the equivalent of 1500 correct chemical events would have to occur, each with a probability of ½. As you now know, we can write out the odds of this as $(½)^{1500}$. That is the same as the odds of flipping a coin 1500 times, and getting heads each time.

For brevity's sake, let's call this molecular machine a *SCESR* – for Simplest Conceivable Evolvable Self-Replicator.

---

[70] C.G. Langton "Self-reproduction in cellular automata." Physica D 10: 135–144. (1984). doi:10.1016/0167-2789(84)90256-2.

What are the odds of a SCESR (simplest conceivable evolvable self-replicator) forming in our universe?

I first read a probability calculation which utilized Golay's estimate in the late Henry Morris' book, *The Scientific Case for Creation.* [71] It made a striking impression on me as a young man. Morris imagined the entire known universe to be packed full of interacting particles the size of electrons. Despite this generous over-estimate of the number of chemical events that could have taken place , the odds of any one *particular* SCESR forming came out incredibly low, $1/10^{280}$. Since for the reasons we discussed in the previous chapter, Golay's figure is almost certainly an *underestimate* of the complexity required, in order to give biopoesis the benefit of the doubt I will also utilize Golay's figure, but will take into account the possibility of other replicator designs with the same degree of information and higher complexity, current indications of the size of the universe and a few other different assumptions that for the sake of argument, are unrealistically in favor of biopoesis.

Using Golay's figure, since the bit is useful for determining the odds of information correctly assembling by chance, the odds of any given sequence of chemical events producing one *particular* working "design" of a SCESR would be $\frac{1}{2}^{1500}$, which equals $1/(3.51 \times 10^{451})$, but for simplicity's sake we will bring it down to $^{1}/_{10}{}^{450}$.

However, *more than one SCESR design may be possible*, and this would increase the odds of a SCESR forming. With that in mind, we can say that...

> ... *T* equals the *Total* number of SCESR designs that would work.
> ... *C* equals the number of those designs that could not form, or could not survive due to chemical and environmental *Constraints.*
> ... *T - C = P*, the number of *Possible* SCESR designs which could potentially form and survive in our universe.

---

[71] Henry Morris, *The Scientific Case for Creation*, Creation-Life Publishers, San Diego, 1977.

The odds of any given sequence of chemical events forming *any* possible SCESR design that could survive in our universe would therefore be $P/10^{450}$. (We will take more complex designs into account later.)

If I flip a coin ten times, only a small fraction of the possible flips will have an orderly pattern, such as HHHHHHHHHH, HTHTHTHTHT, HTHTTHTTTH, etc. Of course, we need not only an orderly or meaningful pattern, but a *self-replicating, evolvable* pattern for a SCESR to form. That would only be a very tiny subset of the meaningful or orderly patterns. And so, although we cannot know exactly what the value of *P* is, we do know that it is an *extremely* tiny fraction of the 10^{450} possible chemical arrangements.

Despite that, let's be generous and assume that *P* equals 10^{37}, which is more than one trillion times the number of stars in the known universe. I believe that this is a very liberal number to assign to *P*, because this number is probably much higher than the number of meaningful designs, and considerably higher than the number of self-replicating designs, that could be produced with such a low information content, for the following reasons:

- Despite the incredible chemical variety found on earth, no replicator simpler than life that does not depend upon life to survive, has *ever* been found in nature.
- Because all life on earth is fundamentally similar, only *one* replicator design is thought to have led to life on earth. If other survivable designs were just as likely to form under those conditions, we would expect to see fundamentally different forms of life on earth exhibiting dissimilar means of replication. But we do not. All of them utilize DNA to replicate. Since the evidence indicates that if biopoesis occurred, only one design survived and evolved into life on earth, assigning an average of one trillion different possible survivable SCESR designs for every star system seems overly generous.
- No one has ever been able to experimentally induce the spontaneous formation of an evolvable molecular self-replicator capable of surviving in the wild, or to determine how one might have formed in an experimentally verifiable way.

- A self-replicating molecule like the protein molecule Golay mentioned would have all of the parts it needs to replicate right beside it, inside the cell. But could something that simple survive in the harsh wild, outside of the nurturing environment of a living cell? We do not know. Most likely, there are *no* possible self-replicating designs that simple which could survive in the wild!
- No human has been able to *intelligently* design and build a molecular self- replicator simpler than life which can survive in the wild to demonstrate that one can exist. If we cannot *intelligently* design one yet, how likely is it that one would form by *unconscious* natural processes?
- Most of the stars in the universe are outside of their own galaxy's habitable zone (GHZ), making them inhospitable to life.
- Most planets are outside of their solar system's circumstellar habitable zone (CHZ), which is the right distance from their sun to sustain life.
- Most planets within the hospitable zones do not have the right composition of elements to nurture life.
- Many planets are exposed to sterilizing gamma ray bursts.
- Many planets are exposed to supernovae.
- Planets without a shielding magnetosphere such as the Earth's will also be exposed to sterilizing radiation from the solar winds. The Earth's magnetosphere is formed by its unique core of circulating molten iron and nickel.

Assigning this very generous value to *P*, the odds of *any* given sequence of chemical events in our universe producing *any* SCESR design would therefore be $10^{37}/10^{450} = 1/10^{413}$.

What is the likelihood of this having happened somewhere in the universe?

The latest estimate of the number of stars in the *observable* universe is 70 sextillion stars. CNN reported that Dr. Simon Driver, when asked "if he believed the huge scale of the universe meant there was intelligent life out there somewhere," replied: 'Seventy thousand million million million is a big number ... it's inevitable." [72]

The number Dr. Driver mentioned is such a large number of stars (70 followed by 21 zeroes, which we can write in shorthand as $70 \cdot 10^{21}$) that this conclusion *sounds* quite convincing, doesn't it? But let's do the math to see whether or not he is right.

If you still remember how to multiply fractions and exponents from high school math, then you should be able to follow what's next.

Our universe has been measured to be flat within an error range of 0.2 percent.[73] A flat universe is *Euclidean*, meaning that two parallel lines are so perfectly straight within it, that they will never merge or diverge. A recent application of Bayesian model averaging to the size of the universe has suggested that if we live in a finite flat universe, it is at least 251 Hubble volumes in size.[74]

So let's liberally increase the estimate of stars in the observable universe to an amount much, much higher than that, to more than *one quadrillion times* what can be observed: 10^{38} stars. That is a *vastly* larger universe than what we are able to observe or to determine exists.

Of course, as we mentioned in the preceding chapter, Golay's machine must have all of the parts it needs to make a copy of itself right beside

---

[72] CNN.com/Science & Space, " Star survey reaches 70 sextillion." Wednesday, July 23, 2003 Posted: 12:29 AM EDT (0429 GMT). http://www.cnn.com/2003/TECH/space/07/22/stars.survey/ (Last accessed 03/11/2019)

[73] N. Aghanim (Orsay, IAS) et al., "Planck 2018 results. VI. Cosmological parameters, Planck Collaboration" . Jul 17, 2018. 71 pp. e-Print: arXiv:1807.06209 [astro-ph.CO] | PDF. They write, "The joint results suggests our Universe is spatially flat to a 1 sigma accuracy of 0.2 %." p. 40.

[74] Mihran Vardanyan, Roberto Trotta, and Joseph Silk. "Applications of Bayesian model averaging to the curvature and size of the Universe." Monthly Notices of the Royal Astronomical Society: Letters, Volume 413, Issue 1, 1 May 2011, P.s L91–L95, https://doi.org/10.1111/j.1745-3933.2011.01040.x (Last accessed 3/11/2019)

it, without pre-existing life to provide those parts. Again we ask, how often does that happen in nature? Let's assume it happens *vastly more often than it actually does*, and suppose ...

... *every* star has *75 earth-sized planets* orbiting it.

... *and* these 75 planets are composed of nothing but a prebiotic soup containing all of the *unassembled* parts needed for all possible SCESR designs to form. (Note that we are presupposing an environment completely hospitable to the *formation* of a SCESR design. But this SCESR *must be of a design that could survive in the actual inhospitable wild* to be a viable candidate that could have led to life.)

We will round the total number of atoms contained in these groups of 75 planets up to 10^{52}, which is a little more than 75 times the approximately $1.33*10^{50}$ atoms on earth.[75]

Enzymes speed up chemical reactions. Carbonic anhydrase is one of the fastest, if not the fastest, of the enzymes known to man. A single molecule is able to catalyze up to 10^6 chemical reactions per second. Let's bump that figure up tremendously and suppose that each of the atoms on these planets takes part in 10^{20} chemical reactions per second.[76]

Multiply that by 10^{21} seconds of cosmic history (an amount higher than 1000 times the current estimated age of the universe, which is 13.8 billion years or $4.35 \cdot 10^{17}$ seconds[77]), and you get $10^{38} \cdot 10^{52} \cdot 10^{20} \cdot 10^{21}$

---

[75] Drew Weisenberger, "How many atoms are there in the world?" Jefferson Lab, http://education.jlab.org/qa/mathatom_05.html (Last accessed 03/11/2019)

[76] Berg JM, Tymoczko JL, Stryer L. Berg JM, Tymoczko JL, Stryer L. *Biochemistry. 5th edition.* New York: W H Freeman; 2002. Section 8.1. They write, "In fact, carbonic anhydrase is one of the fastest enzymes known. Each enzyme molecule can hydrate 10^6 molecules of CO_2 *per second.* This catalyzed reaction is 10^7 times as fast as the uncatalyzed one."

[77] Dr. Edward J. Wollack, "How Old Is The Universe?" WMAP's Universe, wmap.gsfc.nasa.gov., 12-21-2012. http://wmap.gsfc.nasa.gov/universe/uni_age.html (Last accessed 03/11/2018)

= 10^{131} possible chemical reactions that could have been tried out on these planets since the universe began. We must divide this by the number of selections required (1500) to get the number of attempts to form the SCESR that could have taken place. That equals $6.7 \cdot 10^{127}$ attempts, which we will generously "round" up to 10^{128}.

Given these *extremely* generous assumptions, the odds of the simplest conceivable self-replicating molecular system arising would therefore be ($6.7 \cdot 10^{128}/10^{414} = {}^1/_{10}{}^{286}$.

To summarize:

	Odds of the Formation of a 1500-Bit Molecular Replicator (SCESR – Simplest Conceivable Evolvable Self-Replicator)
	10^{38} stars in a universe more and one quadrillion times the Hubble volume,
x	10^{52} atoms in 75 earth-sized planets per star which are all giant nutrient baths,
x	10^{20} chemical reactions per second (higher than the rate induced by the fastest catalyst known to man),
x	10^{21} seconds (greater than 1000 times the age of the universe),
=	10^{131} chemical reactions that would have occurred on these planets.
/	1500, the number of selections required to produce a 1500 bit SCESR,
=	6.7×10^{127} attempts at formation in the observable universe since it began, which we will generously "round" up to 10^{128}.
x	$1/10^{413}$, the probability of one random attempt (sequence of chemical events) producing a SCESR,
=	$1/10^{285}$, the probability of all chemical events on planets since the universe began producing *any* viable SCESR design with an information content of only 1500 bits.

That's only one chance in

1,000,000,000,000,000,000,000,000,000,000,000,000,000,000,000,00
0,000,000,000,000,000,000,000,000,000,000,000,000,000,000,000,00
0,000,000,000,000,000,000,000,000,000,000,000,000,000,000,000,00
0,000,000,000,000,000,000,000,000,000,000,000,000,000,000,000,00
0,000,000,000,000,000,000,000,000,000,000,000,000,000,000,000,00
0,000,000,000,000,000,000,000,000,000,000,000,000,000,000,000,000!

Even if our universe were a *quadrillion* times larger than can be observed, the odds of a simple self-replicator forming by chance in it are so low that they are next to impossible.

ANSWERING OBJECTIONS

1st Objection: "More Complex Replicator Designs Could Exist."

This is true, but not a valid objection, because *each additional bit of information halves the odds of chance formation.* Because of this, the sum of the chance of *all* replicating designs of greater complexity forming will still result in odds that are less than $1/10^{284}$.

This can be represented by the following:

$$[1/(10^{285}) + \frac{1}{2}(10^{285}) + \frac{1}{4}(10^{285}) + \frac{1}{8}(10^{285})...] < 1/10^{284}$$

The first addend represents the odds of all designs with 1500 bits of information forming, the second with 1501 bits, the third 1502 bits. The sum will forever approach $1/10^{284}$, but never reach it. (This is based upon the reasonable assumption that the ratio of survivable replicator designs to all other possible arrangements remains the same.)

2nd Objection: "You Are Not Taking Other Replicator Designs Into Account."

That objection could only be made by someone who either has not completely read, or does not understand what I have written above. These calculations *do* take multiple replicator designs into account. They are represented by the letter *P,* which is intentionally a *gross over-estimate* of the possible number of replicator designs.

3rd Objection: "This is the probability of only a single attempt at a replicator forming, whereas random chemical events are going on all over the universe."

That is simply not the case. In the table on page 94, the third row from the bottom represents all of the attempts that could have taken place since the universe began.

4th Objection: "Simpler Replicators Could Exist."

Again, this objection could only be made by someone who either has not read or does not understand the full argument. In Chapter Five and at the beginning of this chapter I discuss the many reasons why 1500 bits (the amount used for the calculations) is much smaller than a real-life replicator would need to be.

5th Objection: "Any 1500-Bit Arrangement Is Just As Unlikely."

A very common objection often raised by naturalists to improbability calculations like this is that in a poker game, one hand of five cards is as likely as any other, since the probability of any hand is $(1/52)^5$. However, in a card game, the number of possible hands with discernible patterns such as a straight flush is much lower than those without. Likewise, the number of self-reproducing molecular patterns is only a tiny fraction of those that cannot reproduce.

"But we are the ones who discern those patterns and assign value to them," the naturalist further argues. However, *the hand of cards must already have some preexisting mathematical or symbolic relationship for us to discern*. Plus, in this illustration, a discernible card pattern is analogous to a functioning self-replicator, which requires no human discernment. So this counter-argument applies only to the illustration, not to the reality that the illustration represents.

Suppose you saw on my kitchen table a line of Scrabble® pieces spelling the sentence,

"WHERE DOES INFORMATION COME FROM"

Then I told you that something amazing had happened. I had pulled each of those Scrabble® pieces from the dark red velvet bag that came with my deluxe game set one at a time, and remarkably, that sentence came out on the first try! Would you believe my story? Why not? Isn't this combination of 28 Scrabble® pieces as probable as any other combination?

Knowing that highly ordered arrangements like that occur much less frequently than disordered ones do (see chapter 6), you would probably conclude that I was lying to you, and that I had intentionally arranged those Scrabble® pieces to form that sentence myself!

Therefore, a clear relationship exists between the *order* of an arrangement and the likelihood of that arrangement happening by chance. Ordered arrangements, especially highly-ordered arrangements, are much less likely to happen by chance.

Likewise, the set of molecular arrangements that would create an evolvable self-replicator is much, much smaller than the set of arrangements that can't self-replicate and evolve. (To give naturalism the benefit of the doubt, this set of evolvable self-replicators was *grossly* overestimated and represented in the probability calculation above by the value assigned to the letter *P.*)

As this example illustrates so well, isn't the molecular arrangement of life, which is *magnitudes* of complexity more highly ordered than a mere 28 Scrabble® pieces, better explained by it having been assembled by an intelligence than it having happened by chance?

6th Objection: "Some hypothetical environmental conditions would be more conducive than others to the formation of a self replicator."

That's true. However, the probability calculation above is based on bits of information, and therefore takes environmental conditions into account as well. In what way?

Environmental conditions contain information, too. Those most conducive to the formation of a SCESR will contain more of the information required. For instance, when two humans mate, conditions are very favorable for the formation of a new human organism. But this is only because the egg and sperm cells each contain half of the information needed to assemble the genome of that organism! In the same way, synthetic replicators which have been (partly) designed by humans in the lab have always functioned in artificial or natural environments which already contain a wealth of preassembled information, and/or contain partially preassembled parts!

Our calculation is based on an evolvable self-replicator of 1500 bits. If the environment contains one molecule containing 500 bits of information, and another containing 1000, and these join together to form a self-replicator of 1500 bits, the complete odds of chance formation will be $(^1/_2)^{500} \times (^1/_2)^{1000} = (^1/_2)^{1500}$.

So the probability calculation above takes environmental conditions into account.

7th Objection: "Our Universe Could Be Finite, but Incredibly Vast."

A googol is an *incredibly* huge number, 1.0×10^{100}. But our universe must have many times more stars to make the odds favorable for *one single self-replicator* to form by chance. Even given all of the *unreasonably generous* assumptions in this chapter, our universe would need to contain more than a *quadrillion centillion* stars (10^{318}) for it to be likely for a single replicator of only 1500 bits to form by chance. A *true* evolvable replicator would likely need to be much more complex than that. Had we used more realistic assumptions, our universe would have to be much, much larger than even *this* unimaginable number!

The problem with relying upon our universe being *that* vast as an explanation for life is that it is an *unobservable, untestable* hypothesis. In short, just like a religious tenet, it requires *faith* to believe in! For all we know, our universe might be only *slightly* larger than we can observe. Besides, even if the universe *is* that vast, that makes it no more likely that life will form in *our* observable universe.

8th Objection: "You are assuming abiogenesis is a random process. Atoms and molecules follow natural and chemical laws. That is not random."

This argument commits what is known as *the fallacy of equivocation*. This is when a word is used In multiple senses in an argument, leading to a false conclusion. When most people say "random" or 'by chance' they mean "without intelligent agency," not "without natural law." If an explosion happens in a Scrabble factory, all of the Scrabble pieces will follow natural laws as they fall to the ground. But that does not make it likely that they will form the words of a mystery novel when they fall. There are no known natural laws that cause molecules to self-assemble into the correct order to form an evolvable self-replicator where there is no pre-existing life containing instructional information to guide the formation process.

9th Objection: "What if the universe is infinite?"

The next chapter addresses this question.

7 WHY WE CANNOT KNOW THAT THE UNIVERSE IS INFINITE

"Two things are infinite: the universe and human stupidity; and I'm not sure about the universe." — Albert Einstein

"I'm so tired... I was up all night trying to round off infinity." — Steven Wright"

Some infinities are bigger than other infinities." — John Green, *The Fault in Our Stars*

hat if the entire universe (including the unobservable part of it) were infinite? Then wouldn't life be bound to arise naturalistically, trouncing even the miniscule odds given in the previous chapter? As was stated in the previous chapter, even if the universe *were* that vast, that would make it no more probable that life would form in *our* observable universe.

"But it would make it more likely that life would form somewhere, and perhaps our corner of the universe *is* that somewhere," an atheist might respond. So let's consider this question further.

If the universe were infinite, with matter evenly textured throughout, then it would also be a *multiverse* containing many observable universes (Hubble volumes). If we lined them up edge to edge, each of these would be an observable universe to someone at the center of it. However, that observer could only see the galaxies whose light has had time to reach him. Since we cannot see outside of our observable universe, we cannot observe these other hypothetical Hubble volume universes to confirm whether or not they exist.

But there are even more reasons why we cannot know that the universe is infinite. These have to do with the very nature of the concept of infinities. To understand why, let's delve into the fascinating subject of infinities just a little.

Georg Cantor invented the theory of transfinite numbers as well as set theory. He preferred to call infinite numbers *transfinite numbers*.[78] He classified the transfinite numbers into two types: *countable* and *uncountable*. (Many say it makes more sense to think of them as *listable* and *unlistable*.)

THE COUNTABLE INFINITIES

Let's take a few minutes to consider what are called the *countable* infinities. These are also called *aleph_0, aleph-naught, or aleph-null* infinities, and are represented by the symbol $\aleph_0$. These can be listed on a one-to-one correspondence with the set of natural numbers, which is {1,2,3...}. If our universe were infinite, and it contained an infinite number of stars, the set of all of those stars could hypothetically be listed side by side with the set of natural numbers:

Countable (Aleph-Null) Infinities	
Set of Natural Numbers	{1, 2, 3...}
An Infinite Set of Stars	{1st Star, 2nd Star, 3rd star...}
A *countable infinity,* such as a set of infinite stars, can be listed in a one-to-one correspondence with the set of natural numbers. Because of this, both sets have the same cardinality, or number of elements.	

This infinite set of stars would therefore be a countable, or aleph-null infinity. Do true physical infinities such as an infinite number of stars actually exist, or like the set of natural numbers, do we merely conceive of them by making up rules (algorithms) for how to keep counting?

For instance, imagine a man setting out on an infinite nature hike. To conceive of this, in our mind we think something like, "Every time he

---

[78] Jose' Ferreiros, "'What Fermented in Me for Years:' Cantor's Discovery of Transfinite Numbers." Historia Mathematica 22 (1995), 33-42

takes a step, there is always one more step he can take." By doing this, we have made up a rule about how to keep counting the length of his journey. There will never be an *actual* time in which he has taken an infinite number of steps.

"Not true! Someone might object. "After an infinity of time, he will have walked an infinite number of steps!"

But we can reply to him, "How can there ever be a time "after" an infinity of steps? There is always one more step that can be taken in this journey of infinite steps!"

In short, when we symbolically represent an infinite set, we are actually placing an *algorithm* in brackets, such as {1,2,3...}. This algorithm is not an *actual* number, but rather a concept. Furthermore, we cannot ever translate that symbolic infinite set into a set of written numbers, because once we start listing the numbers, we will never arrive at a place where we can put our ending bracket "}"!

And so how can we ever be certain that the abstract concepts of an infinite number of stars or universes truly corresponds to reality? *That is a matter of faith.* Since we are finite creatures constrained by finite time and space, it is not possible for us to truly observe or list an entire infinite set. Only a divine being with an infinite nature that transcends smaller infinities could do that, and that is exactly what Cantor thought God could do.

So *does* our universe contain an infinite number of stars? That, Cantor probably would have said, is something only God knows!

THE UNCOUNTABLE INFINITIES

Did you know that some infinities are bigger than others? Next let's consider what are called the *uncountable infinities*. These are designated by the symbols c, $2^{\aleph_0}$, or $\beth_1$ (beth-one). The set of real numbers is an example of this. The real numbers can be associated with all of the points on a continuous line. Since for every two points, you can always think of another point in-between them, the quantity of real numbers cannot be counted. This kind of an infinity is called a *continuum*, and since its elements cannot be listed, it has *infinitely higher cardinality* than an aleph-null infinity.

In light of this, we can now make an important observation. Some argue that not only would life be bound to form if our universe were infinite, but that it would form in an identical way an infinite number of times. However, in their paper entitled, *About the Infinite Repetition of Histories in Space,* Francisco José Soler Gil and Manuel Alfonseca point out that the number of worlds in an infinite universe is a countable, aleph-null infinity. But the number of possible history lines is much greater, an uncountable infinity. Because the uncountable infinity is infinitely larger than the countable one, the odds of a history line repeating itself would be zero.[79] This is because any number divided by an infinitely larger value equals zero.

SOME PECULIAR CHARACTERISTICS OF INFINITIES

Countable Infinite Sets With the Same Cardinality (Number of Elements)				
Cubic Meters of Empty Space	{	Ist cubic meter of empty space,	2nd cubic meter of empty space,	3rd cubic meter of empty space, ...}
Cubic Meters of Atoms	{	Ist cubic meter of atoms,	2nd cubic meter of atoms,	3rd cubic meter of atoms, ...}
Natural Numbers	{	1,	2,	3, ...}

---

[79] Francisco José Soler Gil and Manuel Alfonseca, "About the Infinite Repetition of Histories in Space." *Theoria: An International Journal for Theory, History and Foundations of Science.* Vol. 29, No. 3 (81) (September 2014), pp. 361-373. http://arxiv.org/ftp/arxiv/papers/1301/1301.5295.pdf (Last accessed 3/12/2019)

Next let's look at some unusual aspects of infinities. Let's suppose that the universe is infinite and it contains infinite galaxies textured evenly throughout. Common sense tells us that the volume of empty space *should* be larger than the volume occupied by the atoms in these galaxies. However, as the table on the previous page shows, both sets have the same cardinality, or number of elements, because they can both be listed in one to one correspondence with the set of natural numbers!

Next, please take a minute to read my retelling of *Hilbert's Grand Hotel* on the next page. As Hilbert's Hotel illustrates, mathematicians consider it possible to add to an infinite set. But unless you add a higher cardinality infinity to it, adding to it does not increase the number of elements it contains. Infinity plus one equals infinity, they believe. Since that's the case, they consider infinity minus one to equal infinity, too. This inspired the humorous little song,

> "Aleph-null bottles of beer on the wall, aleph-null bottles of beer, take one down, pass it around, aleph-null bottles of beer on the wall!"

(As a friend of mine remarked, "It had better be good beer!")

However, if we add two infinite sets that are just alike to each other we get infinity, but if we subtract one from another, we get zero!

Because of paradoxes like this, some argue justifiably that there cannot be an actual countable infinity of material things in our universe. One *certain* conclusion we can draw from this however, is that in the realm of transfinite numbers, one countable infinity can contain another countable infinity within it. Are such counter-intuitive qualities of infinities *really* transferable to the actual physical universe? Or should we take them as a sign that our physical universe cannot be infinite?

Cosmologists who hypothesize that the universe is both infinite and expanding accept (or at least like to play around with) not only the idea of infinities in math, but also in the physical universe. Since so many aspects of abstract math are applicable to reality, they choose to

Hilbert's Grand Hotel

In an infinite universe far, far away, there was a hotel containing an infinite number of rooms. But one night, all of the rooms were occupied! And to make matters worse, an infinite number of new guests showed up, wanting to be checked in! What was the poor desk clerk to do? Rather than turn them all away, he had a clever idea. On the phone PA system, he announced the following:

"Honored guests of the Grand Hotel, we apologize for this inconvenience, but due to unforeseen circumstances, all guests, with no exceptions, must immediately move into the room whose number is twice that of the room they currently occupy. For instance, the guest in room one must move into room two, the guest in room two must move into room four, and the guest in room three must move into room six. You will find fresh linens and towels, if needed, in the closet. To make up for this inconvenience, we will give each of you a thirty-five percent discount when you check out."

Although the guests grumbled, they all obeyed because of the discount and the guests who come knocking on their door. This freed up an infinity of odd-numbered rooms, so the clerk was able to check in all of the new guests!

"I have made an infinite profit for you," the desk clerk said to the owner the following day, "so don't I deserve a big raise?"

"I was infinitely rich before, and I am infinitely rich now. So how have you made me any richer?" the owner replied.

"True," the brilliant desk clerk replied. "But if adding to your wealth makes you no richer, subtracting from it will make you no poorer."

ignore these paradoxical aspects of infinities, and reason, "Why not transfinite math, too?"

Imagine an infinite 3-D space that is a continuum—an uncountable infinity—because for every two planes that I select within it, I can always select another plane in-between them. Each of these planes would be what in theoretical physics is called a *brane* (short for membrane). Think of an infinitely high stack of sheets of paper of varying thicknesses as an illustration of this. Interestingly, even a space of finite size can be an infinite continuum. For instance, you stack an infinite number of planes of varying thicknesses into a box that is only one meter high.

A brane can have any number of allowed dimensions. A brane can be a line, a plane, or a three dimensional space. Every brane occupies its own unique space. If our universe exists within a fourth dimension of space, then it too may occupy a brane.

Is it really possible for an infinite universe to expand (as seems to have happened to Hilbert's Hotel in the story above, when everyone moved to the room number that was twice that of the one they currently occupied)? What would it be expanding into? Doesn't it seem like it would already take up all of the room that there is in the brane that it occupies?

When asked what the universe is expanding into, some cosmologists avoid this difficulty by suggesting that the universe is all that there is, so that it is expanding into *absolutely nothing at all* (not even a quantum vacuum field), and creating new space as it expands. [80]

But if the universe dwells within absolute nothingness, that raises the question, "Absolutely nothing can't cause *anything* to happen! So how could the universe have begun from nothing?"

---

[80] Fraser Cain, "What is the universe expanding into?" podcast. Nov 28, 2013. http://www.universetoday.com/1455/podcast-what-is-the-universe-expanding-into/ (Last accessed 3/12/2019)

Another interesting explanation can be found at the *Curious About Astronomy? Ask an Astronomer* website:

> However, if you just want a short answer, I'll say this: if the universe is infinitely big, then the answer is simply that it isn't expanding into *anything*; instead, what is happening is that every region of the universe, every distance between every pair of galaxies, is being "stretched", but the overall size of the universe was infinitely big to begin with and continues to remain infinitely big as time goes on, so the universe's size doesn't change, and therefore it doesn't expand into anything.[81]

But this raises the question, how can something infinitely big get "stretched" and yet remain the same size?

Do *you* find either of those two answers to be completely satisfying?

Because of these strange peculiarities of infinities, some mathematicians argue against using infinities in math, adhering instead to a philosophy of mathematics known as *finitism*. But an even *stronger* argument can be made that these paradoxes and conundrums mean that no infinity could *actually* exist within our universe.

Not only that, but the question arises, where would the infinite energy required to produce an infinite universe come from? (We will consider this question later in the book.)

And so, *is* our universe contained within an infinite continuum? That, it may justifiably be argued, is also a matter of faith.

Since as finite creatures, we cannot observe an infinity, belief in an infinity *requires* faith. It takes just as much faith to believe in an infinite universe as an explanation of the formation of life, as it does to believe in a Creator. For that matter, it takes faith merely to believe in a finite universe that is vaster than what we can observe as an explanation of

---

[81] Dave Rothstein, "What is the universe expanding into?" *Curious about Astronomy? Ask an Astronomer,* 2003. https://web.archive.org/web/20150116043745/http://curious.astro.cornell.edu/question.php?number=274 (Last accessed 3/12/2019)

life! This means that hypotheses which include anything that we cannot observe as an explanation for life or the universe, are venturing outside of science into the very same realm that religious beliefs lie in: *into the realm of metaphysics.*

WHETHER OR NOT OUR UNIVERSE IS INFINITE IS A MATTER OF METAPHYSICS

Georg Cantor considered the matter of speculating as to whether or not infinities actually exist to be a matter of metaphysics. In his book *Georg Cantor: His Mathematics and Philosophy of the Infinite*, Joseph Warren Dauben wrote:

> "Whenever Cantor spoke of metaphysics he meant the philosophical study of the relations between the constructs of mind and the objects of the external world. Thus the study of the abstract theory of the transfinite numbers was the business of mathematics, but the study of the realization or embodiment of the transfinite numbers in terms of the objects of the phenomenological world was the concern of metaphysics."[82]

Similarly, Leibniz, one of the co-inventors of calculus, regarded infinities as "ideal entities, not of the same nature as appreciable quantities".[83] Also recognizing this distinction, Russian philosopher of science Dr. Andrey Pavlenko writes:

> "In other words, all steps cosmology has made in the direction of acquiring the status of a natural science are inversely proportional to its steps in the direction of allowing infinite values of

---

[82] Joseph Warren Dauben, Georg Cantor: His Mathematics and Philosophy of the Infinite. Harvard University Press, 1979. http://www.math.dartmouth.edu/~matc/Readers/HowManyAngels/Cantor/Cantor.html (Last accessed 3/12/2019)

[83] Douglas M. Jesseph, "Leibniz on the Foundations of the Calculus: The Question of the Reality of Infinitesimal Magnitudes." MIT Perspectives on Science 6.1&2 (1998) 6-40.

cosmological features: the more resolutely cosmology eliminated infinite values, the more assuredly it could be looked upon as a full-fledged natural science (relativistic cosmology was the first here), and vice versa, the greater was the number of infinite values allowed by a cosmological theory, the more inevitably it fell away from the realm of "natural science".[84]

In their paper, "The topology of the universe: the biggest manifold of them all," Janna Levin, Evan Scannapieco, and Joseph Silk of the Center for Particle Astrophysics provide us with some good reasons to suspect that the universe is not infinite:

- Everything we see around us is finite. If the universe if infinite, it is an exception to this rule.
- The theory of relativity is a geometric theory, because gravity curves space. Yet an infinite universe has no definitive shape!
- Inflation (the expansion of space) would predict that the universe is so large we cannot detect it's curvature.[85]

In a 2013 panel discussion at the World Science Festival, theoretical cosmologist Andreas Albrecht, who switched to a finite cosmological model, said to his colleagues, "I find the finite universe rather exciting. Although I have to say, having early in life thought very much along the lines of my colleagues on the right here, I found it actually claustrophobic to switch from the infinite universe to the finite one, but I –I'm glad I did. It's a much, much more..." At this point his colleagues laughed, presumably at his relief over no longer having to deal with infinities,

---

[84] Andrey Pavlenko, "Why Cannot the Theory of the Infinite Universe be Realized?" Ontology Studies 9, pp. 65-78, 2009. https://www.aca-demia.edu/8365509/Why_Cannot_the_Theory_of_the_Infinite_Universe_be_Realized (Last accessed 3/11/2019)

[85] Janna Levin, Evan Scannapieco, and Joseph Silk, "The topology of the universe: the biggest manifold of them all." arXiv:gr-qc/9803026v1 6 Mar 1998. https://arxiv.org/pdf/gr-qc/9803026.pdf (Last accessed 3/24/2019)

and the moderator said, "It's just beautiful. There's twelve steps [as in Alcoholics Anonymous]!"

"It's working out well for me," Albrecht added with a smile. [86]

And physicist George Ellis writes:

> The often claimed existence of physical infinities in the multiverse context — of either universes or spatial sections of universes (Vilenkin 2006) — is dubious. What has been forgotten here is that infinity is an unattainable state rather than a large number — its character is totally different from any finite number and it is a mathematical rather than physical entity. According to David Hilbert (1964): "The infinite is nowhere to be found in reality, no matter what experiences, observations, and knowledge are appealed to." Even if there *were* an infinite number of galaxies, and we could see them all (which we could not), we could not count them in a finite time. So there is no way the existence of an infinity can ever be proven correct by observation or any other test. The concept of physical infinities is not a scientific one if science involves testability by either observation or experiment. The claim of infinites in the multiverse context emphasizes how tenuously scientific that idea is. *It is a huge act of hubris to extrapolate from one small domain to infinity when infinity is never attainable.*[87] (Emphasis mine.)

On the same basis by which some argue God should be excluded from consideration in science because He cannot be empirically detected by repeatable experiment, scientists such as Pavlenko and Ellis argue that hypotheses of an infinite universe or multiverse lie outside of the realm of science. Though infinite cosmological models may contain sound math based upon assumptions, some of those assumptions are

---

[86] "Multiverse: One or Many?" Video of World Science Festival Panel Discussion, Dec. 2013. http://www.worldsciencefestival.com/2013/12/multiverse_switching_to_the_finite/ (Last accessed March 12, 2019)

[87] George Ellis, "Opposing the Multiverse." Astronomy & Geophysics, Volume 49, Issue 2, 1 April 2008, pp. 2.33–2.35, https://doi.org/10.1111/j.1468-4004.2008.49229_1.x (Last accessed 3/17/2019)

essentially metaphysical in nature. That places such cosmologies in the same philosophical category as religious cosmologies, because as some of the theistic cosmologies we will discuss in chapter nine illustrate, someone can make theistic metaphysical assumptions and make accurate mathematical calculations based upon them, too.

In short, if we base our reasoning only upon those things that *we know exist,* then the only reasonable conclusion is that life has been designed by an extremely wise intelligence. We have to suppose something that *we cannot possibly know is true*, that the universe is *incredibly* vaster than what can be observed or infinite, to hope to adequately explain the chance formation of life without God. Even then, the Principle of Insufficient Local Tries is nipping at our heels:

Even though 1024 coin flips makes it probable you will get ten heads in a row, that makes it no more probable that you will get it in only ten flips!

8 WHY A FLAT UNIVERSE IS NOT NECESSARILY INFINITE

"No one likes to be flat-out wrong. It's as disheartening as a flat tire and as embarrassing—if you will pardon the pun—as flatulence. But if you are a popular science writer who has been telling people that a flat universe must be infinite, you simply *are* flat-out wrong." – *Anonymous*

 he impression is often conveyed in popular science media that since space appears to be flat, it therefore must be infinite, like an infinite plane. But is this true?

HOW COULD 3-D SPACE BE "FLAT"?

Astrophysicist Ethan Seigel writes, "We also know that the Universe is really, really flat in terms of its overall spatial curvature. By combining the Planck data with the data from large-scale structure formation, we can state that the curvature of the Universe is no greater than 1-part-in-1000, indicating that the Universe is indistinguishable from perfectly flat."[88]

This means that our universe must be at least 1,000 times larger than can be observed if it's *not* flat. However, if it *is* perfectly flat, it could be much smaller than that.

Why is space in our universe, which is three-dimensional, considered to be "flat"? Because as best as we can tell, it is *Euclidian.* In Euclidian space, the three angles of a triangle will *always* add up to 180 degrees,

---

[88] Ethan Seigel, "How The Planck Satellite Forever Changed Our View Of The Universe," Medium.com, It Starts With a Bang! Column, Jul 26, 2018. https://medium.com/starts-with-a-bang/how-the-planck-satellite-forever-changed-our-view-of-the-universe-3b94484f376d (Last accessed 3/26/2019)

and two parallel lines will *always* remain the same distance apart, neither merging nor diverging.

However, what if space were curved, rather than flat? If the curvature of the lines were very slight, space might *appear* Euclidean even if it actually is not. For example, think of how ancient man thought that the world was flat. That was because it is so large that they could not discern its curvature.

Imagine a tiny, two-dimensional creature living inside the two dimensional surface, or infinitely thin "skin" of a huge balloon. For the sake of convenience, let's call her Toodee (2D), since she is two dimensional. The surface of that balloon would be Toodee's entire universe. To her, there would be no up or down; only width and length. Unlike us, she would live in two-dimensional space. Like the universe in which Toodee lives, the "skin" of any geometric shape, no matter how many dimensions that skin has, is called a *manifold.*

Since Toodee lives inside the two-dimensional surface area of a balloon, the kind of space she resides in is called a *two-manifold.* Likewise, since we live in three dimensional space, the space in which we live is called a *three-manifold.* We are thought to live inside that three-manifold, which is the "skin" of the geometric shape of the universe, just as Toodee would live inside the surface space of that balloon.

What if Toodee lived inside the surface space of an inflatable egg or a doughnut-shaped swimming tube instead of a spherical balloon? Although the *global* geometry of the universe she lived in would then be different, she would still live in a two-manifold. Likewise, the 3D space in which we live could have any number of global shapes and it would still be a three-manifold.

An interesting characteristic of all manifolds is that just as the face of the earth seemed flat or Euclidean to ancient man, all manifolds appear Euclidean to a small enough observer living inside that space, whether or not they really are globally flat. As an example, think of how a football field seems flat to us, although the world is round. This means that if our universe is very big, the space that we live in could actually be globally curved, despite the fact that as far as we can tell with our *local* measurements, it is flat.

Have you ever noticed how on model globes of the earth, lines drawn as straight as possible, which are far apart from each other where they cross the equator, converge at the north and south poles? These lines, which we call *meridians*, are geodesics. To an outside observer, the bending path of a line drawn as straight as possible inside a manifold is called a *geodesic*.

THE DIFFERENCE BETWEEN TOPOLOGY AND GEOMETRY

A manifold's *local geometry* is simply whether or not parallel lines drawn within it remain straight, merge, or diverge.

A manifold's *global geometry* is the appearance of its over-all *shape* to an outside observer, such as whether it is a cube, a sphere or a toroid. Global geometry is what is changed by deforming the shape of a manifold.

As you might guess, since light and lines bend along with the shape of a manifold, the continuity of a manifold is very important. This continuity is called its *topology*. Topology is what is unaffected by deforming the shape of a manifold. Even though their global geometry is different, a cube, an egg, and a cylinder all have the same topology, because one could be deformed into the other. Likewise, a square, a triangle, and a circle all have the same topology.

The only way to change the topology of a manifold is to change the number of holes it has going through it. Because of this, topological shapes are classified according to the number of holes they have, which is called their *genus.* This means that a glass bead and a glass ball have different topologies, because one has a hole and the other does not. Though they look quite different, a doughnut and a coffee cup have the same topology, because both have one hole going all of the way through them. In the coffee cup, this hole is the handle, not the depression that holds the coffee. Tear all of the way through a doughnut to its hole and you will have changed its topology, because then it will no longer have a complete hole.

Geodesics could take *very* different paths on the surface of a ball and a glass bead. That is why topology is so important when we are considering the shape of space. Topologies can either be *simply-connected* or *multiconnected*. Simply put, if a topology does not have a hole going all of the way through it, it is simply-connected. Simply-connected means that you can shrink any ring drawn on it down to a point without penetrating the surface (assuming it is sliding across the surface as it is shrinking). A doughnut, for instance, is multiconnected because if you draw a circle that goes in and out of the hole, it cannot be shrunk down to a point with penetrating the surface. There are only three simply connected topologies, but an infinity of multiconnected topologies. This means that our universe could have a multiconnected topology that explains the strange anomalies that the WMAP and Planck satellites found in the cosmic microwave background radiation, but we simply have not it recognized yet.

The cosmic microwave background. Though most of the variations in it can be explained according to the standard model of cosmology, some can't be. Credit: ESA & Planck.

If we can be certain we are taking *global,* large-scale measurements, and we find that two parallel lines never intersect no matter what direction they point, then we can safely say the local geometry of the space we live in is flat or Euclidean. If those parallel lines eventually intersect on both ends, then space is positively curved like a sphere. If they diverge on both ends, it is negatively curved like the underside of a saddle.

Believe it or not, it is possible for manifolds with different global geometries to be Euclidean. For instance, the local geometry on the surface of a doughnut and a flat sheet are both flat (Euclidean)! Here is an illustration that will help you to understand why.

Let's suppose that I gently placed Toodee on the surface of a perfectly flat, two dimensional rubber sheet. However, I did not want her to fall off, so to keep that from happening, I decided to make her universe *closed* (finite and having no edges). From the rubber sheet she now lived on, I made a doughnut shaped swimming tube, so that when she traveled, she would not come to an edge and go off.

To do this, I took the rubber sheet, curved it around so that the two long sides touched, and then glued them together. Then, I curved it around again so that the two short sides touched, and glued them together also, blowing up the newly created inner tube just enough to keep from stretching it. This would form a doughnut shape, called a *toroid.* After that, Toodee would be living in a *closed universe* from which she could not fall off.

The space she lived in would still be Euclidean, because parallel lines would not diverge. But from our perspective, the *global geometric shape* of the universe in which she lived in would have drastically changed. The topology would have changed, too, because the global geometry of her universe would now have a hole going through it, whereas it did not before.

What if Toodee was very curious, industrious and intelligent, and able to make tools from two-dimensional materials she found within the two-dimensional space of her new universe? And what if she wanted to determine the topology and the geometric shape of the new universe in which she lived? How could she do this? Remember that a manifold is something that *seems* Euclidean if you zoom in far enough, whether its local geometry truly is or not. Toodee could try to mentally "zoom out" by measuring the three angles of a huge triangle across her little universe (see the **Figure 8** below).

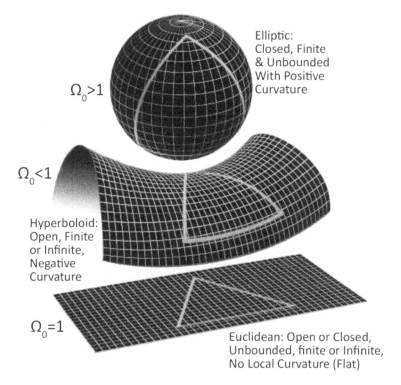

Elliptic:
Closed, Finite
& Unbounded
With Positive
Curvature

$\Omega_0 > 1$

$\Omega_0 < 1$

Hyperboloid:
Open, Finite
or Infinite,
Negative
Curvature

$\Omega_0 = 1$

Euclidean: Open or Closed,
Unbounded, finite or Infinite,
No Local Curvature (Flat)

Figure 8. The local geometry of the universe is determined by the value of the Omega density parameter. Credit: NASA (Green text and blue coloration added by author.)

If the angles did not add up to *exactly* 180 degrees, then she would know that her universe has a positively or negatively curved global geometry, like a balloon or a saddle. However, in this case, since Toodee would now live on a toroid or doughnut shaped universe, she will find the sum of the angles to be exactly 180 degrees. She will then know that the *local* geometry of the space she lives in is flat, but she will not be able to tell its *global* geometry from that alone. This is because there are multiple global shapes in which the topological space will be Euclidean, such as an infinite plane, a torus, or a cylinder.

So how could she determine the *global* geometry of her universe? If she looked through a 2-D telescope to the left and saw the back of her head, and then looked straight ahead and saw the back of her head again, but it appeared to be farther away, she could determine that she lives on a toroid (assuming that a very intelligent 2D creature could get some idea of a 3D shape). If she lived in a manifold of another shape that was Euclidean, she could also determine its global geometry by analyzing what she observed.

Like Toodee, scientists have also attempted to decipher the global shape of our universe by looking for similar visual clues in the sky. They have determined that the local geometry of the 3-manifold we live in is *approximately* flat, but cannot yet determine the global shape of it. They have found no conclusive evidence *yet* of some particular finite global shapes that would result in Euclidean space, but that does not mean it's not the case.

What Is the Global Geometry of Our Universe?

In the example above, I glued the ends of Toodee's universe together to give her universe its global shape and its topology. There are things that give our universe its shape, too. One is its gravitational mass, and the other is the force with which it is expanding. You might recall that Einstein's theory of relativity predicts that gravitational mass curves space. Just how it curves it depends upon an important number called *Omega*, represented by the Greek letter Ω. Omega is also called the *Density Parameter*. Here's why it's called that.

Density is simply mass divided by volume. The *metric*, or unit by which density is typically measured, is kilograms per cubic meter. The *actual* density of the universe is its average mass per cubic meter, and it is represented by the symbol ρ. The *critical* density is the density which is just enough to keep the universe from ever collapsing back in on itself due to gravity. It's represented by the symbol ρ_c. Omega equals the actual density of the universe divided by the critical density:

$$\Omega = \rho/\rho_c.$$

Omega can tell us whether or not we live in Euclidean space, and help us to narrow down the possible global geometric shapes our universe might have. It can even tell us how our universe could come to an end!

GEOMETRY CAN DETERMINE DESTINY

If dark energy does not continue to accelerate the galaxies apart from each other, then **If Omega is greater than 1,** the galaxies in the universe will stop moving apart, and the universe will collapse back in upon itself due to gravity. **Figure 8** illustrates how space might be curved if Omega equals 1, or is less than or greater than 1.

If Omega is greater than one, then because gravity curves space, space has a shape that closes back in upon itself, such as a sphere, and it is *elliptic* because it has positive curvature (see the top drawing in **Figure 8**). An elliptic universe will eventually come to an end, because it will collapse under its own gravity. An elliptic universe is also closed and unbounded (having no edge) from the perspective of someone inside its manifold.

If space is closed and unbounded, then just as you can keep walking in what seems like a straight line around the earth forever, if you traveled in a warp-speed star ship through space in what seemed to be a straight line forever, you would find no end to space, even though it is finite! And depending on your direction and the topology of the universe, you might eventually end up where you started from! Just as the earth has no end from our perspective, an unbounded universe would also seem to have no end to those living inside it. Please keep in mind, however, that an infinite flat universe would be unbounded, too, because it would also have no edge. And yet it would not be closed.

Since a positively curved, elliptic universe is "closed," it therefore must be finite. The most natural elliptic shape to think of is that of a sphere. If our universe has a spherical shape, then it is simply so large that we can't detect it's curvature.

If Omega is less than 1, then space has a *hyperboloid shape* that does not close back in upon itself. The saddle shaped middle drawing in Figure 8 is one such possible hyperboloid shape. Note that the saddle shape in this illustration does not close back in upon itself like a toroid would. If space has a hyperboloid shape, then it has negative curvature. It will never collapse back in upon itself due to gravity.

One very important thing to note is that if the universe were finite in volume to begin with, then *it must remain finite in size, since it is expanding at a finite speed.* Certain hyperboloid shapes have finite volume because of their unique geometry. One of these that is very interesting is called the *Picard Horn.*[89]

If Omega equals one, then space is *flat* and has zero local curvature. It will also never collapse due to gravity. In Figure 8 you will see that the first two triangles have curved lines, but the third one does not. In the third one, space is Euclidean or flat.

Since the latest observations from the Planck satellite indicate that space is flat within an error range of .2 percent,[90] and a flat plane is normally thought of as infinite, it's common, especially in popular science media, for people to mistakenly assert that the universe must be infinite. At the time of this writing, even the writer of a page on the NASA WMAP website conveys this misconception, stating "If the

---

[89] Aurich, Ralf & Lustig, Sven & Steiner, Frank & Then, Holger. (2004). "Hyperbolic universes with a horned topology and the cosmic microwave background anisotropy." Classical and Quantum Gravity. 21. 4901. 10.1088/0264-9381/21/21/010. https://www.researchgate.net/profile/Holger_Then/publication/230909639_Hyperbolic_universes_with_a_horned_topology_and_the_cosmic_microwave_background_anisotropy/links/00b7d52a9930eb3ff4000000/Hyperbolic-universes-with-a-horned-topology-and-the-cosmic-microwave-background-anisotropy.pdf?origin=publication_detail (Last accessed 3/11/2018)

[90] N. Aghanim (Orsay, IAS) et al., "Planck 2018 results. VI. Cosmological parameters, Planck Collaboration." Jul 17, 2018. p. 71. e-Print: arXiv:1807.06209 [astro-ph.CO] | PDF "The joint results suggests our Universe is spatially flat to a 1 sigma accuracy of 0.2 %." p. 40

density of the universe exactly equals the critical density, then the geometry of the universe is flat like a sheet of paper, and infinite in extent." [91] But is this conclusion necessarily warranted?

No, and here's why. As long as the expansion energy is just enough to prevent eventual gravitational collapse, Omega will equal one even if the universe has finite mass. This would mean that the universe must have a shape which is *both* flat and finite. What follows are two shapes that have those qualities.

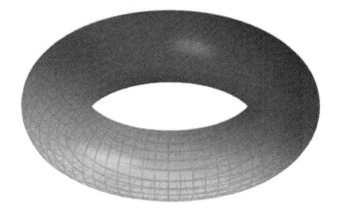

Figure 9. A torus. Credit: Leonid_2

A *torus* (doughnut-shape), which we have already discussed, is a global topology which is a likely shape for a finite flat universe. Joseph Silk, head of Astrophysics at the University of Oxford, explained this in an interview:

"We do not know whether the Universe is finite or not. To give you an example, imagine the geometry of the Universe in two dimensions as a plane. It is flat, and a plane is normally infinite. But you can take a sheet of paper and you can roll it up and make a

---

[91] "Will the universe expand forever?" Universe 101: Our Universe. wmap.gsfc.nasa.gov. http://wmap.gsfc.nasa.gov/universe/uni_shape.html (Last accessed 3/11/2019)

cylinder, and you can roll the cylinder again and make a torus [like the shape of a doughnut]. The surface of the torus is also spatially flat, but it is finite. So you have two possibilities for a flat Universe [though these are not *all* of the possibilities]: one infinite, like a plane, and one finite, like a torus, which is also flat."[92]

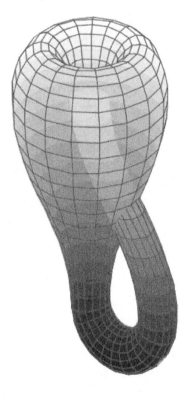

Figure 10. A Klein Bottle. Credit: Tttrung.

Another shape that could result in a finite flat universe is a klein bottle. The various finite flat shapes that our universe could have are called *Riemannian manifolds*. Among these are the Picard Horn and the Poincaré Dodecahedron.

---

[92] ESA, "Is the Universe Finite or Infinite? An Interview with Joseph Silk." Space Science, esa.int. http://www.esa.int/Our_Activities/Space_Science/Is_the_Universe_finite_or_infinite_An_interview_with_Joseph_Silk (Last accessed 3/17/2019)

Interestingly, a new model of the universe that we will briefly discuss in another chapter neatly solves what is called the cosmological constant problem, but requires that the universe be finite.

CONCLUSIONS

And so, we cannot conclude that space is infinite based on the available information; only that it is very big. The NASA WMAP website page quoted above does go on to correctly say, however, "All we can truly conclude is that the Universe is much larger than the volume we can directly observe."

Just as Darwinism was, of course, very quickly accepted by those who preferred to believe that there was not a God, the idea of an infinite universe or multiverse is very popular among those with similar philosophical preferences, and is growing in acceptance. This acceptance, however, is premature, and here's why:

First of all, it is quite possible that the Universe is so large that we simply cannot accurately detect its curvature. In fact, if it is finite but 100 times larger than can be observed, it would still appear flat to us within the Planck error range of 0.2 percent.

Secondly, there is the very real possibility that our universe is *smaller* than what we appear to observe. If space has one of the flat finite closed shapes above, then we could be observing *two* images of many galaxies, but be unaware of it because each image is a snapshot of that galaxy in an earlier location and at a different stage of its formation. [93]

Thirdly, the universe can only be infinite in extent and have infinite mass if it had been infinite in space and mass to begin with. Otherwise, it could not have expanded from finiteness to infinity within the estimated age of the universe. It would have been expanding forever in that case, and be infinitely old, but observations indicate that it is of finite age. Popular science depictions of the universe being smaller

---

[93] http://www.khanacademy.org/science/cosmology-and-astronomy/universe-scale-topic/big-bang-expansion-topic/v/a-universe-smaller-than-the-observable

than an atom before the big bang are referring to the *observable* universe, not the entire universe.

In a *Scientific American* article, cosmologists Jean-Pierre Luminet, Glenn D. Starkman and Jeffrey R. Weeks wrote:

> "...there is preliminary work in quantum cosmology, which attempts to describe how the universe emerged spontaneously from the void. Some such theories predict that a low-volume universe is more probable than a high-volume one. An infinite universe would have zero probability of coming into existence. Loosely speaking, its energy would be infinite, and no quantum fluctuation could muster such a sum." [94, 95]

That means one of three things:

1. **Space is flat and finite, and the mass within it is finite, too.** As previously mentioned, a flat topology can be achieved with finite mass as long as the expansion is *just enough* to keep it from collapsing again. This would mean that space probably has an exotic finite global topology such as a torus.
2. **Space is negatively curved and finite, and the mass within it is also finite.** This can also be achieved with finite mass as long as the expansion energy is *more than enough* to keep it from collapsing again. If so, it probably has a finite shape such as a Picard Horn.
3. **Space is positively curved and finite, but so huge that it has an undetectable curvature.** In such a case, it will appear flat when we measure it (just as the earth appeared to be flat to ancient man), but in reality will be very slightly curved.

---

[94] Jonathan J. Halliwell , "Quantum Cosmology and the Creation of the Universe." *Scientific American*, December 1991, Volume 265, Issue 6. In this article, Halliwell describes the probability of an infinite fluctuation as virtually zero.

[95] Jean-Pierre Luminet, Glenn D. Starkman and Jeffrey R. Weeks, "Is Space Finite?" Scientific American, April 1999. https://web.archive.org/web/20160303203130/http://cosmos.phy.tufts.edu/~zirbel/ast21/sciam/IsSpaceFinite.pdf (Last accessed 3/12/2018)

Commenting on the results of the latest 2018 Planck satellite data analysis, Astrophysicist Ethan Siegal writes,

"All we can see is the part of the Universe accessible to us, which allows us to place constraints on what its topology is allowed to be. As far as we can tell, it's flat, non-repeating and possibly (but not necessarily) infinite. Perhaps, as time goes on, and more of the Universe slowly reveals itself to us, or as our curvature measurements get more precise, we'll discover a departure from what we've concluded so far. After all, we're limited by what we're capable of observing, but those limits will continue to change as the Universe ages. The possibility of a Universe that's vastly different from what we've concluded thus far might lie just beyond the cosmic horizon."[96]

Cosmologist Jean-Pierre Luminet also writes:

"While the last CMB (Planck) data fit well the simplest model of a zero-curvature, infinite space model, they remain consistent with more complex shapes such as the spherical Poincaré Dodecahedral Space, the flat hypertorus or the hyperbolic Picard horn." [97]

And so, contrary to the popular but ill-informed misconception often conveyed in popular science media that if the universe is flat, it must also be infinite, it's quite likely that although space appears flat, our universe is finite.

---

[96] Ethan Siegal, "If You Traveled Far Enough Through Space, Would You Return To Your Starting Point?" Forbes (Science), Starts With a Bang contributor group, Oct 12, 2018 https://www.forbes.com/sites/starts-withabang/2018/10/12/if-you-traveled-far-enough-through-space-would-you-return-to-your-starting-point/#488846e16d52 (Last accessed 3/22/2019)

[97] Jean-Pierre Luminet, "The Status of Cosmic Topology after Planck Data" Universe 2 (2016) no.1, 1 (2016-01-15) DOI: 10.3390/universe2010001. https://arxiv.org/ftp/arxiv/papers/1601/1601.03884.pdf (Last accessed 3/11/2019)

9 JUST HOW FAR CAN NATURAL SELECTION GO?

"Regardless of one's point of view, it's quite easy to see that Darwinism is not in the same league as the hard sciences. For instance, Darwinists will often compare their theory favorably to Einsteinian physics, claiming that Darwinism is just as well established as general relativity. Yet how many physicists, while arguing for the truth of Einsteinian physics, will claim that general relativity is as well established as Darwin's theory? Zero." — William Dembski

"Natural selection eliminates and maybe maintains, but it doesn't create." — Lynn Margulis

"Natural selection is the editor, rather than the composer of the genetic message." – Jack Lester King and Thomas H. Jukes

t this point, you might be thinking, "OK, so the universe probably is not infinite. And the odds of biopoesis are extraordinarily low unless our universe is *vastly* bigger than can be observed. But let's suppose that it *is* vast enough. Can't evolution by natural selection explain the rest?"

First of all, as we discussed in the chapter on infinities, believing that the universe is incredibly vaster than is warranted by observations and measurements is a matter of faith, and therefore *a metaphysical belief akin to religion.*

Secondly, not only must improbability be surmounted to explain the origin of an evolvable self-replicator, it also must be surmounted to explain the many kinds of life we find on our planet. Here's why.

As we discussed in chapter 4, DNA contains instructional information, which is a form of semantic language. To date we have observed no *inventing* source of semantic languages other than intelligences. We referred to this as *the law of linguagenesis.*

Let's suppose that the universe were vast enough that blind chance *did* produce the information required for a simple evolvable self-replicator, as an *extremely rare* exception to the law of biogenesis. Once that happened, could it have evolved into the first cell, including the protein-assembly instructional information that we find in life today? The cell is of such a magnitude of complexity that even human intelligence cannot yet completely comprehend it.

Despite our doubts, let's suppose that the first reproducing cell has come into existence. Once that has happened, can natural selection combined with variation and mutation produce all of the complex forms of life we find on Earth today?

There are some important things to be taken into account before embracing natural selection as an explanation for the information found in the genomes of organisms. Let's consider some of them.

Many of the variations chosen by natural selection, especially those that govern complex behaviors or systems, are explained not by new mutations, but by the genetic information that is *already* stored in a genome.

We tend to see more variation in a species population when intense survival pressures are *not* at work.

Despite the miraculous powers often attributed to natural selection in popular media and by zealous naturalists, it is *not a creative force at all.* It does not create anything; it merely selects what is already there.

In their paper *The Eve Mitochondrial Consensus Sequence,* scientists Robert Carter, Dan Criswell, and John Sanford compared over 800 available sequences of human mitochondrial DNA. From this, they determined the *consensus sequence,* which is the approximate sequence that Mitochondrial Eve had. (We are all descended from Mitochondrial Eve.) The researchers found that over 83 percent of the mitochondrial genome *has not changed at all.* Furthermore, the 17 percent that has mutated in some populations represents *all* changes found, *not* the average change.

The authors point out that this could also be explained by an extreme genetic bottleneck 100,000 to 200,000 years ago. But then given the high mutation rate of the mitochondrial genome, the *average* variation from the consensus ought to be much higher than it is. **They found that the average human differs from the consensus sequence *by only 21.6 nucleotides.*** Because the mitochondrial genome is subject to high mutation rates, this is evidence that the consensus sequence is very young. Mitochondrial Eve's approximate age is therefore consistent with the Genesis account found in the Bible.[98]

Since then, Carter, Sanford and S.S. Lee have written a new research paper that takes a "historical reconstruction" instead of a "consensus" approach. In it, they examine not only the thousands of mitochondrial (chrM) chromosome sequences of humans around the world that have been sequenced and are now made publicly available, but also the Y (chrY) sequences! Using this data, they were able to determine the approximate sequence of Y chromosome Adam/Noah and Mitochondrial Eve, and estimate the time that they lived. In the article abstract of this fascinating paper, they write,

> Both individuals lived less than 10,000 years ago, which is most consistent with a biblical timeframe. Lastly, recurrent mutations are extremely common, and many of them are associated with epigenetic CpG sites, meaning mutation accumulation is not free of environmental influence and many mutations may have accumulated in different lineages in parallel. The genetic evidence strongly suggests that Y Chromosome Adam/Noah and Mitochondrial Eve were not just real people, they were the progenitors of

---

[98] Robert W. Carter, Dan Criswell, John Sanford. "The 'Eve' Mitochondrial Consensus Sequence." In A. A. Snelling (Ed.) (2008). Proceedings of the Sixth International Conference on Creationism (pp. 111–116). http://www.icr.org/i/pdf/technical/The-Eve-Mitochondrial-Consensus-Sequence.pdf (Last accessed 03/12/2019)

us all. In this light, there is every reason to believe that they were the Adam/Noah and Eve of the Bible.[99]

A few simple, beneficial mutations resulting from single point mutations have been found and demonstrated, such as some that confer immunity to certain antibiotics in bacteria. These are very simple changes. But can major changes, such as those that are thought to have emerged during the Cambrian Explosion, be accounted for in this way? During the Cambrian Explosion, which is thought to have lasted 10 million years at the most, almost all of the major phyla emerged. That short time span presents a problem, because as Susumu Ohno of the Beckman Research Institute wrote,

> "Assuming the spontaneous mutation rate to be a generous 10^{-9} per base pair per year and also assuming no negative interference by natural selection, it still takes 10 million years to undergo 1% change in DNA base sequences. It follows that 6-10 million years in the evolutionary time scale is but a blink of an eye. The Cambrian explosion denoting the almost simultaneous emergence of nearly all the extant phyla of the kingdom Animalia within the time span of 6-10 million years can't possibly be explained by mutational divergence of individual gene functions."[100]

This forced Ohno to hypothesize that all of these phyla had nearly identical genomes! However, the form of these phyla is *extremely varied*, and many of their body plans are very unique!

---

[99] Carter, R.W., S.S. Lee, and J.C. Sanford. "An overview of the independent histories of the human Y-chromosome and the human mitochondrial chromosome." 2018. In Proceedings of the Eighth International Conference on Creationism, ed. J.H. Whitmore, pp. 133–151. Pittsburgh, Pennsylvania: Creation Science Fellowship. http://creationicc.org/2018_papers/15%20carter%20Y%20chromosome%20final.pdf (Last accessed 3/18/2019)

[100] Susumu Ohno, "The notion of the Cambrian pananimalia genome." Evolution Vol. 93, pp. 8475-8478, August 1996. http://www.ncbi.nlm.nih.gov/pmc/articles/PMC38696/pdf/pnas01520-0331.pdf (Last accessed 03/12/2019)

Most of the examples that evolutionists point to that involve major changes to a species involve a *loss* of genetic instructional information, such as the ancestors of horses losing two of their three toes, fish and salamanders that have become trapped in caves losing their eyes, and the ancestors of birds losing tiny teeth in their beaks or claws on the tips of their wings. These things are often pointed to as examples of evolution, and it is true that they can easily be explained by natural selection. But do not be misled by these examples, because they are *just the opposite* of a net gain in functional information! It would be more fitting to call these adaptive examples of *degeneration*. We would expect natural selection to harness genetic entropy (the increasing loss of information) for adaptive purposes. But how did the information that was lost get there?

The vast majority of mutations to the DNA of an organism are harmful or neutral. By way of analogy, let's consider the programming code which controls an assembly line robotic arm at the Tesla automobile factory. This seems fitting, since the DNA code is also an instructional code for assembling proteins. What if we were to randomly change the programming code for the robotic arm by means similar to the kinds of mutations that we know of?

- **Point Mutation**: Randomly change or delete a character of the code for the robot here and there.
- **Deletions:** Randomly delete portions of the instructional code for the robot.
- **Nonsense:** Add stop characters to prematurely stop reading portions of the code.
- **Missense:** Cause the code to insert an entirely different part than was intended by the programmer.
- **Horizontal Gene Transfer**: Take entire paragraphs out from the code that controls another robot at the assembly line, and randomly place them into the code for this robot.
- **Translocation:** Randomly exchange sections of code. **Splice site:** Remove comment marks, so that the programmer's comments get added to the robot's commands.

- **Reverse Transcription:** Read some of the sections of the code in reverse sequence.
- **Duplication:** Copy a portion of the code and paste it in randomly.

What are the odds that these "mutations" in the programming code will result in an improved Tesla automobile? Consider, for instance, that the most common cause of cystic fibrosis is the deletion of a *single codon.*

In order for a beneficial mutation to become a distinct characteristic of a species, enough time must pass for it to substitute for the base pair it replaces in the entire breeding population. This is called the *rate of substitution.* The rate of substitution for humans was calculated by geneticist J.B.S. Haldane to be so slow (one per 300 generations at the most), that only 1667 substitutions could have occurred in the ten million years said to have passed since humans diverged from the hypothetical ape ancestor that we share with chimpanzees. By contrast, even if humans and chimpanzees are only one percent different, halving this amounts to a difference of 1.5 million base pairs between our supposed ape ancestor and us. How then do we explain this huge gap between 1667 substitutions and 1,500,000 base pairs? This is known as *Haldane's Dilemma,* and according to Walter Remine, who conducted a thorough analysis of Haldane's Dilemma in his book, *The Biotic Message,* it has never been satisfactorily resolved. [101] [102] [103] [104]

---

[101] B. S. Haldane, J. (1957). Haldane JBS. "The cost of natural selection." J Genet 55: pp. 511-524. Journal of Genetics. 55. 511-524. 10.1007/BF02984069.

[102] ReMine, W.J., The Biotic Message, St Paul Science, St Paul, Minn., 1993.

[103] Responses by ReMine to his internet critics may be read at https://web.archive.org/web/20171017020656/http://saint-paulscience.com/Haldane.htm (Last accessed 03/22/20190

[104] Don Batten, "Haldane's dilemma has not been solved." Journal of Creation 19(1): pp. 20–21, April 2005. http://creation.com/haldanes-dilemma-has-not-been-solved (Last accessed 3/17/2019)

Selective pressures can move one way, and then move in the opposite direction when environmental pressures change. During dry years, Galapagos finch beaks were observed by researchers Peter and Rosemary Grant to get bigger. But later when rainy years came again, and human settlers provided food, the trend reversed itself.[105] In this case, even a minor change such as a larger beak reversed. Are selective pressures *consistent* enough to produce entirely new systems of higher complexity? The fossil record seems to indicate otherwise. Every extinct family exhibits *stasis* in the fossil record. That is, it pops into the fossil record fully formed, and then vanishes from it in essentially the same form, though with minor variations.

> "When we do see the introduction of evolutionary novelty," writes Niles Eldridge of the American Museum of Natural History, "it usually shows up with a bang, and often with no firm evidence that the fossils did not evolve elsewhere. Evolution cannot be forever going on somewhere else. Yet that is how the fossil record has struck many a forlorn paleontologist looking to learn something about evolution."[106]

As biologist Michael Behe pointed out in his book, *Darwin's Black Box*, some biological systems are *irreducibly complex*. An example is the bacterial flagellum. A tiny molecular motor powers it. Take away just one part, and the motor cannot function. How could such systems have evolved in a step-by-step process without originally being *more* complex than the final evolutionary result, which is a greater uphill battle?[107]

---

[105] Peter R. Grant, *Ecology and Evolution of Darwin's Finches*. Princeton University Press, 1986. You may view the datasheet of observed variations in finch beak size at http://www.pbs.org/wgbh/evolution/library/01/6/l_016_01.html (Last accessed 3/18/2019)

[106] Time Frames. *The Evolution of Punctuated Equilibria*, Princeton, Princeton University Press, 1985, pp. 144-45.

[107] Michael Behe, Darwin's Black Box: *The Biochemical Challenge to Evolution*, 1996, New York: The Free Press.

Intense survival pressures will decrease the population of a species. But that will result in more inbreeding. Inbreeding tends to bring out expression of genetic mutations. Most of them are harmful. It is well known that inbreeding is unhealthy for both humans and animals. And yet it is selection pressures that are supposed to enable natural selection to take place, thinning out all but those individuals having a beneficial mutation. This idea is known as "the survival of the fittest." Unfortunately, after the fittest survivors begin to interbreed, not only will this bring out expression of the rare good mutation, but it will bring out expression of the harmful mutations, which vastly outnumber it. But the bad mutations that become expressed because of inbreeding may not all be filtered out by natural selection, for three reasons:

- **First of all,** inbreeding might *eliminate* healthy genes in a population.
- **Secondly,** not all harmful mutations completely destroy functionality. *Fer nstunz, u can stil nderstan this sentans, cant yew?*
- **Thirdly,** not all harmful mutations affect reproductive functionality. They may merely shorten lifespans or make old age much more miserable. As long as the species survives to reproduce effectively enough, these harmful mutations will be passed on. Can the few beneficial mutations that occur overpower the accumulation of the many more slightly harmful but non-fatal mutations that will accumulate in a gene pool? In short, it is difficult to see how a few good mutations can overpower a multitude of harmful ones.

When you continue to make copies of copies, it seems inevitable that copying errors will begin to accumulate despite error correction mechanisms. Try this with a photocopier, and you will see how information tends to degrade over successive generations as a consequence of the *second law of thermodynamics*, which dictates that order tends to erode with time. Try this with a tape recorder, and noise begins to accumulate, and the quality of the recording goes down with each successive copy until it will eventually become unintelligible. This accumulation of noise, which is a loss of information, or an accumulation of disorder, is known as *entropy*.

Mendel's Accountant is the "first biologically-realistic forward-time population genetics numerical simulation" computer program. Utilizing it, researchers John Sanford, John Baumgardner, Wesley Brewer, Paul Gibson, and Walter ReMine ran simulations to see if the natural selection of good mutations could overpower genetic entropy – the accumulation of fitness decreasing disorder in the genome. In *Using Numerical Simulation to Test the Validity of Neo-Darwinian Theory*, they wrote,

> "Since bad mutations outnumber good mutations by many orders of magnitude, even after selection, the bad mutations will still be accumulating much faster than good mutations. Selection only slows this accumulation very slightly—it does not even begin to stop it. Typically we see that selection eliminates substantially less than 10% of the deleterious mutations. All the rest simply build up within the genome at a steady rate. As we will soon see, even when there are some rare beneficial mutations which are also accumulating, these only have a trivial effect on the subsequent fitness decline."

The authors concluded, "At its most fundamental level, evolutionary genetic theory must be about tracking mutations and allele frequencies. It boils down to a very large accounting problem. To objectively test evolutionary genetic theory the thing that has been lacking has been a practical mechanism for tracking each mutation, through large populations, over many generations, in a biologically realistic manner. This has now become possible for the first time, using the numerical simulation program called Mendel's Accountant. This program is a powerful teaching and research tool. It reveals that all of the traditional theoretical problems that have been raised about evolutionary genetic theory are in fact very real and are empirically verifiable in a scientifically rigorous manner. As a consequence, evolutionary genetic theory now has no theoretical support — it is an indefensible scientific model."

This means that genetic entropy could hypothetically reach a threshold, in which the cumulative damage has a fatal effect on the gene pool of an entire species. Could this account for the extinctions of some species? Because of all of the above considerations, we must distinguish between the *special theory of evolution* (also called *microevolution*) and the *general theory of evolution* (also called *mega-evolution.*)

The general theory of evolution was distinguished from the special theory of evolution by Dr. G.A. Kerkut in 1960 in his book, *The Implications of Evolution.* Kerkut was a professor of physiology and biochemistry at the University of Southampton. What he wrote then still applies today:

> There is a theory which states that many living animals can be observed over the course of time to undergo changes so that new species are formed. This can be called the "Special Theory of Evolution" and can be demonstrated in certain cases by experiments. On the other hand there is the theory that all the living forms in the world have arisen from a single source which itself came from an inorganic form. This theory can be called the "General Theory of Evolution" and the evidence that supports it is not sufficiently strong to allow us to consider it as anything more than a working hypothesis. It is not clear whether the changes that bring about speciation are of the same nature as those that brought about the development of new phyla. The answer will be found by future experimental work and not by dogmatic assertions that the General Theory of Evolution must be correct because there is nothing else that will satisfactorily take its place.[108]

Microevolution is indeed a fact and is observed all around us. It happens due to small genetic variations, which, because of selective pressures, can become predominant in a breeding population, such as the average length of a finches beak.

---

[108] Kerkut, G.A. (1927–2004), Implications of Evolution, Pergamon, Oxford, UK, p. 157, 1960. http://ia600409.us.archive.org/23/items/implicationsofev00kerk/implicationsofev00kerk.pdf (Last accessed 03/22/2019)

On the other hand, *macroevolution* is evolution beyond the level of the species. Since speciation of *very similar* kinds of organisms has been observed, we know that *limited* macroevolution does take place. Creationists acknowledge this, and so rather than a Darwinian tree of life, they envision what is called a *Creationist Orchard*, in which God created original kinds of animals (the canines, the felines, etc), and similar kinds of animal species developed from those that were originally created.

However, what about the general theory of evolution, which holds that all of the different kinds of organisms are descended from a single-celled ancestor? Has this kind of evolution really occurred?

Until recently, the general theory of evolution was supported primarily by three assumptions:

Assumption 1: *Close homology (similarity) indicates common descent.* This is not always true for several reasons:

- There are species that are homologous in striking ways, but obviously cannot be related. The placental southern flying squirrel and the marsupial honey glider are examples of this.
- Homology can reflect a common designer utilizing a preferred way of doing things rather than common descent.
- There are many species which appear on the surface to be closely related, but their embryological development unfolds in *strikingly different ways*. British evolutionary embryologist Sir Gavin DeBeer called this "the unsolved problem of homology."[109]

Assumption 2: *Microevolution and limited macroevolution can be extrapolated into mega-evolution.* We have found that there are limits to the features can be expressed through selective breeding. Breeders have succeeded in getting the sugar beet to produce only so much sugar by weight, and no breeder has ever succeeded using artificial

---

[109] Sir Gavin De Beer, "Homology: An Unsolved Problem." Volume 11 of Oxford Biology Readers, Oxford Biology Readers, Oxford University Press, 1971

selection to change a bacterium, a fruit fly, a mouse or a dog into a different kind of creature. Just as the human body is so finely tuned that the malfunction of a single part can cause great pain and suffering, there are limits to how much a complex, finely tuned organism can be changed without adversely affecting that creature.

Assumption 3: *Comparisons of selected portions of the genome are indicative of the overall homology between organisms.* Now that we are sequencing the complete genome of many species, we are discovering striking sequence differences among what we thought were closely related species, and incredible similarities among unrelated ones. Unrelated species share segments of DNA in common, and species thought to be related have sequences which are not in common. We are not as similar to the great apes as was previously thought, and some of the differences are impossible to explain by common descent.[110]

Humans, for instance, have 140 "alien" genes, which we do not share with our supposed ancestors.[111] Given that the average human gene is 1000 codons in length, that amounts to 140,000 new codons! How do we explain this, when as mentioned above, only 1667 substitutions could have occurred in the ten million years said to have passed since humans diverged from the hypothetical ape ancestor that we share with chimpanzees?

This strikes one as very strong evidence for a Creator, but evolutionary biologists believe that they have an hypothesis to explain this, and it is horizontal gene transfer (HGT).[112] They believe that cross-species viral

[110] Kerri Smith, "Gorilla joins the genome club." Nature, Mar 7, 2012. doi:10.1038/nature.2012.10185. http://www.nature.com/news/gorilla-joins-the-genome-club-1.10185 (Last accessed 03/22/20190

[111] Alastair Crisp. et al., "Expression of multiple horizontally acquired genes is a hallmark of both vertebrate and invertebrate genomes." Genome Biology 13 March 2015, 201516:50. https://doi.org/10.1186/s13059-015-0607-3

[112] Graham Lawton, "Why Darwin was wrong about the tree of life." New Scientist, January 2009. https://www.newscientist.com/article/mg20126921-600-why-darwin-was-wrong-about-the-tree-of-life/ (Last accessed 03/22/2019)

and bacterial infection is primarily responsible for it. HGT has been observed to most commonly happen, as one would expect, in prokaryotes (single-celled life forms without a cell nucleus), and much less often in single-celled eukaryotes (life forms with a cell nucleus). However, it occurs even less often than that in multi-cellular organisms, since it is only likely for it to happen through infection of the gametes (male and female germ cells).

Just as it is common for computer programmers to reuse a very useful piece of code many times, one would expect an intelligent designer to reuse an optimal piece of code many times. Scientists are discovering *so many common pieces of code* among unrelated species, that Darwin's tree of life is *undetectable* on the phylogenetic level. Instead, what we are discovering is more like a "web" of life. This prompted researchers investigating this phenomenon to write in *Molecular Biology and Evolution*,

> "Sequence comparisons suggest recent horizontal transfer of many genes among diverse species including across the boundaries of phylogenetic 'domains'. Thus determining the phylogenetic history of a species cannot be done conclusively by determining evolutionary trees for single genes".[113]

It is only through statistical analysis that some researchers believe they can possibly detect Darwin's tree of life behind it all, but the old engineering design adage, "form follows function" may also be the explanation for these statistical commonalities. Apart from these statistical analyses, which could be explained by "form follows function," phylogenetic sequence comparisons appear to be very strong evidence of design.

In the past it has merely been *assumed* that mutations combined with natural selection are sufficient explanations for the origin of the new

---

[113] Pierce, S.K.; Fang, X.; Schwartz, J.A.; Jiang, X.; Zhao, W.; Curtis, N. E.; Kocot, K.M.; Yang, B.; Wang, J. (2011). "Transcriptomic Evidence for the Expression of Horizontally Transferred Algal Nuclear Genes in the Photosynthetic Sea Slug, Elysia chlorotica." Molecular Biology and Evolution 29 (6), pp. 1545–1556. doi:10.1093/molbev/msr316. PMID 22319135.

kinds of life and biological organs on our planet. Since the ages required for this to happen would be too vast, the fossil record too fragmentary and incomplete, and soft tissue in fossils too decayed to perform genetic analysis, it has been impossible for us to observe the general theory of evolution taking place in a verifiable way. And until recently, it has not been possible to perform a rigorous mathematical analysis by means of computer to test whether or not this is possible.

In other words, natural selection has been accepted by faith and assumption, not because of rigorous evidence. Now that we can test this hypothesis in verifiable ways, although we can confirm that the *special* theory of evolution is true, the results are not boding well for the *general* theory of evolution.

Because of all these things, unlike the special theory of evolution, the general theory of evolution is not at all an undisputed hypothesis that deserves accepted theory status, despite the efforts of overly zealous metaphysical naturalists to conflate the two. Although it is popular and widely accepted as the *only* way to *naturalistically* explain the origin of life without an intelligent designer, it is *still* an unconfirmed hypothesis. For although natural selection has been observed to account for speciation among very similar kinds, there is now very good reason to be skeptical that it can adequately explain the origin of entirely new *kinds* of organisms and biological systems (at the family level and higher), or that it can adequately explain the development of new, highly complex organs.

So when someone tells you, "Evolution is a proven fact," question further. If he or she is referring only to the special theory of evolution, most of us would agree. But if he or she is claiming that *the general theory of evolution* also is a proven fact, there are very good reasons for you to disagree.

10 A Survey of Models of the Universe and Interpretations That Reconcile Genesis One With Scientific Observations

Through space the universe encompasses and swallows me up like an atom; through thought I comprehend the world. — Blaise Pascal

hen you read about cosmological models, there are several terms that come up a lot which all refer to the same cosmological model. We have already mentioned that the ΛCDM (Lambda Cold Dark Matter) model is also called the *Standard Model* of *Big Bang* cosmology. But you may also hear it referred to as the *FLRW model*. It's called this because it follows the Friedmann–Lemaître–Robertson–Walker (FLRW) metric. A *metric* is an exact solution to Einstein's field equations of general relativity.

But it's important to understand that the ΛCDM model, though it is the most popular, rests upon some assumptions, which *may not be true*. One of these assumptions is that dark matter actually exists. Dark matter was conceived of to explain the spiral motion of galaxies according to *Newtonian* gravitational theory. Dark matter and dark energy are hypothetical ingredients which are added to the mass of the universe to make Omega equal one, so that it will match measurements which indicate that space is (as best as we can tell) Euclidean.

But there are other possible explanations for the motions of galaxies. F. I. Cooperstock and S. Tieu of the Department of Physics and Astronomy at the University of Victoria found that when they analyzed the motion of the galaxies according to Einstein's theory of *general relativity* instead, there was no need for dark matter.[114]

There is also a cosmological model that builds upon Einstein's theory of relativity called *Cosmological Special Relativity*. It was developed in the early 1990s by the late Dr. Moshe Carmeli, who was Albert Einstein Professor of Theoretical Physics at Ben Gurion University in Israel and president of the Israel Physical Society. His theory matches current observations of our universe, and does not require dark energy or dark matter, though he does introduce an additional dimension of space. It predicted the accelerating expansion of the universe two years before it was observed. The time dilation effects predicted by this theory also have profound theological and philosophical implications.[115]

RECONCILING GENESIS 1 WITH SCIENTIFIC OBSERVATIONS

Many are under the mistaken impression that Genesis 1 is not reconcilable with scientific observations concerning our universe. That is simply not the case. There are in fact *many* Judeo-Christian creationist cosmological models and interpretations which reconcile the two. I am going to share them with you, but will not push a particular one. (It will be obvious which ones I favor the most, though.) Instead, this chapter is intended to be *survey* of them, so that you can decide for yourself which you believe is best.

But before I share some of them with you, it will be useful to note three similarities between the Biblical account of creation and the standard model.

---

[114] F. I. Cooperstock and S. Tieu, "General Relativity Resolves Galactic Rotation Without Exotic Dark Matter." Astrophysical Journal, 07/2005, arXiv:astro-ph/0507619. http://arxiv.org/pdf/astro-ph/0507619.pdf (Last accessed 03/22/2019)

[115] See his book, Cosmological Special Relativity: The Large-Scale Structure of Space, Time and Velocity, Second Edition

Three Similarities Between the Standard Model and the Biblical Account

The First Similarity: A Beginning

First of all, both the standard theory and the Biblical account hold that the universe had a beginning:

> **In the beginning, God created the heavens and the earth. – Genesis 1:1**

The Second Similarity: A Primordial Mass

Secondly, like the standard model, the Bible begins the creation of the universe with a huge, indeterminate amount of mass.

> **The earth was without form and void, and darkness was over the face of the deep. And the Spirit of God was hovering over the face of the waters. – Genesis 1:2**

Was this water created outright, or formed? At least one Christian cosmologist (Humphreys) has proposed that all of the universe was created from this great mass of water, and this idea does seem to fit the Biblical account. If so, this raises many intriguing questions:

Verse 2 begins with a pre-existing mass of water. How long had it been there? Since the days of Genesis were delineated by cycles of evening and morning, how long did the first evening last, before God began organizing the universe, starting with the creation of light? How long was the first morning? Since the days were delineated by evening and morning, not hours, doesn't leave room for the idea that the first day could have been *very* long?

What were conditions like within this great mass of water before cosmic inflation (expansion) began? Could this explain the long ages obtained by radioactive dating? Or if all of the days of Genesis were 24 hour days, rather than date rocks based upon conventional assumptions, how much would fusion within the primordial mass of waters alter the radioactive dating of the ages of rocks?

According to both Genesis 1 and 2 Peter 3:5, our planet is not made of stardust, but "water-dust." This might presumably be the case with many other planets, too.

"But they deliberately forget that long ago by God's word the heavens came into being and the earth was formed out of water and by water." – 2 Peter 3:5

Recent observations lend support to this idea. Scientists have only just come to believe that three times the volume of the earth's oceans is locked away in a layer of rock known as *ringwoodite*. [116]Also, seventy to ninety percent of the gases released by volcanoes is water vapor. [117]

In addition, scientists believe that water is pervasive throughout our universe, especially in the form of ice. Recently a vast reservoir of water was discovered in space.[118] Comets are also made up mostly of ice, as are the Kuiper belt and Oort cloud from which they are thought to come.[119]

The Third Similarity: The Stretching Out of the Universe

Thirdly, both the Bible and the big bang theory include an expanse (space) separating the earth from the heavenly bodies.

And God said, "Let there be an expanse in the midst of the waters, and let it separate the waters from the waters." And God made

[116] Brandon Schmandt et. al, "Dehydration melting at the top. of the lower mantle." Science 13 Jun 2014: Vol. 344, Issue 6189, pp. 1265-1268. DOI: 10.1126/science.1253358

[117] "How Volcanoes Work," geology.sdsu.ed. http://www.geology.sdsu.edu/how_volcanoes_work/Volcanic_gases.html (Last accessed 03/22/2019)

[118] Whitney Clavin and Alan Buis, "Astronomers Find Largest, Most Distant Reservoir of Water." Nasa.gov, Jul 22, 2011. https://www.nasa.gov/topics/universe/features/universe20110722.html (Last accessed 03/22/2019)

[119] Matt Williams, "What is the Oort Cloud?" Universe Today, August 10, 2015. https://www.universetoday.com/32522/oort-cloud/ (Last accessed 03/22/2019)

> **the expanse and separated the waters that were under the expanse from the waters that were above the expanse. And it was so. And God called the expanse heaven. – Genesis 1:6-8a**

We know that the "expanse" or "firmament" was space, because we are later told that God created the stars within it. This separating of the waters sounds very much like cosmic inflation, doesn't it? But it may not be. It may be that God simply separated the mass of the universe, rather than expanding space itself. Did God cause this expansion of the universe before "black hole" gravitational collapse could take place? Or did gravitational collapse take place in another universe, and is ours a "white hole" on the other side?

These waters were likely used to form the other heavenly bodies. One can easily imagine that the initial expansion took place so fast that it overpowered most of the nuclear bonds, and this is why now the most predominate element we detect in the observable universe is hydrogen.

Spreading out this mass throughout and above the space of our observable universe would have left the earth with just the right amount of mass to nurture life. What is fascinating is that we do not know what lies beyond our observable universe. Is there a thin layer of water at the outer fringes of space, beyond the observable universe?

The big bang model leaves unresolved the cause of cosmic inflation. The Bible, however, does not:

> "It is I who made the earth, and created man upon it. I **stretched** out the heavens with My hands and I ordained all their host." – Isaiah 45:12

There are *17* references in scripture to God stretching out the heavens![120] Edwin Hubble, who discovered the redshift of the galaxies and

---

[120]https://web.archive.org/web/20171111131158/http://www.creationists.org/God-streched-out-the-universe-bible-verses.html (Last accessed 04/28/2019)

concluded that this is due to a Doppler effect because they are receding from us, abandoned his first conclusion that our galaxy must lie near the center of the universe. He did this for the sake of following the Copernican principle (the idea that there is nothing special about the earth). Instead, Hubble proposed that the universe is isotropic (the same in all directions), and that the galaxies appear to receding solely because of the expansion of space. This, however, was entirely a philosophical choice. If our galaxy is near the center of the universe, that idea matches observations, too.[121]

What if Hubble was wrong in this assumption, and the Copernican principle is only true as it applies to our solar system? What if our galaxy is located near the center of the gravitational mass of the universe? This idea is known as *galactocentrism*.

24-HOUR DAY CREATIONIST COSMOLOGIES THAT RECONCILE STARLIGHT TRANSIT TIME

The three similarities we have discussed between big bang cosmology and the Bible make it possible for creationist cosmologists to develop 24-hour scriptural cosmologies that match observations just as well and in some cases even better than the standard model. Dr. Russell Humphreys developed one of the earliest that was promising, when he was a physicist at Sandia National Laboratories.

One major objection to the cosmology of the Bible has been the time that it takes for starlight to travel to the distant galaxies. How can billions of light years be reconciled with the six creation days of Genesis? As we have already discussed, it is possible that the first days were not 24 hour days. But if they were 24 hour days, Humphrey's first model utilizes the gravitational time dilation predicted by Albert Einstein's

---

[121] Edwin Hubble, *The Observational Approach to Cosmology*, Oxford: The Clarenden Press, 1937. pp. 50-59.

theory of General Relativity to reconcile seven 24-hour days with distant starlight.[122]

Since then, Dr. Humphreys has begun work on a second cosmological model, which utilizes a new type of relativistic time dilation he calls *achronicity*, or 'timelessness'. This model includes a new solution to Einstein's field equations that describe the gravitational field. Such solutions are called *metrics* because they describe how measuring devices (such as clocks and rulers) behave under different conditions. Metrics are difficult to solve and new ones are not published often, so it will be interesting to see how Dr. Humphrey's new cosmological model continues to develop.[123]

Another new model, developed by physicist John Hartnett and described in his book *Starlight, Time and The New Physics*, takes into account the time-dilation implications of Carmeli's Cosmological Special Relativity to reconcile six 24-hour creation days with the time required for starlight to reach us. However, in this model, time dilation arises from the velocity of the expansion of the universe, not from gravitation. Hartnett, a physics professor and cosmologist, was awarded the 2010 IEEE UFFC Society W.G. Cady Award "For the construction of the ultra-stable cryogenic sapphire dielectric resonator oscillators and promotion of their applications in the fields of frequency metrology and radio-astronomy." He is also an ARC DORA research fellow in the Institute of Photonics and Advanced Sensing and the School of Chemistry and Physics at the University of Adelaide. You may read more about

---

[122] Russell Humphreys, *Starlight and Time,* 1994. Green Forest, AR: Master Books, 2010.

[123] Russell Humphreys, "New time dilation helps creation cosmology." Journal of Creation 22(3), pp. 84–92, December 2008. http://creation.com/new-time-dilation-helps-creation-cosmology (Last accessed 3/18.2019)

his model at JohnHartnett.org, and through the link available through the following footnote: [124]

Alternatively, in his paper *Anisotropic Synchrony Convention—A Solution to the Distant Starlight Problem*, astronomer Dr. Jason Lisle has pointed out that the starlight problem may not be a problem at all.[125] Via email correspondence, Dr. Hartnett kindly provided the author with a nice little summary of Lisle's idea of *anisotropic synchrony convention*:

> We normally describe the speed of light across the universe by assuming that the clocks at the origin and destination of the light are synchronized according to the Einstein synchrony convention (ESC). But Einstein chose this convention as it simplified his Special theory of relativity. And we are free to choose how we synchronize clocks that are used in different parts of the universe. It is not imposed on us by nature itself. From this convention we measure the speed of light (c), which is a two way measure, as it always involves reflecting or resending a light beam from one 'clock' to another and back again, where we have assumed those clocks are synchronized by the transmission of a two-way light signal.
>
> We can alternatively adopt a convention called anisotropic synchrony convention (ASC), and assume that the clocks are synchronized by the one-way light signal. In this case the one-way speed of light is not physically a measurable in the universe (only the two-way speed is) and we are free to choose its value, since this is a

---

[124] A good link with a descriptive video of Dr: Hartnett's model is at http://johnhartnett.org/important-message-youtube/my-cosmology-from-my-book-starlight-time-and-the-new-physics/. Thanks to Dr. Hartnett for some valuable feedback and corrections to these paragraphs of the book. (He has only read a few portions of the book pre-publication, I should add.)

[125] Jason P. Lisle, "Anisotropic Synchrony Convention—A Solution to the Distant Starlight Problem." Answers Research Journal 3 (2010), pp. 191–207. www.answersingenesis.org/arj/v3/anisotropic-synchrony-convention.pdf (Last accessed 3/25/2019)

convention. That means the incoming light from the cosmos has an infinite one-way speed, but a return or outbound speed of 1/2 c. Another way of saying this is that with the ASC we time all events starting with when we first see the light signal from that event. Whereas with the ESC the event is timed from when we see the light signal but one then allows for the finite travel time of the light signal back to the source.[126]

It is also possible that Hartnett and Lisle's theories could both be combined in some ways.

Lisle has pointed out that the Big Bang theory has a light speed travel problem, too. It is called the *Horizon Problem*. The cosmic background radiation is remarkably uniform in all directions. Opposite ends of the universe could only have gotten to be about the same temperature if they have exchanged energy. That exchange could not have happened any faster than the speed of light. But opposite regions of the universe are further apart from each other than light could have traveled since the universe began! The theory of cosmic inflation has been proposed to explain this, but it leaves us with many unanswered questions, including what might have caused the inflation to start, and what might have caused it to end.[127]

Literal Interpretations of Genesis

We have already mentioned the time-dilation cosmologies, which permit literal 24-hour days in interpreting Genesis chapter 1. But many Christians hold to literal interpretations of Genesis 1 that also reconcile starlight transit time. These are presented below, beginning with a new one I would like to propose.

---

[126] Also see http://johnhartnett.org/2013/12/26/how-do-we-see-distant-galaxies-in-a-6000-year-old-universe/ and http://en.wikipedia.org/wiki/One-way_speed_of_light

[127] Lisle, Jason. Taking Back Astronomy, Master Books, 2012, pp. 48-49.

A New Literal Interpretation of Genesis One That Reconciles Starlight Transit Time: *The Day Delineation Hypothesis*

Christians and Jews have long puzzled regarding what the source(s) of light were before the sun was created on day four of the creation week. This hypothesis suggests some possible answers to that question.

In Genesis 1 the days are delineated by evening and morning, not by hours, though the days must have been 24 hours long once the sun was fully created on day four. This means that the first three days could have been longer than 24 hours, provided there were temporary sources of light to the earth from all sides that were unaffected by the earth's rotation. Here I suggest possible sources of that light.

I am not proposing this because I am persuaded it must be correct. It is just a hypothesis. I am quite happy with six 24-hour creation days combined with a time-dilation cosmology. I am simply sharing this interpretation because I regard it as worth considering. Note that it also utilizes time-dilation.

1. **First Day:** The first evening begins with darkness over the combined primordial mass of the earth and the rest of the universe, which is called "the waters." Fusion causes the creation of light within the event horizon of this huge mass of water, ending the first evening. The heavy elements of the earth and solar system are fused during this time.[128]

2. **Second Day:** On the second day, by means of a tremendous input or release of energy, God causes cosmic inflation to occur faster than light, bringing on the next evening. This creates the expanse or firmament of space. It also provides the universe with its gravitational potential energy, which like a

---

[128] I first encountered the idea of the entire universe being created from the primordial mass of water in Russell Humphreys' book *Starlight and Time*. (Green Forest, AR: Master Books, 2010.)

wound-up clock, powers the motions of the planets and fusion within the stars.

The force of the expansion separates nuclear bonds within most of the elements, especially the water, making hydrogen and helium the predominate elements in the rest of the universe. Since space did not expand throughout all of the primordial water mass, beyond the observable universe and the expanse of space there now lies a layer of water (which by now may be very thin), meaning that the universe is finite.

Inflation is much gentler near the center of the primordial mass, and this provides the material for our solar system that accretes into the other planets and our moon. The earth is left with just the right mass and heavier elements formed by fusion within the primordial mass to nurture life.

Interestingly, in a 2006 Edge.org article, physicist Lawrence Krauss is quoted as saying,

> But when you look at CMB map, you also see that the structure that is observed, is in fact, in a weird way, correlated with the plane of the earth around the sun. Is this Copernicus coming back to haunt us? That's crazy. We're looking out at the whole universe. There's no way there should be a correlation of structure with our motion of the earth around the sun – the plane of the earth around the sun – the ecliptic. That would say we are truly the center of the universe. [129]

We may one day find an explanation for this, but if not, it would fit with the idea of the universe being created from a primordial mass of which the earth was the center.

---

[129] "The Energy of Empty Space That Isn't Zero." www.edge.org. 2006-05-07. Retrieved 2018-08-05. https://www.edge.org/conversation/the-energy-of-empty-space-that-isn-39t-zero (Last Retrieved 3/25/2019)

Small water-ice particles drawn to the still-forming sun and planets begin to bombard the earth's atmosphere. The many tiny ice particles striking the Earth's atmosphere, and the many comets formed by the water-ice cause light, and the second morning begins.

3. **Third Day**: Night comes again when most of the ice particles have finished bombarding the earth and sun. During this long evening God causes the continents to rise above the oceans, and the still-cooling continental plates drift into their current locations.

   Then when *light from the brilliance of cosmic inflation* finally reaches the earth, the third morning begins. During this long period of daylight, God creates land plant life and it spreads throughout the earth. Since they are not mentioned in Genesis, perhaps during this long period of daylight God also created the first forms of single-celled life.

4. **Fourth Day:** This is the first 24 hour day. When the light from cosmic inflation dies out, evening comes again, marking the beginning of the fourth day. Then when the first light from fusion within our sun begins, the fourth morning comes. The planets and moons of our solar system are now fully formed.

   Due to gravitational time dilation, time has been passing by more slowly near the center of the universe, so the most distant stars and galaxies have already formed. ("He also made the stars" may not indicate on what day the stars were formed.) Light from them has been traveling for a long time, and it may have begun to arrive on this day.

5. **Fifth Day:** Evening comes again. This is also a normal 24 hour day, during which God creates all of the creatures of the sea and the birds of the air.

6. **Sixth day:** God creates the creatures of the land. The earth is now ready for man to inhabit it, so He creates man and woman.

7. **Seventh Day:** On the seventh day, God rests from creating the universe, setting the example for mankind of six days of work followed by a day of rest.

The Apparent Age Interpretation

Another literal interpretation of Genesis 1 is the *Apparent Age* interpretation. Those who hold to this view believe that just as God created Adam fully grown, he created the universe with the appearance of age. This view has mostly fallen out of favor among Christians and Jews, because of the problem posed by distant starlight. It would mean that the explosion of supernovae we can observe with our telescopes, for instance, never actually happened!

The Gap Interpretation

Another very common interpretation of Genesis is called the *gap theory*. Adherents of the gap theory hold that there were indeterminate ages between the first and second sentences of the book of Genesis:

> **1:1** In the beginning God created the heavens and the earth. **2** Now the earth was formless and empty, darkness was over the surface of the deep, and the Spirit of God was hovering over the waters. – Genesis 1:1-2

Young earth creationists believe that Genesis 1:1 is a summation of the creation week, and the verses that follow provide the details of how God created the earth and the rest of the universe. Those who hold to the gap theory, however, believe that verse one describes God's initial act of creation, and the verses that follow describe either a recreation of the earth or a renewal of the earth.

The Delayed Creation Week Interpretation

Similar to the gap theory is the *Delayed Creation Week* interpretation. In it, the very first verse of Genesis chapter one describes God's creation of the universe and the earth, but the seven 24-hour days of verses 2-31 begin billions of years later. In other words, the universe and the earth are described as already having been created in verse one, and only the *completion* of the formation of the earth and the universe is described in verses 2-31.

The Six 24-Hour Days Interpretation

Lastly, a high percentage of evangelical Christians hold to another interpretation, that *both* the earth and the universe were created in *Six 24 Hour Days*. Dr. Jason Lisle's Anisotropic Synchrony Convention hypothesis, which was previously described, nicely complements this interpretation to explain starlight travel. Both young earth creationists *and* old-earth creationists who ascribe to one of the literal interpretations of Genesis believe that the flood of Noah and other geologic phenomena (such as the rising of the continents from the sea during the creation week) described in the book of Genesis explain many of the fossils and geologic formations found within the earth.

If the idea of 24-hour creation days sounds unreasonable to you, consider the following. Why should we be surprised that an omnipotent, omniscient God who dwells outside of time, within whom the entire universe dwells and is sustained, and who has absolute control over it, could create a multitude of complex life forms in a single 24 hour day, when a time-bound computer programmer of limited power and intellect has similar control over a computer game universe? When we consider the power, intelligence, and awesomeness of God, the more valid question is, why would God create the universe in six days, when He could have created it all *instantly*? (I believe that it was to set a pattern of rest and work for mankind.)

In support of their views, among other things old-earth creationists point to the ages of the earth's rocks obtained by radiometric dating, the commonly accepted methods of dating sedimentary rocks, and the layers of ice found in Arctic ice core drillings.

Young-earth creationists have published replies to these and other objections, and as counter-evidence point to more indications of a young earth than one might expect, including carbon 14 in diamonds and coal, the short lives of comets (which led to the hypotheses of the Oort cloud and Kuiper belts), earth's rapidly decaying magnetic field (which led to the hypothesis that the poles reverse), the puzzlingly low salinity of the oceans, soft tissue recently found in dinosaur fossils, helium in radioactive rocks, and the young faint sun paradox.[130]

Old Earth/Old Universe Views

In addition to young earth creationist models that hold to a young earth but an old universe due to time dilation, there are also interpretations of the book of Genesis that posit an old earth and an old universe.

One of these, which those who interpret Genesis more literally typically reject, is called the *Framework Hypothesis.* It holds that the creation week is not intended to specify how long God's creative act took, but is simply figurative, metaphorical, and semi-poetic language intended to encourage mankind to imitate God's creative cycle of work and Sabbath rest. As evidence of this, they claim that there is a literary parallelism between days one to three, and days four to six. They call these the "two triads" of days.

More common is the *Day-Age* interpretation, which holds that each of the days of Genesis represents a long time period. One explanation for day four is that atmospheric conditions allowed the sun to be perceived only during that age.

---

[130] Danny R. Faulkner, "The Young Faint Sun Paradox and the Age of the Solar System." Journal of Creation 15, no 2 (August 2001): 3-4. https://answersingenesis.org/astronomy/sun/the-young-faint-sun-paradox-and-the-age-of-the-solar-system/ (Last accessed 3/25/2019)

Similar to it is the *Analogical Days Interpretation,* which holds that the days of creation week are God's consecutive workdays of unspecified length, analogous to the human workweek.[131]

The *Punctuated 24-Hour Theory* holds that God created light on the first day, waited billions of years, created the dry land on the second day, waited billions of years, and so on.[132]

The Framework, Day-Age, and Analogical Days interpretations of Genesis are those most often chosen by theistic evolutionists. Some theistic evolutionists believe that God guided the process of evolution. Others hold that God created the universe and earth in such a way that biogenesis and evolution happened by natural processes.

Those who accept a more literal interpretation of Genesis have several objections to these views, however:

- They do not fit the plain reading of the text.
- Other places in the Bible either directly or indirectly affirm that God's creative activity took six days (Exodus 20:11, Job 33:6, Mark 10:6, Acts 17:26, Romans 1:20, Romans 5:12, 1 Corinthians 15:21-22, 1 Corinthians 15:45).
- According to Genesis 1:31, After God finished creating the heavens and the earth, He "saw all that He had made, and it was very good." It is hard to imagine God saying that regarding a world in which billions of animals were suffering and dying as they evolved!
- Romans 5:12 indicates that sin and death entered the world through Adam. That does not fit evolutionary theory.

---

[131] Hugh Ross, "Four Views of the Biblical Creation Account." Reasons to Believe, August 8, 2000.
https://web.archive.org/web/20151208042322/http://www.reasons.org/articles/four-views-of-the-biblical-creation-account (Last accessed 3/25/2019)

[132] "Nine Views of Creation." BlueletterBible.org, undated.
http://www.blueletterbible.org/faq/creation.cfm (Last accessed 3/25/2019)

All of these examples of how believers interpret Genesis chapter one serve to illustrate that many rational and informed minds find harmony between the Bible and the cosmos we observe.

How Will the Universe End?

We have been comparing modern cosmologies with how the Bible tells us that the universe began. But how does the Bible compare with modern ideas about how it will end? If Omega is less than one, the big bang model possibly predicts a cataclysmic end to the universe, called *The Big Crunch*.

But there are also ideas about how the universe might end that could apply even if Omega is greater than or equal to one. In their paper *Phantom Energy and Cosmic Doomsday,* Robert R. Caldwell, Marc Kamionkowski, and Nevin N. Weinberg proposed what they call *The Big Rip.*

> Cosmologists have long wondered whether the Universe will eventually re-collapse and end with a Big Crunch, or expand forever, becoming increasingly cold and empty. Recent evidence for a flat Universe, possibly with a cosmological constant or some other sort of negative-pressure dark energy, has suggested that our fate is the latter. However, the data may actually be pointing toward an astonishingly different cosmic end game. Here, we explore the consequences that follow if the dark energy is phantom energy, in which the sum of the pressure and energy density is negative. The positive phantom-energy density becomes infinite in finite time, overcoming all other forms of matter, such that the gravitational repulsion rapidly brings our brief epoch of cosmic structure to a close. The phantom energy rips apart the Milky Way, solar system, Earth, and ultimately the molecules, atoms, nuclei, and nucleons of

which we are composed, before the death of the Universe in a "Big Rip".[133]

Another end of the universe prediction is called the *Vacuum Metastability Event.* In keeping with the humorous tradition of combining colorful metaphors about the beginning and end of the universe with the word "big," this theory is called *The Big Slurp.* A 2013 article in the NBC News Cosmic Log, entitled *"Will Our Universe End in a 'Big Slurp'? Higgs-like Particle Suggests it Might"* begins with the following:

> BOSTON — If the "Higgs-like particle" discovered last year is really the long-sought Higgs boson, the bad news is that its mass suggests the universe will end in a fast-spreading bubble of doom. The good news? It'll probably be tens of billions of years before that particular doomsday arrives.
>
> That's one of the weirder twists coming out of the continuing analysis of results from Europe's Large Hadron Collider, which produced the first solid evidence for the existence of the Higgs boson last year. Current theory holds that the Higgs boson plays a role in imparting mass to other fundamental particles. Confirming the discovery of the Higgs would fill in the last blank spot in that theory, known as the Standard Model.[134]

It is fascinating to compare these three end-of-the-universe scenarios with how the Bible says that the universe will end:

> But the day of the Lord will come as a thief in the night; in which the heavens shall pass away with a great noise, and the elements

---

[133] R. Caldwell, Marc Kamionkowski, and Nevin N. Weinberg, "Phantom Energy and Cosmic Doomsday." arXiv:astro-ph/0302506v1 25 Feb 2003. https://arxiv.org/pdf/astro-ph/0302506v1.pdf (Last accessed 3/25/2019)

[134] "Will our universe end in a 'big slurp'? Higgs-like particle suggests it might." NBC News Cosmic Log, Feb 18, 2013 2:02 PM. http://cosmiclog.nbcnews.com/_news/2013/02/18/17006552-will-our-universe-end-in-a-big-slurp-higgs-like-particle-suggests-it-might?lite (Last accessed 3/25/2019)

shall melt with fervent heat, the earth also and the works that are therein shall be burned up. – 2 Peter 3:10

And all the host of heaven shall be dissolved, and the heavens shall be rolled together as a scroll; and all their host shall fade away, as the leaf fadeth from off the vine, and as a fading leaf from the fig tree. – Isaiah 34:4

Finally, although the end of the universe is not a pleasant prospect, the Bible promises us a new universe to replace the old one:

And I saw a new heaven and a new earth: for the first heaven and the first earth were passed away; and there was no more sea. – Revelation 21:1

Long ago You laid the foundation of the earth. Even the heavens are the works of your hands. They will come to an end, but You will still go on. They will all wear out like clothing. You will change them like clothes, and they will be thrown away. But You remain the same, and Your life will never end. – Psalm 102:25-2

11 IS THE UNIVERSE A "FREE LUNCH"?

"Nothing comes from nothing. Nothing ever could." – Maria in the *Sound of Music*

ll things that begin have a cause. Our universe began. Therefore, our universe must have a cause. But what was it? While the theist believes that the cause of the universe was God, another explanation is required for naturalists. The possible naturalistic explanations fall into four broad categories:

1. **An infinite regress.** This explanation conveniently avoids the need for an uncaused first cause. However, as we will discuss in the upcoming chapter on the first cause, this proposition is logically problematic.

2. Related to the above is the idea of **an eternal static universe.** This idea once predominated among naturalists in the form of the *steady state theory*, but since it does not match observations of our expanding universe, it has fallen out of favor.

3. **A causeless first cause.** Perhaps there was a causeless first cause, but it was unintelligent. However, as we will discuss in the chapter on the first cause, there are some good arguments that if there was a first cause, it must have been intelligent. Perhaps that is why I have yet to come across a naturalist who promotes this idea. Perhaps the association of a first cause with God makes this idea distasteful to many atheistic minds.

4. **A way for nothingness –** *all on its own* **- to make itself into something.** Are what are called the *Free Lunch* models the answer that naturalists have been hoping for? Historically, the idea that the universe could have sprung into being from nothingness has struck most of mankind as ludicrous. But surprisingly, in the last few decades, this "ludicrous" idea has been gaining traction. The idea, which takes several forms, is called

the *universe-from-nothing* hypothesis in a book of the same name by theoretical physicist and cosmologist Lawrence Krauss.

We can classify universe-from-nothing theories into two kinds: universe from *absolutely* nothing (UFAN) models, and universe from intangibles (UFI) models. In UFAN models, the universe arises from sheer non-existence. But in UFI models, the universe arises through intangible things that we once thought of as nothing, but now know to be something - typically a fluctuation in a quantum vacuum field.

Did God Create the Universe From Nothing?

Universe-from-nothing proponents might be surprised to learn that their ideas share some traits in common with the Judeo-Christian doctrine called *creatio ex nihilo,* which means "creation from nothing." By contrast with some naturalistic universe-from-nothing proposals, however, in creatio ex nihilo nothing does not make itself into something by its own power. After all, how could *nothing* ever do *anything*? Instead, there is an intelligent agent – God – who creates things where there was nothing before. An illustration of this might be the way that a computer game programmer can add things to a computer game world where there was nothing before. Or the way that an intelligence can mathematically derive minus one and plus one from zero.

Not all orthodox Christians hold to creatio ex nihilo, though it is a popular teaching. This is because it is not to be found explicitly in the creeds, and cannot be conclusively proven from the Bible. What most Christians *do* agree that scripture teaches, however, is that created things are distinct from God, that God was pre-existent before anything else existed, and that all things were brought into existence by Him.

"Through him all things were made; without him nothing was made that has been made." John 1:3

Although the Bible teaches that all things were made by God, it does not explicitly teach that our universe was created from nothing. Instead, it teaches us what it was *not* made from. It was not made, it tells us, from things that can be seen:

> "By faith we understand that the universe was formed at God's command, so that what is seen was not made out of what was visible." Hebrews 11:3

And so according to the New Testament, the universe could have been created by God from nothing, *or* it could have been made out of something currently invisible to us. Could this have been a quantum vacuum field? As we touched on in an earlier chapter, it would be a small thing for the omniscient, omnipotent, and omnipresent God of Judeo-Christian theology to create a quantum vacuum field and then precisely aim a quantum fluctuation to produce a finely tuned universe such as ours in one single "bang."

Or it is conceivable that He created it from an *instanton* (which we will discuss shortly) with precisely tuned values. Perhaps He may have used these methods, but for a precisely tuned and functionally ordered universe such as ours to have happened without any intelligent guidance – as we have been discussing and will ponder even more in later chapters, is extraordinarily unlikely.

There are many other conceivable ways that God could have created the universe, but if He did create it from a quantum vacuum field or an instanton, then according to the Bible, it would have either directly or indirectly been brought into being by Him, for He is described in the Bible as "the God who gives life to the dead and **calls into being things that were not.**" – Romans 4:17

CAN *ABSOLUTELY* NOTHING CREATE A UNIVERSE?

Some universe-from-nothing cosmological models (the UFAN models), such as the *Hawking-Turok Instanton* theory, actually propose that the universe came into existence from *pure* nothingness, in the sense of non-existence, without God. In (the late) Hawking and Turok's model, the instanton is like a seed from which the entire universe grows. Since it has about the mass of a pea and contains dimensional "wrinkles" like a pea, the press affectionately dubbed it a *pea instanton*. Explaining the idea of a pea instanton, Turok wrote:

"Think of inflation as being the dynamite that produced the big bang. Our instanton is a sort of self-lighting fuse that ignites inflation. To have our instanton, you have to have gravity, matter, space and time. Take any one ingredient away, and our instanton doesn't exist. But if you have an instanton, it will instantly turn into an inflating, infinite universe."

This prompted Jack Wong of the University of Victoria to explain to his Physics 303 students:

"So in essence, Hawking and Turok proposed that the universe began from virtually nothing. The two physicists believe that the instanton does not exist "inside" of anything, nor was there anything existing "before" the instanton. The instanton was a combination of gravity, space, time, and matter packed into a rounded miniscule object. They believe the existence and subsequent actions of this object produced the big bang, and subsequently, the universe we live in today." [135]

In his article *God Did Not Create the Universe,* Hawking said the following:

"Because there is a law such as gravity, the universe can and will create itself from nothing. Spontaneous creation is the reason there is something rather than nothing, why the universe exists,

---

[135] Jack Wong, "The Universe From a Pea." Wong's Physics 303 Web Site, Spring 1999. https://web.archive.org/web/20151017101403/http://web.uvic.ca/~jtwong/index.html (Last accessed 3/25/2019)

why we exist. It is not necessary to invoke God to light the blue touch paper and set the universe going."[136]

Of course, curiosity compels us to ask , "How could the pea instanton, or any universe for that matter, have arisen from pure nothingness? How could absolute nothingness have produced the ingredients of an instanton: the law of gravity with it's precisely tuned values, matter with its behavioral laws, space with its dimensional characteristics, and time with its unique directional flow?" Turok wrote,

> "It's very important to realize that this instanton doesn't exist within anything. There is nothing "before" or "outside" of it, and it is just meaningless to ask what came before it or what lies outside it"[137]

But this is not an answer to our question, which is not what came before the pea instanton, or what lies outside of it. Our question is "How could the pea instanton, or any universe for that matter, have arisen from pure nothingness?" That is *not* meaningless to ask, and it is a very relevant question.

If, as the late Hawking and Turok seemed to assume, causality cannot exist without time, then how could a *timeless nothingness* have caused the pea instanton to come into existence? In other words, if there is no causation without time, how could nothingness have been the cause of anything "before" there was time?

And for that matter, even if you did have time, how could *absolutely nothing at all* cause *anything* to happen? In short, the idea that a universe could arise from absolutely nothing at all appears to be philosophically self-refuting.

---

[136] "Stephen Hawking: God did not create Universe" BBC News, 2 September 2010. http://www.bbc.co.uk/news/uk-11161493 (Last accessed 3/25/2019)

[137] Neil Turok, "Before the Big Bang." Cambridge University Website. Undated. http://www.damtp.cam.ac.uk/research/gr/public/daily_tel.ps (This is a downloadable postscript file last accessed 3/25/2019)

However, Hawking appeared to believe that modern cosmological models such as this ought to take precedence over philosophical considerations, having stated "Philosophy is dead. Philosophers have not kept up with modern developments in science. Particularly physics."[138]

Not a few modern-day philosophers took exception to that statement, and Christopher Norris, professor of philosophy at Cardiff University, was one of them. He wrote that

> "...scientists tend to go astray when they start to speculate on issues that exceed not only the current-best observational evidence but even the scope of what is presently conceivable in terms of testability. To speak plainly: one useful job for the philosopher of science is to sort out the errors and confusions that scientists – especially theoretical physicists – sometimes fall into when they give free rein to a speculative turn of mind."[139]

But besides raising the ire of philosophers, some of whom *do* keep up with modern developments in science, there is an even more compelling reason why disregarding philosophy is unwise. As physicist Aaron Wall wrote in *Undivided Looking*, his physics and theology blog,

> "People who dismiss philosophy still end up doing it; they just do it badly, without a critical examination of their premises."[140]

---

[138] Matt Warman, "Stephen Hawking tells Google 'philosophy is dead'." The Telegraph, Home>Technology>Google, 17 May 2011. http://www.telegraph.co.uk/technology/google/8520033/Stephen-Hawking-tells-Google-philosophy-is-dead.html (Last accessed 2/25/2019)

[139] Christopher Norris, "Hawking contra Philosophy: Christopher Norris presents a case for the defense." Philosophy Now, Issue 82, January/February 2011. https://philosophynow.org/issues/82/Hawking_contra_Philosophy (Last accessed 3/25/2019)

[140] Aron Wall , "A Universe from Nothing?" blog post, December 7, 2012. http://www.wall.org/~aron/blog/a-universe-from-nothing/ (Last accessed 3/25/2019)

You can have a cosmological model that contains highly advanced math that is flawless. But if the philosophical premises behind the model are wrong, then the model, no matter how correct and admirable the math within it may be, is wrong.

In an *Astronomy* magazine article concerning the pea instanton (which was humorously entitled "Give Peas a Chance") Tom Yulsman wrote:

> Stanford University cosmologist Andrei Linde dismisses the instanton as a mathematical abstraction with no clear basis in reality. Moreover, he questions whether it's even possible to explain how the universe could have been created from nothing.
>
> "Stephen is an extremely talented person," Linde was careful to say of Hawking. "Sometimes, however -- this is my interpretation -- he trusts mathematics so much that he makes calculations first and interprets them later." Linde finds this trust in the primacy of the math to be a bit like religious faith.
>
> "You know, it is such an esoteric science, creation from nothing. You can come away with your interpretations and there is no way to check them. It is like a religion."[141]

Linde has very good reason to doubt that something could be created from absolutely nothing. The problem with that idea is one that philosophers have been discussing since the days of Thomas Aquinas:

Something that does not yet exist in any form cannot create itself!

This principle was elucidated long ago by philosophers with the Latin phrase, *ex nihilo nihil fit*, meaning "Out of nothing comes nothing."[142]

William Lane Craig writes,

---

[141] Yulsman, Tom. "Give Peas a Chance," Astronomy magazine, September 1999, Vol. 27 Issue 9, p. 38

[142] "The Caused Beginning of the Universe: a Response to Quentin Smith." British Journal for the Philosophy of Science 44 (1993), pp. 623-639.

The principle *ex nihilo nihil fit* seems to me to be a sort of meta-physical first principle, one of the most obvious truths we intuit when we reflect seriously. If the denial of this principle is the alternative to a theistic metaphysic, then let those who decry the irrationality of theism be henceforth forever silent![143]

CAN A FEW STEPS ABOVE NOTHINGNESS CREATE A UNIVERSE?

The idea that our universe originated from a quantum vacuum fluctuation began with physicist Edward P. Tyron in 1973, when a two-page article that he wrote was published in the journal nature. It was entitled, "Is the Universe a Vacuum Fluctuation?" The abstract for the article read,

The author proposes a big bang model in which our Universe is a fluctuation of the vacuum, in the sense of quantum field theory. The model predicts a Universe which is homogeneous, isotropic and closed, and consists equally of matter and anti-matter. All these predictions are supported by, or consistent with, present observations.[144]

But Tyron was before his time, and his article was mostly ignored. It was not until Alan Guth proposed cosmic inflation and Vilenkin the idea of the universe arising from quantum tunneling that the idea began to catch on.

Unlike the pea instanton theory, in Tyron's model and others like it, "nothing" in reality means something: a quantum mechanical fluctuation in a vacuum field. These models therefore do not really violate the philosophical *ex nihilo nihil fit* principle. According to such models, the universe did not create itself from *pure* nothingness in the sense of non-being.

"We are not calling it 'nothing' to mislead you," proponents of these models would say. "We are just calling it that to grab your attention,

---

[143] Ibid.

[144] Edward P. Tyron, "Is the Universe a Vacuum Fluctuation?" Nature 246, 396 - 397 (14 December 1973); doi:10.1038/246396a0

and because a quantum vacuum field *looks* like nothingness to all of us. In addition, we once used to consider the vacuum of space to be nothingness. We now know that it is a field subject to fluctuations, and that it probably contains energy. And so we are not proposing that the universe came from *true* nothingness in the sense of non-existence, but rather that it came from something *a few steps above that* on the way to the kind of somethingness that we are all familiar with."

"But," theists counter, "your theory does not answer the question of how things came to be. You have just pushed the problem of causation back a step. Where did the quantum vacuum field come from? Why is it fluctuating? Where did the quantum laws come from?"

Acknowledging the validity of such questions, theoretical physicist Alexander Vilenkin stated, "These laws were there even before the universe. The laws are somehow more fundamental than the universe and have some platonic existence."[145]

But where can platonic ideas and forms originate, except within a thinking mind?

Also in reply to such questions, Krauss said in an interview regarding his book, *A Universe From Nothing*, "I don't ever claim to resolve that infinite regress of why-why-why-why-why; as far as I'm concerned it's turtles all the way down."[146]

Could it be "turtles all the way down"? We will examine that question in the chapter on the First Cause.

Most of those who appeal to the idea of the universe arising from a quantum vacuum fluctuation appeal to the phenomenon of

[145] Elizabeth Puccini, Tristan Waldroop. (Producers) Video: "A Universe From Nothing | Prof. Alexander Vilenkin | The Search for the Theory of Everything" Toe Movie, Published on Jan 3, 2014
https://www.youtube.com/watch?v=jHdI4Let27I (Last accessed 3/25/2019)

[146] Anderson, Ross. "Has Physics Made Philosophy and Religion Obsolete?" [Interview with Lawrence Krauss] The Atlantic, April 23, 2012.
http://www.theatlantic.com/technology/archive/2012/04/has-physics-made-philosophy-and-religion-obsolete/256203/ (Last accessed 3/25/2019)

particle/antiparticle pairs as possible evidence this could happen. Of course, there is a big difference between a couple of tiny virtual "particles" (which are not true particles) that quickly disappear and a vast universe containing multitudes of true particles that last for a long time.

How could you get a long-lasting universe like ours from a quantum fluctuation? Astrophysicist John Gribbon replies:

> Quantum uncertainty allows the temporary creation of bubbles of energy, or pairs of particles (such as electron-positron pairs) out of nothing, provided that they disappear in a short time. The less energy is involved, the longer the bubble can exist. Curiously, the energy in a gravitational field is negative, while the energy locked up in matter is positive. If the Universe is exactly flat, then as Tryon pointed out the two numbers cancel out, and the overall energy of the Universe is precisely zero. In that case, the quantum rules allow it to last forever.[147]

Also, we have no way of determining if the energy content of the universe is *exactly* zero, as required by many universe-from-nothing models. Physicist Jake Herbert writes:

> Despite Hawking's blithe assertion, no human being can possibly know the precise energy content of the entire universe. In order to verify the claim that the total energy content of the universe is exactly zero, one would have to account for *all* the forms of energy in the universe (gravitational potential energy, the relativistic energies of all particles, etc.), add them together, and then verify that the sum really *is* exactly zero. Despite Hawking's intelligence and credentials, he is hardly omniscient.[148]

---

[147] John Gribbin, "Inflation for Beginners." aether.lbl.gov. Undated. https://aether.lbl.gov/www/science/inflation-beginners.html (Last accessed 3/25/2019)

[148] Jake Hebert, "A Universe from Nothing?" Acts & Facts. 41 (7): 11-13, 2012. https://www.icr.org/article/6901 (Last accessed 3/25/2019)

If the universe began with zero energy, then because of the law of the conservation of energy, its net energy must remain zero unless something from outside of our universe adds or takes away energy from it. But as we will shortly explain, just because a closed system has zero net energy *does not* mean that zero energy was required to produce it.

PROBLEMS WITH TYRON'S ORIGINAL "UNIVERSE-FROM-NOTHING" PROPOSAL AND OTHERS LIKE IT

There are several difficulties and problematic questions associated with Tyron's original "Universe-from-nothing" model, and one or more of them apply to other "free lunch" models which build upon his idea as well.

To begin with, Tyron and Krauss's models rely upon the universe being perfectly flat (Euclidean, such that two parallel lines never diverge from each other or cross each other). Although our best measurements indicate that the universe is *approximately* flat, it could simply be so large that we cannot detect its curvature, just as the earth appeared to ancient man.

Secondly, in order for our universe to have originated from a vacuum fluctuation, then as Tyron pointed out in his article, it must be embedded in another space - a "hyperspace" with an additional dimension that contains a vacuum field. But is there a quantum vacuum field outside of our universe? We do not know. And where would this hyperspace, and the quantum laws that govern it have come from?

Thirdly, *particle/antiparticle pairs* are actually what are called *virtual* particles. They are not true particles at all, being defined only, in the words of theoretical physicist Matt Strassler ,"in the presence of relatively weak forces." And it is the presence of *other* particles and fields that causes them! As Strassler explains:

> "The best way to approach this concept, I believe, is to forget you ever saw the word "particle" in the term. A virtual particle is not a particle at all. It refers precisely to a disturbance in a field that is

not a particle. A particle is a nice, regular ripple in a field, one that can travel smoothly and effortlessly through space, like a clear tone of a bell moving through the air. A 'virtual particle', generally, is a disturbance in a field that will never be found on its own, but instead is something that is caused by the presence of other particles, often of other fields.... in quantum field theory, quantum fluctuations are sometimes called, or attributed to, the 'appearance and disappearance of two (or more) virtual particles'. This technical bit of jargon is unfortunate, as these things (whatever we choose to call them) are certainly not particles — for instance, they don't have a definite mass — and also, more technically, because the notion of 'a virtual particle' is only precisely defined in the presence of relatively weak forces."[149]

Fourthly, quantum fluctuations that produce virtual particle/antiparticle pairs have been experimentally confirmed to happen in empty space *within* our universe. But do they happen outside of it? We have no way to experimentally confirm this, since we cannot get outside of our universe! Since, as Strassler explained in the quote above, a virtual particle is caused by a quantum fluctuation resulting from the presence of *other* particles and fields, what would have caused the fluctuation that generated our universe, if no other particles existed before?

Only under special conditions do true particles spontaneously come into existence within our universe, such as under experimental conditions in which virtual photons are given enough energy to remain as real photons, [150] or when Hawking radiation emanates from just

---

[149] Matt Strassler, "Virtual Particles: What are they?" Of Particular Significance: Conversations About Science with Theoretical Physicist Matt Strassler." October 10, 2011. http://profmattstrassler.com/articles-and-posts/particle-physics-basics/virtual-particles-what-are-they/ (Last accessed 3/19/2019)

[150] Charles Q. Choi, "Something from Nothing? A Vacuum Can Yield Flashes of Light: 'Virtual particles' can become real photons--under the right conditions." Scientific American, February 12, 2013. http://www.scientificamerican.com/article/something-from-nothing-vacuum-can-yield-flashes-of-light/ (Last accessed 3/25/2019)

outside the event horizon of black holes. Neither of these examples violate the laws of the conservation of energy, however, but are merely a transfer of matter and/or energy that is dependent upon *pre-existent* matter and/or energy to occur. When Hawking radiation is generated, for instance, there is a corresponding reduction in the size of the black hole. Since we do not observe any true particles springing into existence within our universe without preexisting matter and energy to cause this, what is the justification for claiming that this could have happened *outside* of the universe if there was no preexisting matter to provoke it?

Fifthly, Tyron's original paper in *Nature* requires that the universe be closed. In other words, it must close back in upon itself and have no edge, like the surface of a globe does. If it were both closed *and* flat, this would mean that the universe is finite. If it is closed, perfectly flat, and finite, this means that it must have an exotic shape, such as that of a toroid. If so, as we discussed in a previous chapter, it must be *much larger* than what we can observe to explain the chance formation of life. However, it may be only *slightly* larger than what we can observe and still fit within our measurements.

Sixthly, Tyron's, Hawking's and Krauss's models require the universe be to *globally isotropic* – approximately uniform in all directions. The 2015 Planck satellite results reported "Full-sky CMB maps from the 2015 Planck release allow us to detect departures from global isotropy on the largest scales."[151]

In "CMB Anomalies after Planck," Dominiik J. Schwatz et al. write,

> "Despite numerous detailed investigations, we still lack a clear understanding of these large-scale features, *which seem to imply a*

---

[151] Quote from the abstract of the Planck 2015 results. XVIII. Background Geometry & Topology. http://xxx.lanl.gov/abs/1502.01593 (lanl.arXiv.org > astro-ph > arXiv:1502.01593)

violation of statistical isotropy and scale invariance of inflationary perturbations."[152]

Seventhly, Tyron's hypothesis required that the universe be composed equally of matter and antimatter. However, observations made since Tyron wrote his article indicate that antimatter constitutes only a very tiny percentage of the universe. This imbalance of matter and anti-matter in the universe is known as *baryon asymmetry*. Newer universe-from-nothing models do not require this.

Lastly, Vilenkin, who has his own "Creation of Universes From Nothing" model, acknowledged that if the most traditional view of quantum mechanics – the Copenhagen interpretation - is adopted, the odds of our universe occurring as a quantum fluctuation are vanishingly small. Vilenkin conceded that one must adopt the problematic "many universes" Everett interpretation of quantum mechanics for his own proposal to be likely. He wrote:

> "If the Copenhagen interpretation is adopted, then the creation was a one-shot event, with a single universe popping out of nothing. This, however, leads to a problem. The most likely thing to pop out of nothing is a tiny Planck-sized universe, which would not tunnel, but would instantly collapse and disappear. Tunneling to a larger size has a small probability and therefore requires a large number of trials. It appears to be consistent only with the Everett interpretation"[153]

Zero Net Energy ≠ No Energy

Before we go on, it is important to make a distinction between gravitational *field* energy and gravitational *potential* energy. Gravitational field energy is what attracts masses to each other. On the other hand,

---

[152] Dominik J. Schwarz, Craig J. Copi, Dragan Huterer, Glenn D. Starkman, "Cosmology and Nongalactic Astrophysics" (astro-ph.CO), 10.1088/0264-9381/33/18/184001, arXiv:1510.07929 [astro-ph.CO]

[153] Vilenkin, Alexander. *Many Worlds In One: The Search for Other Universes*, 2007, Farar, Strauss and Giroux, p. 117.

gravitational potential energy is the energy that is stored by moving masses apart from each other, kind of like stretching out a rubber band.

Some zero-energy universe models such as that of Lawrence Krauss claim it is the field energy that cancels out the energy contained in the mass. But in the regime of general relativity, gravity is simply considered to be the curvature of spacetime. One must choose to look at things from the standpoint of Newtonian physics in order to regard gravity as a force with a magnitude of energy.

Tyrone's original model , on the other hand, relies on gravitational potential energy, rather than field energy, to cancel out the positive energy of the mass of the universe.

In order for gravitational potential energy to always be considered negative, you have to choose infinity as a reference point, and this is also an arbitrary choice. Physicist and astronomer Danny Faulkner explains,

> In physics, the only negative energies are those encountered with potential energies. Indeed, Tryon used gravitational potential energy in the general form $-GmM/R$ to estimate the total gravitational potential energy of the universe. Using values then current (circa 1973), Tryon found that gravitational potential energy and the energy of matter were roughly equivalent, from which he concluded that the universe had zero energy.
>
> However, potential energies are zero only if we choose an appropriate reference point to make them so (the mathematics is simpler this way).
>
> In classical physics, the choice of reference point is arbitrary, and if we choose a different reference point, all potential energies could be positive. Hence, in an absolute sense, one cannot so easily make the energy of the universe zero. However, some physicists have argued that in non-classical physics this is possible (Berman 2009) or have put forth theories of how certain fields may be present in

the universe that may require negative potential energies. Indeed, the entire motivation for this sort of approach appears to be the bias against the possibility of a Creator rather than some formal requirement based upon observation of the universe or known laws of physics."

In order to hypothetically derive *actual* equal positive and negative energies from nothingness, the two energies must have a relationship: they must be symmetric opposites of one another in some sense. And if they can be derived from nothingness, it ought to be possible to combine them to obtain nothingness again.

However, if stored energy is released when positive and negative energies cancel out, then there is a *potential energy* relationship between the two energies. In fact, considering gravitational energy to be negative *requires* that there be a potential energy relationship, because as physicist Danny Faulkner wrote in the quote above, "In physics, the *only* negative energies are those encountered with potential energies." [emphasis mine.]

Is stored energy released as gravitational field energy and mass interact? Yes, kinetic energy is released, and as gravity pulls matter back together in the stars, work is performed that triggers fusion. Gravity pulls masses back together with *force,* which in this case is a directional pull on the masses.

This means that the nature of the universe is such that there is a *potential energy relationship* between gravitational field energy and mass, and that relationship can be summarized by these three simple principles:

1. It takes energy to separate gravitational masses from each other.
2. As long as there are no interfering factors, the energy required to separate gravitational masses equals the gravitational potential energy gained.
3. As gravity does its work and gravitational masses come back together, potential energy is released in the form of kinetic and other energies.

From a Newtonian perspective, this means that *tremendous energy* was required to separate the masses within our universe and to create gravitational field energy, and that energy had to come from somewhere. Steven Hawking himself said,

> "Since it takes *positive energy* to separate the two pieces of matter, gravity must be using negative energy to pull them together." [emphasis mine]

Since the only negative energies are those encountered with potential energies, there must be a potential energy relationship between the positive energy of mass and the negative energies of the gravitational field and gravitational potential energy. And that brings us to our next point:

It takes energy to create a potential energy relationship.

When it comes to potential energies, if there is a negative energy of -1 and a positive energy of +1, then the stored potential energy is the difference between them, which is +2.

Force is simply a magnitude of energy with a directional push or pull. Suppose one strong man is pulling on your right arm, and another strong man is pulling on your left arm with equal force in exactly the opposite direction. Since they are pulling with equal force, is there zero net force tugging on you? Zero *net* force, yes, but certainly not zero force, or your shoulder sockets would not feel like they are about to dislocate!

If I place an arrow in a crossbow, pull back the string and place it on its latch, then the negative force of the bow will exactly match the restraining force provided by the string and latch, so that there will be zero net force in the system. But does that mean that no energy was required to put the crossbow in that state? When I pull the trigger and release the arrow, it will be obvious just how much energy was placed into that net zero energy system!

And so, it is clear that you can have zero *net* energy, and at the same time have tremendous *potential* energy. But despite the fact that Hawking himself acknowledged that it takes "positive energy" to separate two gravitational masses, he seems to equate *net* zero energy with the universe spontaneously creating itself using *no* energy when he offers this as an explanation for how all of the particles in the universe got here! He wrote,

> "Where did they [the particles in the universe] all come from? The answer is that, in quantum theory, particles can be created out of energy in the form of particle/antiparticle pairs. But that just raises the question of where the energy came from. The answer is that the total energy of the universe is exactly zero. The matter in the universe is made out of positive energy. However, the matter is all attracting itself by gravity. Two pieces of matter that are close to each other have less energy than the same two pieces a long way apart, because you have to expend energy to separate them against the gravitational force that is pulling them together. Thus, in a sense, the gravitational field has negative energy. In the case of a universe that is approximately uniform in space, one can show that this negative gravitational energy exactly cancels the positive energy represented by the matter. So the total energy of the universe is zero. "[154]

Alex Vilenkin says essentially the same thing:

> "The way the universe gets around that problem [of how to create itself from nothing] is that gravitational energy is negative," Vilenkin says. "Therefore, creating a closed universe out of nothing does not violate any conservation laws." [155]

---

[154] Hawking, Stephen. 1998. A Brief History of Time. New York: Bantam Books. p. 129.

[155] Steve Nadis, "What Came Before the Big Bang?" Discover, September 2013. http://discovermagazine.com/2013/september/13-starting-point (Last accessed 3/25/2019)

As we discussed earlier, a cosmological model may be mathematically correct. But if the premises behind it are wrong, then the model, no matter how mathematically brilliant or elegant it is, must be wrong. In this case, the highly questionable presupposition underlying most universe-from-nothing proposals is that 'total" or "net" zero energy in the universe means that no energy was required to create it.

But as we have already discussed, zero net energy does *not* equal no energy! It's a simple principle that energy must be expended to create a potential energy difference between positive and negative energies. Here are some simple examples to illustrate this:

- In order for me to lift a large stone into the air and give it gravitational potential energy, I have to expend energy. Apart from the friction of air, if I let go of it, the kinetic energy obtained at impact *will equal the energy required to raise it to that height.*
- If I blow up a balloon and tie it off, then the positive push of the air within it will exactly equal the negative pull provided by the elastic rubber. There will therefore be zero net energy, but does this mean that no energy was expended to blow it up?

In short, net zero energy *does not at all* mean that zero energy went into creating a closed system, contrary to what appears to be a common assumption in "universe-from-nothing" cosmological models. In fact, the greater the difference between the related opposite energies in a net zero potential energy system, the more energy was required to create that system!

It therefore makes sense that the greater the difference between the positive matter and the negative gravitational potential energy in our universe, the more energy was required to place our universe in its current state. And so, the *more* matter our universe contains, the greater the gravitational field energy, and the *more* gravitational potential energy it has, the *more* energy should have been required to place it in its current state.

This means that contrary to what Hawking argued (and as his own words acknowledge), to create a universe with zero net energy that has a great deal of gravitational potential energy, a great deal of energy is required, or the conservation laws *will* be violated. Therefore, if a quantum vacuum fluctuation can produce a universe containing gravitational potential energy and gravitational field energy that can perform work, that fluctuation *must* have energy.

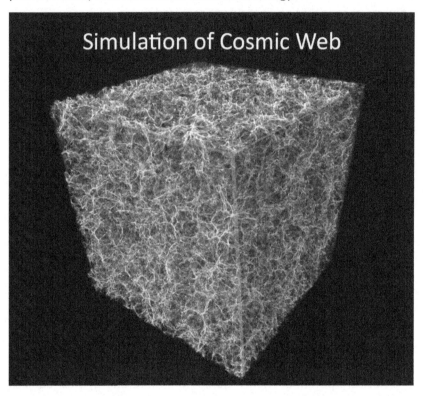

Figure 11. A NASA simulation of cosmic web. According to the Hubble team, "This graphic represents a slice of the spider-web-like structure of the universe, called the 'cosmic web.' These great filaments are made largely of dark matter located in the space between galaxies. The Hubble Space Telescope probed the structure of intergalactic space to look for missing ordinary matter, called baryons, that is gravitationally attracted to the cosmic web."[156] *Credit: NASA*

Just as stretching out a rubber band gives it potential energy, the pulling (or pushing) apart of the matter in the universe gave it gravitational potential energy. We know this because as gravity pulls all of that matter back together, fusion occurs within the stars, powering all of the

---

[156] http://hubblesite.org/image/2348

life on our planet, and the galaxies and planets spin in a dazzling display of kinetic energy.

As gravity performed its work and things started to come back together, the galaxies (and dark matter if it exists) coalesced into a *texture* that looks a lot like the fibers in a natural elastic fabric that has been stretched out. This texture of matter throughout space is known as *cosmic web*. See figure **Figure 11** for a NASA simulation of it.

And so clearly, if the universe has zero net energy, that does nothing at all to explain how it obtained all of its potential energy.

One well-accepted hypothesis is that most of the expansion of space happened in the first moments after the big bang. The idea that space drastically expanded in the first few moments of the universe, proposed in the 1980s by physicists Alan Guth and Andrei Linde, is called *cosmic inflation*. In the cosmic inflation hypothesis, the "explosion" of the big bang was not just an explosion of matter, but of space. As space rapidly expanded, the matter of the universe was stretched apart with it.

And so like a huge elephant in the room, the unavoidable and obvious question is,

> *Who or what put all of this gravitational potential energy and gravitational field energy into the universe?*

That is a great mystery! Is there an answer to it? The ancient prophet Isaiah provided an answer to that question long before the discipline of modern cosmology began. If you have never read *The Book of Isaiah*, then you have been deprived of a great work of literature containing beautiful, soaring, majestic prose of deep meaning. Isaiah recorded God providing the following answer to that mystery, seemingly in anticipation of those who would ask this very question:

> *"It is I who made the earth and created mankind on it. My own hands stretched out the heavens; I marshalled their starry hosts."*
> — Isaiah 45:6

Our discussion has made it apparent that only a highly unlikely quantum fluctuation of tremendous energy could have produced our universe. Since a quantum fluctuation of that magnitude, and that produced a low entropy, finely-tuned universe like ours is so improbable, you would need *a lot* of universes to make it likely for our universe to have formed. That would require our universe to be imbedded in a multiverse containing a vast number of universes, and it leaves us with many unanswered questions about the origin of that hypothetical hyperspace, it's energy, and it's laws. In short, instead of avoiding creation by God, such universe-from-nothing models merely push back the problem of causation.

Is No Energy Required for the Expansion of Space?

The concept of the expansion of space is used by Hawking and Vilenkin to avoid the problem of the energy required to create the gravitational potential energy of the universe. Although these men deny that the conservation laws are violated through this by claiming that the net energy of the universe is zero, physicist Sean Carroll believes that is the wrong approach. He simply claims that when it comes to the expansion of spacetime, the energy conservation laws do not apply! He writes,

> "...in my experience, saying "there's energy in the gravitational field, but it's negative, so it exactly cancels the energy you think is being gained in the matter fields" does not actually increase anyone's understanding — it just quiets them down. Whereas if you say "in general relativity spacetime can give energy to matter, or

absorb it from matter, so that the total energy simply isn't con- served," they might be surprised but I think most people do actually gain some understanding thereby.

Energy isn't conserved; it changes because spacetime does. See, that wasn't so hard, was it?" [157]

Carroll uses the energy that a photon loses as it is redshifted as an ex- ample of energy not being conserved when space expands. But it may actually be conserved. Although photons are massless, they are still affected by gravity, since they must travel though the curved space created by the gravitational mass of the universe. As a photon moves away from a gravitational mass, it loses energy and red shifts, but as it travels towards one, it gains energy and blue-shifts. If no photon can escape the gravitational pull of all of the mass in the universe, then any loss in energy due to the expansion of space will be ultimately regained when the photon is recaptured by the gravity of the universe. This means that the energy lost by a photon as space expands would simply become potential energy. So energy *would be* conserved in that case.

If energy was required to expand space, this means that it would be conserved even if photons are able to escape the gravitational mass of the universe. Since mass gains kinetic and gravitational potential en- ergy as space expands, it seems reasonable to conclude that energy must be required to expand space. After all, we refer to the mysteri- ous force that is *currently* causing the galaxies to move apart from each other at an accelerating rate as dark *energy*!

If black holes – which affect space by dramatically curving it - radiate as much energy in the form of Hawking radiation as they lose while they evaporate, isn't it reasonable for us to conclude that another method of reshaping space – expanding it – also must not violate the conservation laws?

---

[157] Sean Carroll, "Energy Is Not Conserved" February 22, 2010 blog post. http://www.preposterousuniverse.com/blog/2010/02/22/energy-is-not- conserved/ (Last accessed 3/25/2019)

If the conservation laws hold true even on universal scales, then energy must have been required to stretch out space, just like it is required to stretch out the fabric of a tent or a trampoline.

And so, *is* cosmic inflation – the theoretical rapid stretching of space right after the big bang– truly the way in which the matter in the universe became pulled apart, thus giving the universe all of its potential energy? And if so, what caused cosmic inflation to happen?

That is considered to be one of the greatest mysteries in cosmology today. Eric Agol, an astrophysicist at the University of Washington, remarked "Inflation is an extremely powerful theory, and yet we still have no idea what caused inflation—or whether it is even the correct theory, although it works extremely well."[158]

In short, when some cosmologists appeal to the expansion of space to argue that no energy was required to create the universe, they are really appealing to something shrouded in mystery. They are speculating, because they do not really *know* that zero energy is required to stretch out space. If the conservation laws apply at this scale, then *tremendous* energy must have been required to stretch out space!

The problem with claiming that the law of the conservation of energy does not apply when space expands is that it violates the *law of action and reaction* that most of us learned in grade school. This is also known as *Newton's Third Law of Motion*:

> For every action, there is an equal and opposite reaction.

If the expansion of space resulted in all of the gravitational potential energy of the universe being created from zero energy, or even from very low energy, then from a very small or nonexistent input of energy, a much, much greater reaction occurred – the *vast* gravitational potential energy our universe!

---

[158] Ker Than, "Greatest Mysteries: How Did the Universe Begin?" Live Science, August 13, 2007. http://www.livescience.com/1774-greatest-mysteries-universe.html (Last accessed 3/25/2019)

Does that make sense to you? Doesn't disregarding the law of action and reaction in order to explain the creation of the universe without God seem rather dubious?

But beyond that, there are unanswered questions regarding the concept of the expansion of space.

1. Was the matter which formed the galaxies moved apart *because* of the expansion of space (EoS), or
2. Was the matter propelled apart *within* space?
3. Or as physicist and cosmologist John Hartnett has proposed, is space defined by the average density of the matter within it, in which case space was moved apart *with* the galaxies? He calls the idea of such a space the *cosmic substratum*.

All three of these ideas would match observations. Hartnett writes:

"I argue that this hypothesis [the EoS, or expansion of space] is invalid and that no local or global experiment could detect expansion of space, or *even of the cosmic substratum*. *Relativity simply will not allow that.* And that puts *cosmology firmly into the realm of metaphysics.*

"Often, the rubber balloon analogy is used—galaxies stuck on the surface as the balloon is blown up—which illustrates space expanding and the galaxies being pushed apart from each other (and also that there is no centre, no special place uniquely for us in the universe).

"Nowadays, the expanding big bang universe is considered to be established dogma, but it has its own problems. The biggest is the problem of kinetic energy of the galaxies driven apart by massless space. Do they have kinetic energy? Those with the EoS "surface of the balloon" analogy cannot have kinetic energy because they are *not moving through space*, but if they *move with the cosmic substratum* they do. In the case of the former, the universe has been called the "ultimate free lunch" (Stenger 1990), but really it just adds more questions.[159]

And so, as Hartnett indicates, in answer to the question, could the expansion of space *alone* have provided the universe with all of its gravitational potential energy, the answer is no, not unless the law of the conservation of energy does not apply, or unless the expansion of space was caused by an amount of energy equal to the resulting gravitational potential energy. This is because if the laws *do* apply, the law of the conservation of energy demands that the total net energy in our universe must remain constant.

If zero energy drove cosmic inflation, then if the law of the conservation of energy applies, the matter being carried along by the expansion of space should have no kinetic energy!

However, observations make it plain that the galaxies contain tremendous potential and kinetic energy. Papers, books and computer simulations have been written about the tremendous kinetic and gravitational interactions that occur when galaxies collide.

In fact, our own galaxy is currently on a collision course with its nearest galactic neighbor, the Andromeda galaxy (M31). The collision is anticipated to produce a new merged galaxy called "Milkdromeda."[160] The European Southern Observatory has provided us with a beautiful photograph (see **Figure 12**) of two galaxies merging entitled, "A Cosmic Embrace."[161]

---

[159] John G. Harnett, "Expansion of Space—A Dark Science." Answers Research Journal 7 (2014):pp. 453:458. http:// www.answersingenesis.org/arj/v7/expansion-of-space.pdf (Last accessed 3/25/2019) Also see http://www.johnhartnett.org.

[160] Fraser Cain, "When Our Galaxy Smashes Into Andromeda, What Happens to the Sun?" Universe Today, May 10, 2007. http://www.universetoday.com/1604/when-our-galaxy-smashes-into-andromeda-what-happens-to-the-sun/ (Last accessed 3/25/2019)

[161] http://www.eso.org/public/usa/images/ngc2207/

Figure 12. Galaxies NGC 2207 and IC 2163 in a cosmic merger. The smaller galaxy's shape is being distorted by the larger one, throwing out streamers over 100,000 light years long. If no energy was required to move the matter that formed the galaxies apart, then why do we see kinetic interactions like this when galaxies merge? Credit: ESO

But how could kinetic interactions like this occur when galaxies collide, if zero energy was required to separate the matter from which these galaxies originally were formed?

If something is not really moving through space, then how can it have kinetic energy? If zero energy was expended to separate the matter of the universe, then why is so much energy being released as gravity pulls the matter back together? Doesn't it make sense that the energy being released must have come from the energy required to separate it?

In a previous chapter, I quoted cosmologists Jean-Pierre Luminet, Glenn D. Starkman and Jeffrey R. Weeks. That quote bears repeating:

> ...there is preliminary work in quantum cosmology, which attempts to describe how the universe emerged spontaneously from the void. Some such theories predict that a low-volume universe is more probable than a high-volume one. An infinite universe would have zero probability of coming into existence. Loosely speaking, its energy would be infinite, and no quantum fluctuation could muster such a sum.[162] [163]

From this quote, it is clear that not all cosmologists hold to the idea that a high-volume universe such as ours can be created from a zero or low energy quantum fluctuation. And it is *impossible* for a fluctuation to have zero potential energy, though it *can* have zero net energy. This is because the total energy of the fluctuation is the difference between its positive and negative values. If our vast universe was created from a vacuum fluctuation, where did this tremendous energy come from?

KEEPING OUR SENSE OF WONDER AND HUMILITY

In the preface of his book, *A universe-from-nothing*, Krauss writes,

> Moreover, all signs suggest that this is how our universe *could* have arisen. I stress the word *could* here, because we may never have

---

[162] "Quantum Cosmology and the Creation of the Universe," by Jonathan J. Halliwell; Scientific American, December 1991, describes the probability of an infinite fluctuation as virtually zero.

[163] Jean-Pierre Luminet, Glenn D. Starkman and Jeffrey R. Weeks, "Is Space Finite," Scientific American, April 1999. https://web.archive.org/web/20170317045828/http://cosmos.phy.tufts.edu/~zirbel/ast21/sciam/IsSpaceFinite.pdf (Accesed 3/25/2019)

enough empirical information to resolve this question unambiguously. [The emphasis in this quote is Krauss's, not mine.][164]

Likewise, Vilenkin acknowledged at the end of his "Spontaneous Creation of Universes" essay,

> "The ideas discussed in this essay are of metaphysical nature; they are not subject to experimental tests and can only be tested by an overall consistency of our picture of the universe."[165]

Let's keep in mind that Intelligent Design proponents also "test" the validity of their hypotheses by examining the overall consistency of our picture of the universe. They find the complexity of life and the low entropy state of the universe to be consistent with their hypothesis. Clearly, as Vilenkin acknowledged, "universe-from-nothing" models are metaphysical proposals, placing them in the same class as Intelligent Design cosmologies, in that they are based upon presuppositions that cannot be directly verified by experiment. There is no scientific evidence that our universe created itself from nothing. In fact, as Krauss himself admits, there may never be!

Even though we are learning and discovering, humility should compel us to admit just how much we do not know about the underlying nature of our universe or the means by which it was brought into being. The philosopher CEM Joad wrote,

> "Intellect can light up only a small area of the universe. For my part, I should subscribe to the familiar paradox that the more we know, the more we are conscious of our ignorance - the further the intellect has traveled, the smaller it seems relatively to the distance still to be traveled."

---

[164] Lawrence M. Krauss, *A Universe-from-nothing*, Free Press, NY, 2012, p. xiii

[165] Alexander Vilenkin, "Spontanaeous Creation of Universes." Honorable Mention Essay submitted to the Gravity Research Foundation, 1983. http://www.gravityresearchfoundation.org/pdf/awarded/1983/vilenkin.pdf (Last accessed 12/25/2015)

Even biblical theists such as myself find the Bible sketchy on most of the fine details of exactly *how* our universe was created. We are given only broad generalities of information. Our universe is an object of tremendous fascination to us primarily because it is still shrouded in so much mystery. This brings to mind some poetic prose from what is probably the oldest book in the Bible, the book of Job. God spoke this challenge to Job:

> *"Can you bind the chains of the Pleiades? Can you loosen Orion's belt? Can you bring forth the constellations in their seasons or lead out the Bear with its cubs? Do you know the laws of the heavens?"*
> *Job 38:31-33a*

Doesn't that ancient challenge still apply to us even today? We are still figuring out the laws and nature of our own universe. And though we may speculate that perhaps our universe lies within a sort of hyperspace containing a quantum vacuum field, we do not *truly* know the laws of the realm that lies immediately outside of our universe – much less any "heavens" that may lie above that! Even today, despite all of our scientific progress, if we are honest, we must humbly admit that we can only speculate about these things. The *hundreds* (or perhaps even thousands) of different modern cosmological models that we have is evidence of this.

To summarize, some "free lunch" cosmological models violate the time honored and sensible philosophical principle of *ex nihilo nihil fit*, which means, "out of nothing, nothing comes." Secondly, all of them assume that zero net energy means no energy. However, there appears to be a potential energy relationship between the positive energy of the mass, and negative field and potential energies of the universe. Lastly, the expansion of space is used to explain how the mass of the universe could have become separated without an input of energy. By doing so, they are in effect claiming that the *law of action and reaction* also does not apply to the origin of the universe. If the universe was created using zero or very little energy, then a small action produced a *much* greater reaction!

If a closed system has tremendous *potential* energy while at the same time having zero *net* energy, then if these three common sense principles apply, this state could only have been achieved by putting tremendous energy into the system.

Nearly all of us received free bag lunches when we were children, but they did not just pop into existence on their own. Someone (typically a caring mom) expended energy to make them for us!

12 RICHARD DAWKINS' PROBABILISTIC ARGUMENT AGAINST GOD

"That deep emotional conviction of the presence of a superior reasoning power, which is revealed in the incomprehensible universe, forms my idea of God." — Albert Einstein

ware of probability arguments such as those presented in this book, and in order to escape the obvious implication of them that there is a God, some metaphysical naturalists have raised interesting counter-arguments to the existence of God.

In his book *The God Delusion*, Richard Dawkins writes:

> "However statistically improbable the entity you seek to explain by invoking a designer, the designer himself has got to be at least as improbable. God is the Ultimate Boeing 747."[166]

Here Dawkins was referring to a statement astronomer Fred Hoyle made regarding the odds of life forming by chance, which I quoted in chapter five, but will repeat again:

> "A junkyard contains all the bits and pieces of a Boeing 747, dismembered and in disarray. A whirlwind happens to blow through the yard. What is the chance that after its passage a fully assembled 747, ready to fly, will be found standing there? So small as to be negligible, even if a tornado were to blow through enough junkyards to fill the whole Universe."[167]

---

[166] Richard Dawkins, *The God Delusion* (London: Bantam Press, 2006), p. 114.

[167] Fred Hoyle, *The Intelligent Universe: A New View of Creation and Evolution,* (1983), p. 19. You may read Hoyle's quote in context at http://www.charliewagner.net/hoyle.htm. (Last accessed 3/25/2019)

By the "Ultimate Boeing 747" Dawkins is of course referring to the omniscient, omnipotent, and omnipresent God of Judeo-Christian theology. Dawkins' argument appears to rest upon certain presumptions. Let's identify what they might be.

PRESUMPTION 1: THE SIMPLEST HYPOTHESIS THAT EXPLAINS OBSERVATIONS IS ALWAYS THE ONE TO BE PREFERRED.

The idea that if all other factors are equal, the simplest explanation is the one to be preferred, is known as *Ockham's razor* (also spelled *Occam's Razor)*. It is quite fashionable for naturalists to claim that theism is a more complex explanation than naturalistic mechanisms, and therefore violates Ockham's razor. But although He is infinitely complex in intellect, God's underlying nature may be very simple. Shortly we will discuss the reasons for this, and they are compelling.

But even if God is complex, Ockham's razor is merely an heuristic rule of thumb, not evidence. It serves as a general guideline for choosing between competing hypotheses. There are several justifications for it. First of all, if the evidence can be explained equally well by both a simple idea and a more complex one, the simplest explanation is often (but not always) more likely to have happened. Secondly, simple explanations are more practical for us to use.

However, unless competing explanations explain the evidence equally well, Ockham's razor is not intended to be the sole criterion for choosing between them. The reason for this can be illustrated with the little story, *Shaving with Ockham's Razor.*

Obviously, these aliens have nicked quite badly by shaving with Ockham's Razor. But why? For two reasons:

1. Sometimes the most reasonable explanation is not the simplest.
2. *Ockham's razor does not trump evidence.* The aliens gave more weight to Ockham's razor than they did the evidence that the teacup was intelligently designed!

Shaving With Ockham's Razor

A race of aliens living in a nearby solar system had their own version of Ockham's Razor, and adopted it as a guiding principle of science. In accordance with it, they believed that among competing scientific hypotheses, the simplest and most elegant one that fits the evidence should be chosen.

One day, an automated probe from their planet landed in a field on Earth. Unfortunately, during its long journey, the probe was damaged by interstellar dust particles and lost camera and communication functionality. However, it was still able to automatically collect soil and mineral samples. While gathering a soil sample, it happened to scoop up a long lost, small white ceramic teacup from a little girl's toy tea set. Then it returned to the planet from whence it came.

After much consideration, the aliens concluded that despite the fact that the teacup *appeared* to be intelligently designed, it was not designed by an intelligence, but was formed by volcanism and natural erosion, because this would be the simplest and least complex explanation.

Ockham's Razor is a good guideline, and it is useful when we must choose between one hypothesis that is simple, and another that is complex, *but only if both explain the evidence equally well.* It's not a hard and fast rule though, because sometimes, even when two ideas seem to explain the evidence equally well, the most complex idea is the true one. Ockham's razor should therefore never be given more weight than observational evidence, logic, or sensibility. Unfortunately it is often misapplied by those who do not understand this, as though it amounted to evidence!

PRESUMPTION 2: GOD SHOULD BE REJECTED AS AN EXPLANATION FOR LIFE BECAUSE HE WOULD BE MORE COMPLEX THAN WHAT HE IS BEING USED TO EXPLAIN. SINCE HE IS MORE COMPLEX, HE IS LESS PROBABLE TO HAVE FORMED.

First of all, the Bible does not teach that God formed by chance from chaos, but rather that He was preexistent as the uncaused first cause.

Secondly, *sometimes a more complex explanation explains the evidence better.* Despite their technological sophistication, the aliens in our little sci-fi story ignored and suppressed the plain fact that the teacup they found appeared to be intelligently designed.

We humans also intuitively recognize it when something is created by an intelligence, and we are quite good at it. Until modern times, most if not all of the peoples of the world came to the conclusion that the universe was created by an intelligence because of the complexity of life. Although I have not located the source, years ago I read that children who had never heard of God were asked if they thought that everything was made by someone, or just happened. Most of them thought that the universe had been made by someone, but they did not know who.

Most primitive people who have been taught nothing about God also come to this conclusion. They are not certain *who* created things, however, and so naturally, some imaginative minds will attempt to come up with explanations, thus explaining primitive tribal creation myths. In fact, this instinctive recognition and belief that life is intelligently designed is so pervasive that Dawkins himself was forced to acknowledge it from the very beginning in his book, *The Blind Watchmaker.* On the very first page he wrote:

> "Biology is the study of complicated things that give the appearance of having been designed for a purpose."

Dawkins then goes to great lengths to argue that this appearance of design for a purpose in living things is deceptive.

Should we still trust this basic, instinctive recognition we have a Maker? Are we doing the right thing by discarding our gut instincts and

Tonto Gives the Lone Ranger an Indian IQ Test

The Lone Ranger and Tonto went camping in the desert. They were extremely exhausted after trailing a gang of outlaws all day, so after they got their tent all set up, both men fell into a very deep sleep.

Hours later, Tonto woke the Lone Ranger and said, "Kemo Sabe, look at sky. What you see?"

The Lone Ranger replied, "I see millions of stars."

"What that tell you?" asked Tonto.

The Lone Ranger pondered for a minute and then said, "Astronomically speaking, it tells me there are billions of stars and potentially many more planets. Astrologically, it tells me that Saturn is in Leo. Philosophically, it tells me that we are small and insignificant compared to this vast universe. Time-wise, it appears to be approximately a quarter past three in the morning. Meteorologically, it seems we will have a beautiful day tomorrow. What's it tell you, Tonto?"

"Mmmmn. Now Tonto *know* why white man need Indian scout. It tell me someone stole tent!"

concluding that life was not formed by an intelligence? As we discussed in chapter 6, there are sound mathematical reasons to believe that this gut instinct is correct.

As this joke about the Lone Ranger and Tonto illustrates, sometimes "uncivilized" men and children are able to plainly recognize something that is true which many "civilized, educated and sophisticated" people have lost the ability to see, because we collectively take such pride in our knowledge. In the words of the apostle Paul: "Knowledge puffs up, but love builds up." In this matter, we are living proof of the saying, "A little knowledge is a dangerous thing."

194

Should we disregard the fact that we *appear* to be designed simply because our Designer must (in some respects at least) be more complex in intellect than we are?

If so, then let's reject the idea that a painting has a designer, because the painter is more complex than the painting!

PRESUMPTION 3: GOD IS THE MOST IMPROBABLE THING CONCEIVABLE, AND SO HIS FORMATION IS HIGHLY UNLIKELY.

Jews and Christians hold that God is omniscient (all knowing and all-wise), omnipresent (present everywhere), and omnipotent (all powerful). And so when Dawkins speaks of God as the "Ultimate Boeing 747," he appears to be referring to the Judeo-Christian God, the God of the Bible.

Certainly, the formation of a being like God in and from *our* universe would not only be improbable, but impossible. Does the Bible teach us that God owes His origin to our universe? Let's have a look. In order to evaluate Dawkins' claim that the God *of the Bible* is improbable, we need to take into account what *the Bible* teaches about God and His nature.

In the very first verse, the Bible teaches that our universe owes its existence to God, not vice versa.

> In the beginning God created the heavens and the earth. – Genesis 1:1

Obviously, if God created our universe, He must exist independently of it. And so probabilities that would apply inside of our universe would not apply outside of it, in the likely case that the metaphysical realm where God dwells is different from our own universe.

So what does the Bible teach us about this realm where God dwells?

> He who is the blessed and only Sovereign, the King of kings and Lord of lords, who alone possesses immortality and **dwells in**

unapproachable light, whom no man has seen or can see. To Him be honor and eternal dominion! Amen. – I Timothy :15a-16.

A realm of light would be quite different from our own universe, perhaps consisting of interacting waves. But the realm where God dwells may have another quality that is different from that of our own universe. It may exist independently of time as we know it.

Many cosmologists tell us that time began when our universe did. If they are correct, then the cause of our universe must not have been subject to time (at least as we know it), or to the precise laws of our universe. Long before many modern cosmologists came to the conclusion that time began with the universe, Jewish and Christian theologians came to the conclusion that God is not subject to time, because of verses such as Isaiah 57:15:

"For thus said the high and lofty One that **inhabits eternity**, whose name is Holy; I dwell in the high and holy place, with him also that is of a contrite and humble spirit, to revive the spirit of the humble, and to revive the heart of the contrite ones."

The Hebrew words translated "inhabits eternity" here can alternately be translated "dwells forever" or "inhabits forever." While this verse in and of itself could merely be speaking of the eternal duration of the life of God, there are other scriptures which lead us to believe that God transcends time and dwells in eternity. First of all there is the fact that God chose to call himself by a name which indicates that He always exists in the present:

"And God said unto Moses, 'I AM THAT I AM:' and he said, 'Thus shalt thou say unto the children of Israel, I AM hath sent me unto you.'" – *Exodus 3:14, KJV*

In John 8:58, Jesus, indicating that He was divine, said that he also existed in the present with God before Abraham was born:

"Jesus said unto them, 'Verily, verily, I say unto you, Before Abraham was, I am.'" – *John 8:58, KJV*

The phrase "from everlasting" seems to indicate that God existed, and will exist, before and after all of the ages of time:

> "*Art* thou not from everlasting, O LORD my God, mine Holy One?" — *Habakkuk 1:12a, KJV*

> "Before the mountains were brought forth, or ever thou hadst formed the earth and the world, even from everlasting to everlasting, thou *art* God." — *Psalm 90:2, KJV*

According to the Pulpit Commentary, the words translated 'before time began" in 1 Corinthians 2:7 literally mean "before the ages". This seems to indicate that God existed before time itself did.

> "No, we declare God's wisdom, a mystery that has been hidden and that God destined for our glory before time began."- *1 Corinthians 2:7*

Taking these verses to mean that God transcends time, what exactly *is* this realm called *eternity* that God inhabits? Book XI of the *Confessions* of Augustine and Book V of Boethius's *The Consolation of Philosophy* are widely recognized as the two greatest treatises on this subject.[168] Theologians and philosophers use the word eternity in two different senses.

Sempiternity

The first of these senses is called *sempiternity* or *everlastingness*. This means that God has existed, and will exist throughout all of the ages of time.

However, most theologians and philosophers believe that there is more to eternity than simply everlasting time. Philosopher David Braine points out, "...if we understand eternity as mere

---

[168] Deng, Natalja, "Eternity in Christian Thought," *The Stanford Encyclopedia of Philosophy* (Fall 2018 Edition), Edward N. Zalta (ed.), https://plato.stanford.edu/archives/fall2018/entries/eternity/ (Last accessed 3/25/2019).

everlastingness, then it seems that we are in danger of reducing Him who is worshipped to the level of the creature."[169]

Atemporality

That leads us to the second sense of the word eternal, which is called *atemporality*. It is typically understood to mean that God is not subject to time as we know it, but created it and transcends it. This idea is based upon Bible verses such as the following:

> "For a thousand years in Your sight Are like yesterday when it passes by, Or as a watch in the night." – Psalm 90:4

> "But do not let this one fact escape your notice, beloved, that with the Lord one day is like a thousand years, and a thousand years like one day." - 2 Peter 3:8

> "Before I formed you in the womb I knew you, before you were born I set you apart; I appointed you as a prophet to the nations." – Jeremiah 1:5

> "For those whom He has known beforehand He has also predestined to bear the likeness of His Son, that He might be the Eldest in a vast family of brothers;" – Romans 8:29, *Weymouth*

The gospel of John tells us that Jesus created all things. This, presumably, would include time itself.

> "In the beginning was the Word, and the Word was with God, and the Word was God. He was with God in the beginning. Through him all things were made; without him nothing was made that has been made." – *John 1:1-3*

---

[169] David Braine, "God, Eternity and Time—An Essay in Review of Alan G. Padgett, God, Eternity and the Nature of Time." EQ 66:4 (1994), pp. 337-344. http://www.biblicalstudies.org.uk/pdf/eq/1994-4_braine.pdf (Last accessed 3/25/2019)

Assuming that God created time as we know it, then as these Bible verses seem to indicate, then He must transcend it. That means that He is not limited to it as we are, though He certainly can work within it, and even think and reason within it if He so desires, since the Bible teaches us that He fills all things. In Psalm 139, which is a wondrous contemplation of God's omnipotence, omnipresence, and omniscience of past, present and future events, King David wrote,

O LORD, you have searched me and you know me.
You know when I sit and when I rise;
you perceive my thoughts from afar.
You discern my going out and my lying down;
you are familiar with all my ways.
Before a word is on my tongue,
you know it completely, O LORD.
You hem me in--behind and before;
you have laid your hand upon me.
Such knowledge is too wonderful for me,
too lofty for me to attain.
Where can I go from your Spirit?
Where can I flee from your presence?
If I go up to the heavens, you are there;
if I make my bed in the depths, you are there.
If I rise on the wings of the dawn
if I settle on the far side of the sea,
even there your hand will guide me,
your right hand will hold me fast.
If I say, "Surely the darkness will hide me
and the light become night around me,"
even the darkness will not be dark to you;
the night will shine like the day,
for darkness is as light to you.
For you created my inmost being;
you knit me together in my mother's womb.
I praise you because I am fearfully and wonderfully made;
your works are wonderful, I know that full well.

My frame was not hidden from you
when I was made in the secret place.
When I was woven together in the depths of the earth,
your eyes saw my unformed body.
All the days ordained for me
were written in your book
before one of them came to be.
Precious to me are your thoughts, O God!
How vast is the sum of them!
Were I to count them,
they would outnumber the grains of sand.

Not being subject to time as we know it might mean that God can think innumerable thoughts during every moment of our time, devoting incredible attention to each person moment by moment. Similar to how a computer programmer can "pause" the execution of a program and then resume it, God could from His perspective effectively 'freeze frame" time, or move slowly or quickly through it, not unlike how we can with a Blu-ray movie using a remote. Of course, we would not be conscious of these pauses or slow-downs in God's perception.

Conceivable Reasons For God's Atemporality

The reason for God's atemporality is debated among theologians and philosophers. Here are some conceivable reasons for it:

Omnitemporal Presence

Some theologians speculate that to God, all times are present. We could call this idea *omnitemporal presence.* An argument for God's omnitemporal presence can be made from the concept of time dilation. Time dilation is a consequence of Einstein's theory of relativity. The closer a clock is to the speed of light, or to a large gravitational mass, the more it slows down compared to clocks further away. If clocks are moving differently throughout the universe, then is there something that *all* of the clocks are moving relative to besides each other?

Another argument for God's omnitemporal presence can be made from the fact that the present moment is constantly moving from the past to the future. In each place within the universe, what is it that the present moment, or "now" is moving through? Perhaps this is the timeless eternity in which God dwells.

If so, does timeless eternity serve as the reference frame for all time rates? For us, the movement of the present moment through time is like a vector ray that points in one direction only. We are not its masters but its slaves, forced to march by it in one direction only, from the past to the present. But since God transcends time, perhaps for Him time may be accessed at any point. Would this mean that God *could* change the past? Yes, but it stands to reason that since the decisions he made in the past were perfect, He would make the very same ones again, so He *would* not change it.

Timelessness

If eternity is timeless, what exactly does that mean? How can we really understand what timelessness might be if we do not even know what time is?

Augustine wrote, "For what is time? Who can easily and briefly explain it? Who even in thought can comprehend it, even to the pronouncing of a word concerning it?"

The quest for a satisfying answer to that question continues to this day. Most, if not all definitions of time are somewhat circular in that they include some direct or indirect reference to time. For instance, as Augustine also pointed out, we define longer units of time by shorter units of time. What is a minute? 60 seconds. What is an hour? 60 minutes! Merriam-Webster also defines time with some circular references, as "a nonspatial continuum that is measured in terms of events which succeed one another from past through present to future."[170]

---

[170] http://www.merriam-webster.com/dictionary/time (Last accessed 3/25/2019)

We tend to spatially organize past events in our minds. Similarly, in Minkowski spacetime, time is treated mathematically as a dimension that we move through. That serves us well mathematically, but is time *really* another dimension? We cannot move backwards, left or right in it, only forwards. Recently, some scientists have proposed that there is no time at all, and that time is simply the numerical order of change.[171]

Our failure to satisfactorily define time should humble us, because it reminds us of how little we *actually* know about how the universe works.

Since the exact nature of time remains a mystery to us, rather than attempting the elusive task of completely defining what time is, let's confine our consideration to one essential thing that time does. Most of us will agree that "time is what keeps everything from happening at once." [172]

Although this is not a complete definition of time, it does seem to accurately describe a function of it. Many would argue that it is the speed of light rather than time that keeps everything from happening at once, but how could we have the concept of speed *without* time? If the speed of light could not exist without time, then it would seem that the speed of light depends on time, not vice-versa.

So it seems reasonable to conclude that in a timeless realm, a causal chain of events would have infinite velocity. I do not mean "at once" in the sense of an instant that comes and goes. That would be a moment in time. What I mean is "at once" in the sense of events not restrained or regulated by time. If God dwells in timeless eternity, then He simply *is*. He has no beginning and no end in time, though He is the

---

[171] Amrit Sorli, Davide Fiscaletti, and Dusan Klinar. "Replacing time with numerical order of material change resolves Zeno problems of motion." Physics Essays, 24, 1 (2011). DOI: 10.4006/1.3525416.

[172] This saying is thought to have originated with Ray Cummings in his 1922 short story *The Time Professor*. It has been repeated by scientists such as John Archibald Wheeler and C.J. Overbeck, and is often mistakenly attributed to Einstein and Feynman.

beginning and the end of all things. All of the events within timeless eternity would not happen at once from our perspective, however, since our universe would be located on a causal chain within eternity. However, if God controls the flow of time, then as many events as He desires - such as his own thoughts - could take place during one of our instants.

If this concept of everything happening at once in timeless eternity is correct, that means that in a timeless realm *innumerable* things would happen at once! Timelessness need not rule out causality, though it would rule out state changes and motion, since something could not exist in two places or in two states at once. Rather, it seems that there would need to be a logical space-based causality than a motion-based causality.

The very page you are reading can serve as an example of causality in a timeless realm. The logical flow of thoughts on this white page are a form of cause and effect. And they are all present at once on this page. The difference between a sequence of cause and effect events in a timeless realm and a time-bound one could be compared to how an old-fashioned printing press would have produced this page (stamping all of the letters all at once) versus how a teletype would have produced it (one letter at a time).

Logical causality in a timeless realm can be compared to a bucket of water being pulled out of a well by a taut chain. Each link in the chain simultaneously pulls the next link in the chain, all the way down to the bucket, which is also being pulled up. Each cause and its effect are all happening at once. (This is not a perfect analogy because there actually is a time interval between the links in a chain affecting each other, but it is close enough for you to get my point.)

Apparently not realizing that causality might exist outside of time, in the first episode of the Discovery Channel TV series *Curiosity* entitled, *Did God Create the Universe?* Stephen Hawking said,

> "So when people ask me if a god created the universe, I tell them the question itself makes no sense. Time didn't exist before the Big

Bang, so there is no time for God to make the universe in. It's like asking for directions to the edge of the Earth. The Earth is a sphere. It does not have an edge, so looking for it is a futile exercise."[173]

In our universe, finite time places a restraint upon the number of events that can happen, and therefore lowers the probability of ordered events happening. For instance, even if a man had been flipping a coin every second from the time the universe began, the odds of him ever getting 1500 heads in a row during that time are next to impossible. Finite time restrains the probability of order. But that would not be the case in a timeless realm.

Infinite Hypertime

You might recall from reading chapter eight that some infinities have more members (i.e. a higher cardinality) than others. In fact, some infinities have infinitely more members than others do. The mathematician Cantor envisioned what is called *The Absolute Infinite,* and associated it with God. It is an infinity that encompasses all other infinities.

This idea opens up to us the concept of *infinite hypertime.* Imagine the thoughts of God propagating at an infinite speed within infinite spaces of lower cardinality that are contained within spaces of higher cardinality. This could conceivably result in a kind of time, but one that is much more wonderful than time as we know it. This would make time-based causality possible, including motion and state-changes.

If we combine this idea with the idea of infinite dimensions, with micro and macro spaces contained within spaces, our tiny finite minds become even more dazzled. Such an idea is too wonderful for us to grasp, and it is probably best not to try to. (Some speculate that spending too much time trying to comprehend infinities contributed to Cantor spending time in and out of mental institutions.) So let's suffice it to

---

[173] Quote of Stephen Hawking appearing at time interval 33:57 in Curiosity (2011) Season 1 Episode 1.
https://www.youtube.com/watch?v=Y0k3ApSN3DU (Last accessed 3/25/2019)

say what this would mean that for every moment of our time, God can think innumerable thoughts regarding us, and devote loving attention to each and every person. This reminds is of what King David wrote:

> Precious to me are your thoughts, O God!
> How vast is the sum of them!
> Were I to count them,
> they would outnumber the grains of sand.

In fact, no matter how we understand the eternal nature of God – as everlastingness, omnitemporal presence with unbounded time, time-lessness, or infinite hypertime, *in eternity, there would be no finite time to restrain probability. Given unending time, timelessness, or in-finite hypertime, even the most improbable things could happen.* And so Dawkins' claim that God is improbable simply does not take into account what the Bible teaches regarding the eternal realm in which he dwells.

However, as mentioned earlier, the Bible does not teach that God formed by chance from chaos, but rather that He was pre-existent as the uncaused first cause. We will discuss some compelling, logical rea-sons for this in the next chapter. Time and eternity, however, are of great relevance to what's next.

PRESUMPTION 4: COMPLEX THOUGHT CAN ONLY EXIST WITHIN A BEING OF COMPLEX COMPOSITION.

Divine Simplicity

There is an historic theological doctrine called *divine simplicity*. It is a doctrine that not all orthodox theologians hold to, and not regarded as an *essential* tenet of the Christian faith. However, it may be traced back to early Christian times, and was held to by Christian thinkers such as Augustine, Anselm, and Aquinas. There are several concepts of di-vine simplicity, but the most popular one is that in His foundational essence, God is not made up of multiple objects, like a human is made of minerals, water, and complex organic molecules. Rather, this concept holds that He is a unitary whole. If God is simple, Dawkins' entire argument fails.

If on the other hand God's essential, foundational nature is not simple but composite, all of His parts must have been pre-existent, necessary, and therefore non-contingent. Although in that case we could say that His total being is contingent on His necessary parts, He would still be the first cause of all other things.

The concept of Divine simplicity *does not* mean that God is simple in intellect. The complexity of God's thoughts and ways are clearly taught in scripture:

> "For my thoughts are not your thoughts, neither are your ways my ways," declares the LORD. "As the heavens are higher than the earth, so are my ways higher than your ways and my thoughts than your thoughts." - *Isaiah 55:8-9*

If God's essential, foundational nature is simple (non-composite), then his essence is a unitary whole that is non-contingent and necessary.

The *Sh'ma* found in Deuteronomy 6:4 in Hebrew is...

> "Sh'ma Yisra'eil Adonai Eloheinu Adonai echad."

It is translated,

> "Hear, O Israel: The Lord our God, the Lord is one" -*Deuteronomy 6:4*

Although the Sh'ma can be understood in other ways, it could possibly mean that God's foundational essence is unitary and non-composite.

How might God's foundational nature be of one simple essence, but conducive to complex thought? Apart from God revealing this to us, there is no way that we can know with certainty, though we can speculate based upon what He has revealed.

So as you read this section, please understand that it is not to be regarded as anything but *theological and cosmological*

speculation. Although trying to figure out mysteries can be fascinating, fun and exciting, speculation should never be regarded as known fact.

If God is of one single, simple essence, something with this quality such as a simple substance or field can contain regions which are in different states. For instance, a magnetic recording can be stored on a continuous length of steel wire (this technology is known as wire recording).[174] An example from theoretical physics is when a wave propagates through a field. That wave is believed to consist of variations in the strength of the field. In other words, different regions of the field are existing in different states. Particle-antiparticle pairs caused by vacuum field fluctuations are another example from theoretical physics of different regions of a field existing in different states.

Regions holding different states can interact with each other, such as when particle-antiparticle pairs cancel out, or coherent light produces interference patterns. The number of possible states and how the regions which hold those states interact depends upon the nature of the substance or field, as well as the nature of the variances within it. If these states form binary bits, these need not be ones and zeros, alternating between somethingness and nothingness. For instance, they could be values of one and two, alternating between something and more of something.

We now know that there are one dimensional elementary cellular automata such as *Rule 110* that are Turing –complete.[175] They are Turing-complete because patterns can exist within them that are capable of universal computation. Regarding this, Stephen Wolfram, who has devoted a great deal of time to studying cellular automata and introduced us to *Rule 110*, states:

[174] "Wire Recorders." Museum of Magnetic Sound Recording website p., 2018. https://museumofmagneticsoundrecording.org/Wire.html (Last accessed 3/25/2019)

[175] Matthew Cook, "A Concrete View of Rule 110 Computation," 2009arXiv0906.3248C, June 2009/.
https://arxiv.org/pdf/0906.3248.pdf (Last accessed 3/25/2019)

> "In the existing sciences whenever a phenomenon is encountered that seems complex it is taken almost for granted that the phenomenon must be the result of some underlying mechanism that is itself complex. But my discovery that simple programs can produce great complexity makes it clear that this is not in fact correct." [176]

Rule 110 is simple enough that it is conceivable something like it could arise by chance even in a realm bound by finite time. But so much more than this is possible in a realm not bound by finite time

Cellular automations such as Rule 110 work based upon *time steps*. In each time step, the ones and zeros change states based on their environment– how many ones or zeroes are next to them. They change states according to the *rules* a programmer has chosen about what those changes should be.

However, it is conceivable that in a timeless realm, time steps could be replaced by each simultaneous logical step of cause and effect. The simple state-change rules could be based on aggregate probabilities or simply the nature of the immaterial spirit substance of God. The state changes would be caused by waves of higher and lower concentrations interacting.

With no true particles, there might be no friction, Brownian motion or entropy, so no energy would be required to produce a variation in the substance. Within a simple, non-quantized substance, an infinitesimally tiny amount of variation would cause a wave to propagate, instantly cascading into an expanding wave of cause and effect. Since a simple substance could be infinitely subdivided, each wave of causality would grow smaller as it expanded, so that the law of action and reaction would not be violated:

> "For every action, there is an equal and opposite reaction."

---

[176] Wolfram, Stephen, *A New Kind of Science* Chapter 1, Section 1, p. 4, second paragraph. http://www.wolframscience.com/nksonline/p.-4-text?firstview=1 (Last accessed /25/2019)

Imagine an interplay of interacting waves and states throughout the infinite spirit substance of God. As previously mentioned, if God's thoughts propagate instantly at a lower cardinality infinite speed, but travel across a higher cardinality space, this could result in something similar to time-based causality, which would be a sort of divine hyper-time. This would not be time as we know it, but something much more wonderful.

But if there is not a divine-time-based causality like that, in a timeless realm in which everything happens at once, each region holding a state could change states only once, because one region could not exist in two states at once. If God is infinite, that would not be a problem because there would be infinite room for the waves of causality to ride on. Not only God's thoughts, but all of God's creation could ride upon this wave of causality as well, as a theistically sustained reality (TSR) or as portions of the expanding causal wave that He has set aside to create from.

A wave of causality with infinite velocity would instantly roll across an infinite space of the same cardinality. But what if it were rolling across an infinity with infinitely higher cardinality? The idea boggles the mind.

What if not one wave, but an infinite number of lower cardinality infinite waves of expanding causal thought are rolling across the higher cardinality infinite essence of God? State changes would result from the interaction of these waves. The waves could have a dimensional character. If two-dimensional and the states are binary, they could roll *as one dimensional elementary cellular automatons* in an expanding circular wave, like a wave from a drop of water in a still pool. If three-dimensional, the waves of causality would exist as 2D surfaces of an expanding sphere. If four-dimensional, the waves could be a form of 3-D space on the surface of a 4-D hypersphere expanding *like an instantaneous explosion of light*, and so on, depending on the number of dimensions.

In such a case, even though God's underlying essence would be simple, the paths of God's thoughts would not be. Thoughts could instantly propagate outwards and horizontally across the waves, which would be one coherent whole. God's consciousness and all that He has created could exist within these waves of causality. Depending on the number of possible states, the state change rules, the number of dimensions, and the geometric shape of the state-change regions, the transmission paths could logically or spatially be variable, multidimensional, phasic, oscillatory, branching, networking, etc., *but have infinite velocity.* This would mean that God could think an infinite number of thoughts about us for every moment of our time!

And so, just as elementary cellular automata are very simple but produce different patterns - some of them very complex - *the nature of God could be very simple, but conducive to complex thought and complex creation.* By way of example, the network of neurons in a human brain are, except for pre-programed instincts, a "blank slate" when a person is born. But by their very nature, they produce highly complex thought and language! Minds of a complex composite nature such as ours require an intelligence to properly explain their origin. But a mind of a simple underlying nature does not.

Imagine a Mind capable of thinking an infinity of simultaneous thoughts for each moment of our time, *with no limit to the depth of reasoning possible.* Such a Being would not only be omniscient, but capable of devoting great attention and love to every human being.

The Trinity

For companionship, this Great Mind could radiate or "beget" personal distinctions within Himself (the Spirit and the Son). Though they would be contingent upon Him, they would be made of the same divine essence, so this would not compromise His *underlying* foundational unity.

> "For as the Father has life in himself, so he has granted the Son also to have life in himself." — *John 5:26*

> "I and the Father are one." — Jesus speaking in John 10:30. NIV

In the last verse quoted above, the Greek word translated "one" is neuter, indicating that Jesus and the Father are of one essence or substance.

The One who dwells outside of time simply *is*. All of the decisions that God makes within time, though they are temporal acts to us, are fixed in eternity.

Does human consciousness arise as a result of different aspects of the human soul (which is composed of the mind, body and spirit) being aware of and communicating with each other? If so, then it seems that a tri-personal, multidimensional, multi-spatial, infinite being capable of instantaneous thought would have ultimate consciousness, awareness and being. (Along this line of thought, see *The Conversing God* by Todd Marshall for a thought-provoking exploration of the idea of knowledge itself having been created through Trinitarian information transfer.[177])

How Could Time Exist Within a Timeless Realm?

How could a subdomain of time be created in a timeless realm? Many think of time as a fourth dimension of space. It is also possible that God has given us a perception of time by granting us a sense of the difference between events that occur in a few causal steps and those that occur in more causal steps. This might function as an internal time clock.

Another idea I like regarding the origin of time is one proposed by John Hartnett. He writes:

> "The quantum vacuum impedes the progress of photons through space to the speed, c, and hence it introduces the first "clock" and

---

[177] Todd E. Marshall, "The Conversing God: Exploring Trinitarian Information Transfer through the Perspective of Gordon Pask's Conversation Theory." SAUonline, Spring Arbor University. https://pdfs.seman-ticscholar.org/a0ca/b7eb70de6a532f1d6e1e52cd1e3441b4fd4d.pdf (Last accessed 3/25/2019)

the forward arrow of time. Empty space would have meant unimpeded photons with infinite speed. By inference then *there never existed a time of empty space.*"[178]

Keeping Tethered to Earth While Exploring the Clouds

There are surely other hypothetical models of God having a simple nature that we can conceive of. Or perhaps the correct model is one that we could not possibly imagine.

But hopefully these speculative ideas will suffice as examples of how the doctrine of divine simplicity *could* be correct even if eternity is a timeless realm in which everything happens at once. If eternity is simply everlastingness or omnitemporal presence with unbounded time, no such explanation would be required.

Regarding this kind of theological speculation, a final word of caution is in order here. Although theological speculation can be stimulating and fascinating, let's be careful not to let it inflate our minds. Even seasoned theologians and philosophers would be foolish to latch on to their speculations and believe in them as though they were a fact.

Though it's fascinating to speculate, let's not come to final conclusions prematurely, *but wait upon God to reveal the mysteries of His true nature to us.* We do not need to have all of the answers prematurely. Let's keep our childlike wonder of the mystery of His nature until then.

If we cannot know the nature of our own universe yet, which we can see, how can we truly understand the nature of the Creator of it, whom we cannot see? I would not at all be surprised if the actual metaphysical reality is much more profound and different in many respects than these speculations.

[178] Hartnett, John, "Expansion of Space—A Dark Science." Answers Research Journal, November 14, 2013. https://answersingenesis.org/astronomy/cosmology/expansion-space-dark-science/ (Last accessed 3/25/2019)

Or the full metaphysical reality could be incomprehensible to our limited minds, trapped as we are within time and only three dimensions of space.

The point is that we do not really know exactly what the foundational nature of God's spirit essence is, and though we may cautiously speculate, we will likely get it wrong, like a primitive tribesman speculating how an iPhone works. If we were to claim that we *did* know, then the words that God spoke to Job would surely apply to us:

> "Who *is* this that darkeneth counsel by words without knowledge?"
> – Job 38:2

And so, let's believe that God is what He has revealed Himself to be. But regarding those aspects of His nature that He has not revealed (such as exactly what the nature of His eternality and spiritual essence are), let's believe that *He is whatever He is*, which is *not necessarily what we think He could be.*

> God said to Moses, "I AM WHO I AM. This is what you are to say to the Israelites: 'I AM has sent me to you.'" –*Exodus 3:14*

When it comes to speculating beyond what God has revealed to us about himself, and even when it comes to taking into account our possible misunderstandings of what He has revealed to us, C.S. Lewis has some very good words of advice. When we attempt to communicate with God, our prayers ought to be directed "Not to what I think Thou art, but to what Thou knowest Thyself to be."

If these *speculations* - and that is all they are intended to be- have opened your mind to the cosmological possibility of God's preexistence and simplicity, then they have served their intended purpose.

The important thing to recognize is that the nature of life and of our Universe points to creation by a divine intelligence. We do not have to completely understand everything about God's nature to love, serve and appreciate Him. By way of example, though I do not always understand the thought processes of the female mind, I still love and appreciate my wife. In the same way, we do not have to completely understand God's nature to believe that the evidence points to Him as the Creator of the universe. How could we even hope to completely understand Him? It is sufficient to know He dearly loves us, and that is what counts most.

When asked how he would summarize all that He had written, the famous theologian Karl Barth replied, "Jesus loves me, this I know, for the Bible tells me so."

And so no matter how we understand eternity, as everlastingness, omnitemporal presence, timelessness, or some combination of these, it seems possible that the doctrine of divine simplicity could be correct.

CONCLUSIONS

We can summarize the weaknesses in Dawkins' probability argument like this:

- The simplest explanation is not always the correct one.
- Some causes are considerably more complex than their effects.
- The first cause of necessity must have been uncaused and preexistent.
- In eternity, there would be no finite time to restrain probability.
- Rule 110 serves as an example for us that great complexity of information can conceivably arise from simplicity. Though complex in thought, in accordance with the historic doctrine of divine simplicity, God may not be of a composite nature, but of a simple one.

Richard Dawkins' objection to the existence of God therefore rests upon uncertain presumptions and a misconception of the eternal nature of God.

Finally, let's close this chapter with a salient observation:

Conditions outside of our universe are likely very different from those within it.

Unless Dawkins has stepped outside of the universe to observe conditions there, he cannot possibly know that God is unlikely to exist!

13 THE FIRST CAUSE

"Imagination is the beginning of creation. You imagine what you desire, you will what you imagine and at last you create what you will."
— George Bernard Shaw

 ome metaphysical naturalists have argued that perhaps there was an infinite past (also known as an *infinite temporal regress*). If so, they contend, God could not have been the first cause. Let's consider this idea.

At one time the "steady state" theory of cosmology was popular, which held that the universe has existed forever. Some cyclical universe and Big Bounce cosmologies also propose that the universe has existed forever, though in previously different forms.

Applying Ockham's razor, a beginning is a much simpler hypothesis than an infinite past or an infinite causal regress. But there is much more reason than merely that to favor a beginning over an infinite regress.

WHY THE 2ND LAW OF THERMODYNAMICS POINTS TO A CAUSE

Let's suppose that an astronaut was standing on a moon with no atmosphere. The moon was one solid rock. He lifted a basketball towards the stars, giving it potential energy. Then he let go of it, releasing that potential energy as kinetic energy. It fell to the moon and began bouncing. Eventually however, it quit bouncing, even though there was no atmosphere. Why? Because the bouncing of the ball caused the ground to vibrate, transferring kinetic energy to it. It also imperceptibly nudged the moon a little in the direction that the ball was falling. The energy was still there, but it had dissipated into other forms, and was no longer available to do any discernable work.

This astronaut was observing the *second law of thermodynamics* in action. According to this law, energy tends to flow from a region of more

216

concentrated energy to a region of less concentrated energy, until a state of equilibrium is reached and there is no longer energy available to perform work. For instance, heat tends to flow from a hot area to a cold one.

This flow of energy from regions of more concentrated energy to more evenly distributed ones can be utilized to perform useful work *if* some means exists of harnessing that flow. The unique composition of the earth, for instance, enables it to harness the power of the sun to keep the atmospheric and water cycles going. Water flows downhill and this flow of energy can be harnessed in hydroelectric dams while it is flowing, but once it reaches the ocean, that potential energy is no longer available to perform work. Photosynthesis in plants harnesses the flow of energy from the sun to produce food energy. Car engines harness the flow of heat from ignited gasoline vapors. Battery powered machines harness the electrical energy in batteries. In a battery, electric current will flow from a higher voltage potential to a lower one, until eventually the battery goes dead. Because of the second law of thermodynamics, *even the Eveready Bunny* will eventually quit "going and going!"

Just as energy tends to flow from a state of high concentration to a more evenly distributed one, particles also tend to evenly distribute themselves when they knock up against each other. For instance, release a pink gas in the corner of a room, and soon the whole room will have a pink haze. The hotter the temperature of the room, the faster that will happen.

This tendency for energy and particles to go from a state of higher concentration to a more evenly distributed one is also what causes things to go from a state of order into a state of disorder. The most handsomely crafted brick wall will eventually fall down. Given enough time, without repairs a stylish house will need to be condemned. A high performance sports car will eventually quit working, rust and fall apart. This state of disorder, equilibrium, or dissipated energy is called *entropy*.

Things which have a high state of order or potential energy are said to have a state of low entropy. Things which have a high state of disorder or dissipated potential energy are said to have high entropy. This statistical tendency for things to move from a state of high order to a state of low order is also a consequence of the second law of thermodynamics.

Probability is also related to entropy. Higher order things, which have lower entropy, have a lower probability of forming by chance. As a highly ordered system degrades into disorder, it moves into a more probable state.

An argument commonly given against this relationship is that any single disordered arrangement is just as unlikely to form as an ordered one. For instance, in a poker game, any particular *disordered* hand of cards is just as unlikely to form as an *ordered* one. For instance, you are just as unlikely to be dealt a hand consisting of a Four of Hearts, Seven of Spades, Jack of Diamonds, Nine of Clubs, and Ace of Hearts as a royal flush of Hearts. However, in poker, we value hands not only by the improbability of a particular hand occurring again, *but also by whether or not the hand has certain discernable patterns.* The number of hands with these discernable patterns is much lower than the total number of possible hands. Likewise, in a thermodynamic system, the total number of discernably ordered arrangements (such as self-replicating ones) is much lower than the total number of disordered ones. Thus, the set of meaningfully ordered arrangements of molecules exhibits less overall entropy than the set of disordered ones. This is also why the argument of naturalists that *any* universe might be able to sustain its own form of life fails. Just as a working cell could not form spontaneously from iron alone, any kind of life will require components of a certain composition and order. The set of universes containing that sort of order will be minutely smaller than the set that does not.

Most scientists believe that the flow of time is closely associated with the flow of entropy. In fact, entropy is often called "the arrow of time."

Heat and light energy will flow from our sun into the surrounding cooler space until our sun eventually burns out. Eventually, it is thought that all of the energy will radiate from the stars and planets, and that the universe will reach a state of equilibrium in which no more energy will be available to perform work.

> "The universe will eventually die, wallowing, as it were, in its own entropy. This is known among physicists as the 'heat death' of the universe. . .The universe cannot have existed for ever, otherwise it would have reached its equilibrium end state an infinite time ago. Conclusion: the universe did not always exist." – Physicist Paul Davies [179]

And so, the second law of thermodynamics testifies against the concept of an eternal universe. If causality went back forever in our universe, then why has an end state of equilibrium not yet been reached because of the second law of thermodynamics? *Why* do we still find ourselves in a low entropy, highly ordered universe?

WHY THERE CANNOT BE AN INFINITE PAST

Suppose that Jaun Ponce de León, the famed early explorer of America whom folklore holds was looking for the fountain of youth, discovered the fountain, drank from it, became immortal, and is living among us to this day disguised as a young college freshman. His history professor is growing suspicious however, because he makes A's without even studying!

If you think about it, at any point in the future, Jaun will have only lived a finite number of years. From Jaun's example, we can draw the following conclusion: If the length of time from now until any point in the future will always be finite, then the length of time from any past moment until now must have been finite, too.

---

[179] Davies, Paul (1984). God and the new physics (1st Touchstone ed.). New York: Simon & Schuster. p. 11

For Juan, living forever will never actually be achieved, because there will always be another day to live. This means that living forever will always be an abstract concept to him, not an achieved reality. But the metaphysical naturalist who claims that there was an infinite past is asking us to believe that forever has already happened! In the Disney film *Toy Story*, Buzz Lightyear's goal was to travel "to infinity and beyond." But those who believe in an eternal past are in effect saying that we have *already* traveled to infinity and beyond!

The *Merriam-Webster Dictionary's* primary definition of the word infinite is "extending indefinitely: endless."[180] If by definition, infinity has no end, how could the present moment, as it is traveling through all of time, have ever reached or gone beyond something that has no end? Such an idea is self-contradicting!

But what if time is a line extending to infinity in both directions, and the present moment is a point on that line moving towards the future? If that were so, would there not have been an infinite past? Yes, if that kind of time were possible, but the very nature of time as we know it precludes a beginningless time from existing. Here's why.

We will use seconds as our units of time. But first, since it is very easy to get confused when discussing this, let's clearly establish some definitions.

- **A Ray.** This is simply a direction and a starting point, and it has infinite length *towards* the direction of travel. An example would be, "He left Albany Georgia headed due northeast." If time has a beginning but will advance indefinitely into the future, then it may be represented by a ray. A time-related example would be "May our journey into a better future begin now."

- **A Converse Ray.** This is a new term invented for this discussion, and although it may seem counter-intuitive, we need it to describe the idea of infinite past time and it's direction of flow. A converse ray would be a direction of travel and an

---

[180] http://www.merriam-webster.com/dictionary/infinite?show=0&t=1420592619 (Last accessed 03/25/2019)

ending point, but unlike a ray, it would have infinite length *away from* the direction of travel. In other words, while an infinite ray travels from a point to infinity, a converse ray travels from infinity to a point. An example would be, "Do you see that river that empties out into the ocean over there? I think it has no beginning, because I could not find it. I think if you travelled upstream forever, you would never reach the source of it." If past time goes back forever, then it must be a converse ray, because it's direction is towards the present moment, not away from it. A time-related example would be, "I am not kidding; it literally took me forever to get here." The question is, can a converse ray of time exist? We will address that question shortly.

- **A Line.** This is two rays joined together at a point, and it is infinite. If all of time can be represented by an infinite line, a converse ray would be the past, an ordinary ray would be the future, and the point where they are joined together would be the present moment. An example would be, "Do you see that line of spaceships travelling past our galaxy towards the outer edge of the Andromeda galaxy? They say that highway has no beginning and no end."

- **A Line Segment.** This is a piece of a line, ending at a point on each side. Unlike a line, it is finite. If time has a point of beginning and a point in which it ends, then it may be represented by a finite directional line.

- **A Scalar.** A scalar is a magnitude without regard to direction. An example is "An hour contains 60 seconds."

- **A Vector**. A *vector* includes both magnitude *and* direction, such as "He drove 60 miles due southeast of Atlanta." A time-based example would be, "I will meet you ten days from now." In the last example, the magnitude is ten days, and the direction is towards the future. By contrast, if you had a time machine, you could travel ten days into the direction of the past.

- **Speed** is the distance traveled per unit of time through the three dimensions of space, without reference to direction. An example is "60 miles per hour."

- **Velocity** is a vector quantity, since it is speed with a direction. An example would be, "The UFO is travelling 600 miles per hour due NorthWest."
- **Now.** This is the present moment as it travels from the past to the future. It is an advancing wave of causality that we ride upon, like surfers on an ocean wave. Its location always coincides with a particular point in time.
- **Nowvelocity.** This is another term invented for purposes of our discussion. It describes a special kind of velocity: the rate at which the present moment travels through time. Einstein's theories of relativity have revealed something strange about time to us. The rate at which time flows for any object in our universe depends upon how fast it is moving, how close that object is to a gravitational mass, and how big that gravitational mass is. The closer you are to a large gravitational mass, or the nearer you are traveling to the speed of light, the more slowly time would advance for you compared to someone on earth.

For instance, in the movie *Interstellar*, astronaut Joe Cooper ends up having to spend more time on a planet near a black hole than he wanted to. By the time he leaves that planet, he is very distressed, because his daughter Murph, who is back on earth, is now 23 years older - the same age as him! The same thing would have happened to Cooper if he had been on a spaceship travelling at close to the speed of light: time would have moved more slowly for him than for his daughter. Since velocity is the distance travelled through *space* per unit of time in a certain direction, we need another term to describe the rate with which one travels through *time* into the future. Let's call the rate at which any object flows into the future its *nowvelocity*, and define it as *how many units of time pass compared to the same unit of time in a chosen frame of reference.* For instance, let's choose Earth as our frame of reference. While Cooper was on that planet near the black hole, his nowvelocity was much slower than his daughters's on Earth.

The present moment travels through time at a finite rate of nowvelocity for all human beings. If it did not, *everything would take place at once* from our perspective. (Exactly *why* the present advances at a finite nowvelocity for human beings is a matter worthy of conjecture, but we do not need to address it for the purposes of the immediate discussion.)

- **Past Time**. This is the distance that the present moment has travelled through time up until the present moment. It is a scalar quantity, such as 10^{100} seconds.
- **Total Time.** This is the total distance that the present moment will have travelled from the past to the future at the end of time. It is also a scalar quantity, like 10^{2000} seconds. If there will be no end to time, then it is an infinite quantity.

And so in precise terms this is the question we are asking: *Is the magnitude in seconds of Past Time infinite?*

Here is a simple logical syllogism to show that it cannot be. (In logic, a *syllogism* is a form of deductive reasoning consisting of a major premise, a minor premise, and a conclusion.) This is based upon and is essentially the same as a syllogism by Christian philosopher William Lane Craig,[181] but for our purposes here, it is stated just a little differently:

> You cannot ever arrive at an infinite sum by successive addition at a finite rate (in this case, a finite nowvelocity).
>
> Past time is the sum of all seconds by successive addition at a finite rate, up until the present moment.
>
> ∴ (Therefore) the sum of all past seconds cannot be infinite.

But since infinity plus infinity equals infinity, isn't it possible to have traversed one "countable" infinity while not yet having reached the end of a second "countable" infinity? No, because the first infinity has

---

[181] William Lane Craig and Michael Murray, Philosophy of Religion: A Reader and Guide, Rutgers University Press, 2002, p. 97.

no end. Therefore, how could you have already travelled beyond something that has no end?

Since past time must be a finite quantity, this leads us to another syllogism known as the *Kalām Cosmological Argument*, which has also been popularized in recent years by Craig. He states the Kalām Cosmological Argument this way:

> Everything that begins to exist has a cause.
>
> The universe began to exist.
>
> ∴ (Therefore) the universe has a cause.[182]

Our arguments for a first cause of our universe have rested somewhat upon the time-bound nature of our universe. However, if time began with our universe, then whatever or whoever caused our universe must exist in a realm that is outside of time, at least as we know it.

If there is some other form of time in the realm in which our universe resides, these arguments will still apply there. Regarding what lies outside of our universe, my grandson Kai said to me the other day, "The earth is inside our universe, our universe is inside of heaven, and heaven is inside of God."

That was something surprising to hear from the lips of a five-year old! It makes me think of the words of King Solomon regarding the temple he built for God in Jerusalem:

> "But who is able to build a house for Him, **for the heavens and the highest heavens** cannot contain Him? So who am I, that I should build a house for Him, except to burn incense before Him?" - 2 Chronicles 2:6, NASB

Wise king Solomon, it appears, had a sophisticated cosmology! And so, if there is some sort of time in the heaven or even heavens (outer realms) that are above our universe, these arguments would

---

[182] Craig, William Lane; Moreland, J. P. , *The Blackwell Companion to Natural Theology*, Oxford: John Wiley and Sons, 2009.

presumably apply there, too. But if that which *ultimately* lies outside of our universe is a timeless realm, will our arguments still apply there? Could there have been an infinite series of causes and effects leading up to our universe in a timeless realm? Let's consider that question next.

WHY THERE MUST HAVE BEEN A FIRST CAUSE

What if our universe (or the realms it dwells within) is an island of time in a timeless realm of cause and effect? Since cause and effect would have infinite velocity in such an environment, wouldn't an infinite chain of causes and effects be achievable in that timeless realm? Yes, but does this mean that there *must have been* an infinite series of causes and effects leading up to our universe within that timeless realm?

No, and here's why. All effects must have a cause, but not all causes need to have a cause. Something pre-existent, for instance, needs no cause. Since not all causes have causes, there need not have been an infinite regress of causes and effects. There may have been a first cause.

Now let's turn our attention to the question, "In a timeless realm, *could* there have been an infinite regression of causes and effects leading up to our universe?"

Here are two simple syllogisms that explain why that cannot be the case.

The Argument From the Radiation of Causality

- All effects radiate from causes.
- Every kind of radiation has a source (such as light).

∴ (Therefore) everything that is caused has a first cause, which is its source. Why the Sum of Events Leading to Our Universe Is Finite

Why the Sum of Events Leading to Our Universe Is Finite

Why do we smile when we hear Buzz Lightyear shout "To infinity and beyond!"? We smile because we intuitively know, "You can't go beyond infinity. Infinity has no end!"

And why do we smile if a loved one tells us, "I'll love you forever and a day!" We smile because we think, "We will never reach the end of forever, so you can't really love me forever and a day!"

This leads us to our next syllogism:

The Argument From the Endless Nature of Infinity

- Since all causes radiate from a source, an infinite magnitude of causes and effects can result only from cause and effect *without end*.

- The events leading up to our universe *ended* when the universe began.

- ∴ (Therefore) the number of events leading up to our universe could not have been infinite, so there must have been a beginning to the events that led up to the formation of our universe.

And so we see that an infinite causal regress could not have existed prior to our universe. This means that the series of causes and effects which led to our current universe must have begun with a first cause!

This logic would also apply to cyclical universe models (including big bounce models) which include an infinite causal regress. There could not have been an infinite chain of cyclical universes prior to ours! Even physicist Alex Vileniken, one of the promoters of *eternal inflation*, which is the idea that one universe can spawn an infinite number of other universes, believes that eternal inflation must have had a beginning.

Vilenkin said in an interview, "For the eternal inflation model, what we can show mathematically is that there is no end to this process. Some people thought maybe you could avoid a beginning, too. But our 2003 theorem shows that [avoiding a beginning] is impossible for this scenario. Although inflation may be eternal into the future, it cannot be extended indefinitely to the past."[183]

WHY THE FIRST CAUSE MUST HAVE BEEN CAUSELESS AND PREEXISTENT

And so we can say the following:

> The first cause could not have been caused. Otherwise, it would not have been the first cause!
>
> Since *nothing cannot do anything*, the first cause must have been something or someone.
>
> The first cause could not have brought itself into existence. This is because it would have needed to exist in some form before it could do anything.
>
> ∴ (Therefore) the first cause must have been something or someone that was both causeless and preexistent.

Even most (but not all) naturalists seem to find the idea of all existence arising from absolutely nothing to be irrational. In order to explain how the universe could have naturalistically sprung into being, they must consider what we commonly call "nothing" – the vacuum of empty space – as "something": a quantum or vacuum field.

We can think of two possible kinds of existent things:

1. Non-contingent things which necessarily must exist and therefore need no cause.

---

[183] By Jacqueline Mitchell, "In the Beginning Was the Beginning: Cosmologist Alex Vilenkin does the math to show that the universe indeed had a starting point." May 29, 2012. https://now.tufts.edu/articles/beginning-was-beginning#sthash.AxTKbHck.dpuf (Last accessed 03/25/2019)

2. Contingent things which do not necessarily exist, and there-fore require a cause in order to come into existence.

And so the first cause, by its very nature, must have been non-contingent: necessarily pre-existing, and requiring nothing to cause it.

WHAT OR WHO WAS THE FIRST CAUSE?

Did time and space begin with the inception of our Universe? Or is our universe imbedded in a realm that also has its own "meta" time and space? Either way, as we have already demonstrated, it cannot be "tur-tles all the way down." Since the events that led to the creation of our universe must be finite in number, even if we must count back, we will eventually arrive at a pre-existent first cause of our universe that is transcendent, existing outside of time and space. Since matter and fields are dependent upon time and space to exist, this first cause must have been immaterial (incorporeal).

Although they perhaps can be regarded as immaterial, the dimensions of time and space are not causative agents. Neither are ideas. The only causative thing that we can conceive of which would be immaterial is an incorporeal mind. At one time an objection to the first cause being an incorporeal mind (i.e. a spirit) was that a mind needs a body in order to produce a material effect. Since we do not know what the nature of spirit is however, that is sheer conjecture. *Being immaterial does not mean having no substance - it simply means having a substance of a different nature than material things.* In addition, since the advent of computer game worlds such as Minecraft, we now know that a pow-erful enough mind could conceivably create a computed reality, so this objection no longer holds. A human mind having a realistic dream is a crude analogy of this.

But this idea actually did not originate with modern computer sci-ence. Xenophanes (565-470 BC) argued for a God who caused and controlled all things by thought:

"Always He remains in the same place, moving not at all: nor is it fitting for him to go to different places at different times... but without toil he shakes all things by the thought of his mind."[184]

Similarly, the even more ancient book of Genesis records that God created by speaking:

And God said "Let there be light," And there was light." – *Genesis 1:3*

Speaking and the execution of computer commands are the closest concepts we have to convey the idea of a thought that produces a material creative effect. The fine-tuning of our universe and the highly ordered complexity of life points to an intelligent cause. In chapter 2, we discussed why it would be next to impossible for an intelligence in another universe to aim a quantum mechanical fluctuation accurately enough to produce our universe. Therefore our universe must have been made by an intelligence that is not a part of any universe, and was pre-existent. In other words, the first cause must have been a conscious, immaterial mind. The God of the Bible matches that description:

"This is what the LORD says-- Israel's King and Redeemer, the LORD Almighty: I am the first and I am the last; apart from me there is no God." – Isaiah 44:6 NIV

"I am the Alpha and the Omega," says the Lord God, "who is, and who was, and who is to come, the Almighty."- Revelation 1:8 NIV

"Through him all things were made; without him nothing was made that has been made." – John 1:3 NIV

We are taught in scripture that God is spirit:

---

[184] Michael Patzia, "Xenophanes (c. 570—c. 478 B.C.E.)" *Internet Encylopedia of Philosophy: A Peer-Reviewed Academic Resource.* http://www.iep.utm.edu/xenoph/ (Last accessed 03.25/2109)

> "God **is spirit**, and those who worship him must worship in **spirit** and truth."

Spirit is typically understood to be an immaterial substance that supports conscious intelligence. We usually think of it as unembodied, but this need not be so. The Bible teaches that the human spirit is embodied until death, unembodied in heaven or hades, and will again be embodied at the day of resurrection. Interestingly, a problem that gives infinite multiverse theorists difficulties is called the *Boltzmann Brain Paradox* – the idea that unembodied minds are more likely to form by chance in a chaotic environment than embodied ones.[185] So why are we embodied? Would it not be more likely that an unembodied intelligence formed us? And would it not also be more likely that this unembodied intelligence is of one simple immaterial essence, and preexistent as the first cause, rather than formed by chaos from contingent things?

God seems to have declared His self-existent, uncreated nature when Moses asked for His name. God's mysterious reply was:

> And God saith unto Moses, "I AM THAT WHICH I AM;" He saith also, "Thus dost thou say to the sons of Israel, '**I AM hath sent me unto you.**'"
> - *Exodus 3:14, Young's literal Translation*

The fact that God speaks of Himself as existing in the present tense may refer not only to His omnipresence throughout time, but to His transcendence of time. Jesus said something very similar:

> Jesus said to them, "Truly, truly, I say to you, before Abraham was born, I am." – John 8:58

Why would God be perfectly good? An evil mind usually flows from the temptations associated with human desires, lusts, and survival strategies. Even a finite spirit such as Satan can be tempted by non-fleshly

---

[185] Matthew Davenport, Ken D. Olum, "Are there Boltzmann brains in the vacuum." arXiv:1008.0808v1 [hep-th] 4 Aug 2010. https://arxiv.org/pdf/1008.0808.pdf (Last accessed 03/25/2019)

desires such as conceit, pride, or the desire to have followers. But since God is incorporeal (spirit), immortal, all-knowing, all-wise and eternal, He could not be tempted by such things. He would therefore always choose what is ultimately best. An all-knowing mind would know better than to engage in evil.

> "When tempted, no one should say, "God is tempting me." **For God cannot be tempted by evil, nor does he tempt anyone**; but each person is tempted when they are dragged away by their own evil desire and enticed. Then, after desire has conceived, it gives birth to sin; and sin, when it is full-grown, gives birth to death. Don't be deceived, my dear brothers and sisters. Every good and perfect gift is from above, coming down from **the Father of the heavenly lights, who does not change like shifting shadows**." -*James 1:13-17, New International Version*

In a previous chapter we discussed the Christian doctrine known as *creatio ex nihilo*, which means that God created all things from nothing.

There are at least three conceivable ways that an immaterial God could have created things from nothing. Our universe could be, as was mentioned in chapter two, a *TSR* (a theistically sustained reality) *completely* detailed to the last particle, computed within the mind of God, similar to how a computer game world is formed within a computer. Every physical phenomenon, including randomness, can in theory be computed on a powerful enough computer or mind.

However, as I mentioned in chapter two, there are other conceivable ways that God could have created our universe. God could have set aside portions of what He is composed of so that it was no longer a part of Him, and created all other things directly or indirectly from that. Since God is infinite, He could take from Himself to form all other things and remain infinite, because infinity minus any finite number or any smaller infinity equals infinity.

This is not to imply pantheism: the belief that God and the physical universe are one and the same thing; only that they were *originally* made of the same substance. A woman can shear the wool off of a sheep, spin it into yarn and make a sweater. Once she has done that, the sweater and the sheep are no longer the same thing.

Or perhaps, just as +1 and -1 equal zero, God pulled apart nothingness to make something, or used something (such as a false vacuum) to create all other things. (In a false vacuum, if +2 is the ground state, then in relation to it, +1 is the same as -1, and +3 is the same as +1.)

Just as the set of even numbers can exist side by side with the set of odd numbers, and each is an infinite set, since matter is mostly empty space, we can conceive of multiple parallel realities existing together in the same volume of space. This is similar to how multiple signals at different frequencies can be transmitted through a conductive metal or transmission medium. Likewise, the three persons of the Christian Trinity could all co-exist together with creation, together filling and pervading one another and all of the smaller creation. Regarding the ascended Christ it is said,

> " For God was pleased to have all his fullness dwell in the Son " – Colossians 1:19, *(NET)*

It is interesting that in the book of Genesis, when God desires to create, He merely *speaks*, and something comes into existence:

> And God said, "Let there be light," and there was light. Genesis 1:3

This reminds us of how a game programmer creates things by issuing commands in a computer language.

In an interview, the co-founder of string theory, theoretical physicist Michio Kaku said,

> "So, the subatomic particles that we see in nature - the quarks, the electrons - are nothing but notes on a tiny vibrating string. What is physics? Physics is nothing but the laws of harmony that you can write on vibrating strings. What is chemistry? Chemistry is nothing but the melodies you can play on interacting vibrating

strings. What is the universe? The universe is a symphony of vibrating strings."[186]

Kaku holds that the mind of God may be "cosmic music resonating through 11 dimensional hyperspace." However, since scripture informs us that God created all things, then if string theory is correct, God must transcend 11 dimensional hyperspace. That would mean, as my friend Peter Whang recently suggested to me, that 11 dimensional hyperspace was brought into existence by, and still resonates to the vibrations of the spoken word of God.

Whatever idea is the correct one, the scripture passages which inform us that God "spoke" things into existence are clear indications of the effortless, absolute control God has over His creation. Either way, scripture is clear that we exist within, and are sustained within God:

> For in Him we live and move and have our being. -Acts 17:28a

> "For by Him all things were created, both in the heavens and on earth, visible and invisible, whether thrones or dominions or rulers or authorities-- all things have been created through Him and for Him. He is before all things, and in Him all things hold together." – *Colossians 1:16-17*

Furthermore, Jesus, whom the Bible teaches created all things, is called "The Word" in the first chapter of the gospel of John:

> In the beginning was the Word, and the Word was with God, and the Word was God. The same was in the beginning with God. All things were made by him; and without him was not any thing made that was made. – John 1:1-4

---

[186] Michio Kaku, "The Universe Is a Symphony of Vibrating Strings." Big Think Video, 25 January, 2011. Quote located at time interval 0.24 seconds https://bigthink.com/videos/the-universe-is-a-symphony-of-vibrating-strings-2 (Last accessed 03/25/2019)

The phrase "The Word" in this verse seems to carry with it connotations of information – in fact, the highest order of information. This idea is conveyed in the title of Dr. Werner Gitt's book, *In the Beginning Was Information.*[187]

Please note that when I suggest that our universe *could* possibly be a reality sustained within the mind of God, I'm certainly not suggesting that God is a computer or a machine. Living minds carry on computations (thoughts or cognitions) too! God is not a machine but a living, personal being, capable of love just as you and I are.[188] In fact, He is capable of much greater love than we are, and his clarity of consciousness far exceeds our own. This means that His personhood far exceeds ours. Compared to Him, *we* are the ones who are the more machine-like, since we are much lower on the scale of intelligence.

What I am saying, however, is that similar to how some human beings can astound us with their computational skills, the mind of the living God is capable of innumerable and instantaneous parallel cognitions far, far beyond the computations of any supercomputer known to man. Furthermore, His methods of cognition may vastly transcend our simple methods of thought and computation. *And these may be cognitions of an entirely different nature than binary computations.*

Within the realm of our known universe, it is highly improbable that life would have formed by chance. Isn't creation by an intelligence the only cause of complex order and semantic information that we have ever observed?

And doesn't it seem more reasonable, and *much more likely* that a creative intelligence of one simple essence would have been preexistent

---

[187] Werner Gitt, *In The Beginning Was Information*, Master Books, 2005. https://answersingenesis.org/answers/books/in-beginning-was-information/ (Last accessed 03/25/2019)

[188] Contrary to the title "God is the Machine," which is a December 2002 article in *Wired*, God is not a digital machine, but a living being. The content of the article nevertheless is thought-provoking. Kevin Kelly, "God Is the Machine." Wired, Dec 2002. http://archive.wired.com/wired/archive/10.12/holytech.html (Last accessed 3/25/2019)

in an eternal realm, than that life arose by chance in our universe, which is constrained by time and the laws of thermodynamics?

We may therefore safely conclude that there was a first cause, and that this cause was pre-existent, immaterial and intelligent.

14 Where Do the Laws of Nature Come From?

"It is evident that an acquaintance with natural laws means no less than an acquaintance with the mind of God therein expressed." — James Prescott Joule

n a previous chapter, we discussed the fact that life has the appearance of design. But it is more than life which appears to be designed. The very principles which govern the universe, the interactions between human beings, and our methods of reasoning also have the appearance of *thoughtful* design.

Where Do the Laws of the Universe Come From?

Imagine that one day, we will be able to create simulated computer game-worlds with truly intelligent AI characters in them. Will these game characters ever begin to wonder where the laws of their universe come from? That would be a very appropriate question for them to consider, wouldn't it? In their case, the answer would *not* be a quantum fluctuation. I think that is an appropriate question for *us* to consider, too.

Another good question to ask ourselves is, 'Why is so much of abstract math applicable to the natural world?" Why does nature seem to be organized in such a uniform way, that we can describe it mathematically?

Consider the physical laws of our universe:

- *Why* is the two-way speed of light 186,282.397 miles per second?

- *Why* is the total energy of a body (its rest mass energy) equal to the mass of the body times the speed of light squared? (This is Einstein's famous equation, $E=MC^2$.)
- *Why* is the gravitational force between two objects proportional to the mass of each, and inversely proportional to the distance between them? And *why* is this relationship *so* predictable, that scientists and engineers are able to use it to send probes to the outer planets and moons of our solar system?
- *Where* did these laws of the universe come from?
- And *why* do matter and energy obey them?
- Lastly, *why* are these laws so precisely tuned, that if they were even slightly changed, life could not exist in our universe?

Do they arise from average patterns of particle behavior? If so, then couldn't exceptions to the laws possibly occur? Why do they appear to be invariable?

WHERE DOES MORAL LAW COME FROM?

But the laws of physics are not the only laws we ought to consider.

- *Why* do we simply *know* that it is wrong to abuse a child?
- *Why* do we simply *know* that it is wrong for a man to beat his wife?
- *Why* do (most of us) feel guilty after we say something that hurts another person's feelings?

These are all instances of violating the *Golden Rule which* Jesus gave us – "Do unto others as you would have them do unto you." Where did this and all other moral laws come from?

Nearly all of us feel the pull of moral law. A person who does not is called a sociopath. This not a person you would want to marry, befriend, or enter into a business relationship with, because they can wrong you and feel no remorse for it. Some sociopaths are too smart for it, but they stand a much higher chance than the general population of ending up in a prison cell or a mental institution.

Some would argue that moral laws are relative, simply a matter of pref-erence, herd instinct programmed into our DNA by millions of years of evolution, what we have been taught, or due to cultural conven-tion. But I had an experience when I was a child which runs counter to these ideas.

I had been taught from my parents and relatives that mice were filthy pests that should be killed. One day, I was exploring in my grand-mother's basement, and I found a plastic bucket that four or five live mice were trapped in. I'm not sure how this happened. Perhaps there was some food in there that had originally attracted them. Or perhaps one fell in and the others, hearing his cries for help, attempted to res-cue him and fell in themselves.

When I saw all of these mice, I decided that I was going to kill those creatures which I had been trained to think were so nasty. I carried the bucket outside beneath my Grandmother's pear tree, found a pear that had fallen to the ground, and threw it at one of the mice, killing him. After I did that, however, something happened which completely surprised me. The other mice fearfully screamed at me, just as human beings might do at the injustice of someone killing them. Realizing that they were sentient beings with emotions and more intelligence than I had expected, I immediately regretted my actions. I tipped the bucket over and let the remaining mice go (probably to go right back into my grandmother's basement)!

Clearly, I came to a moral conclusion that went against what I had been taught to believe.

I am not arguing that killing animals is always wrong. Human life is more valuable, and therefore I believe it can be justifiable, though re-grettable, to *compassionately and humanely* kill animals to protect or sustain human life. Though it would have been justifiable to trap and release, or to humanely kill those mice so that they would not re-infest my grandmother's home, I think that we should never be unnecessarily unkind or cruel to animals, as I recognized that I was being at that time. An ethical hunter, for instance, aims to take his game in such a way that it does not suffer or even realize what is happening. A well designed mouse trap accomplishes essentially the same thing.

The importance of being kind and compassionate to other sentient beings is a moral law which as a child I was able to intuitively recognize. That moral law was not dependent upon what I had been taught; in fact, it went *against* what I had been taught in this instance. But that moral law was real, and it existed, and I *keenly* felt it.

> "The righteous care for the needs of their animals, but the kindest acts of the wicked are cruel." – Proverbs 12:10

If morality were just a matter of convention, what about the terrible things that the Nazis did to the Jewish people prior to and during WWII? Their cultural convention was that the things they were doing were right. But did that cultural consensus really make it right? No! Most of us can look at the tragic photographs of the starving children, women and men which were taken after the concentration camps were liberated and intuitively tell that what was done to these poor people was horribly evil and wrong.

Nearly everyone would also agree that it is wrong to sadistically torture a child, or even a kitten or a puppy. And even the most committed moral relativist will complain that it is not right if you cut him in line, underpay him, or mistreat him in some way. Suddenly, he becomes a person who believes in absolute moral laws!

Moral laws therefore exist independently of cultural consensus. But if they do not come from *us*, where *do* they come from? From instinctive urges pre-programed into our DNA by mutations chosen by natural selection? That is what Richard Dawkins believes. He wrote,

> In the universe of blind physical forces and genetic replication, some people are going to get hurt, and other people are going to get lucky; and you won't find any rhyme or reason to it, nor any justice. The universe we observe has precisely the properties we should expect if there is at the bottom, no design, no purpose, no

evil and no good. Nothing but blind pitiless indifference. As that unhappy poet A. E. Houseman put it:

> For nature, heartless, witless Nature will neither know nor care. DNA neither knows nor cares. DNA just is, and we dance to its music.[189]

CS Lewis made an excellent point in his book *Mere Christianity* which stands in opposition to Dawkins' argument that our morality merely comes from instincts programed into our DNA. Lewis pointed out that when we have competing instincts, it's usually the *weaker* instinct that is the right thing to do!

For instance, if you are hiking and come across a stranger being attacked by a mountain lion, you might feel the compassionate instinct to help. But you will probably feel fear and the instinct to preserve your life even more keenly. If you suppress the stronger of the two instincts, and try to save that person's life if you can, then you have managed to overcome your DNA to do the right thing.

And so moral laws seem to transcend our instincts, and as Kohlberg's Theory of Moral Development illuminates, individuals with the most highly developed morality are able to overcome even their own survival instincts to observe these laws.

Imagine that an ancient city was besieged, and the inhabitants ran out of food. One mother and father hid food from their children and ate it in secret. Then after the food ran out, they secretly killed and ate their children. Two unmarried sisters who had taken in some orphans, however, refused to eat anything, and instead sacrificially gave all of the food that they had to the orphans. These women were able to transcend their own survival needs to fulfill the moral law of love.

Which of these two sets of adults did the right thing? Nearly all of us would say that the two sisters did, and that the parents who ate their children were extremely evil, wrong and selfish. And yet, is what they

---

[189] Dawkins, R., River out of Eden, Weidenfeld & Nicholson, London, p. 132-133, 1995

did evil and selfish simply because *you* think it is? In other words, is it wrong *only* because it violates *your* personal standards? Or just as twenty-two plus twenty-two equals forty-four whether an uneducated man thinks it does or not, is what they did wrong because it violates a standard that holds true no matter what people think?

To argue or teach otherwise is to open up a Pandora's Box of evil, and *that alone is evidence that moral law is true.* In other words, the fact that observing objective, universal moral laws preserves civilization, peace, happiness and life is very strong evidence that these principles are real. If a hypothesis lines up with thousands of years of experience and experimentation, that is pretty good reason to call it a true law! We had best leave the lid on that Pandora's box!

Moral laws are therefore universal, objective truths, which hold true whether some people agree with them or not. And they are different from mere preference, custom, or opinion. If I think that blue is a nicer color than brown, that is a matter of preference, and your opinion regarding that would be just as valid as mine. But "thou shalt not murder" is not a matter of mere preference. If it were, we could justifiably permit serial killers to roam the streets.

In this sense, moral laws are similar to the laws of math. Just as the laws of math are real, universal, abstract truths which apply to the relationships between things, the laws of morality are real, universal, abstract truths which apply to the relationships between human beings, and even to our relationships with animals.

If these moral laws exist independently of preference, opinion, upbringing, instinct, or social convention, then where do they come from? Just as all human laws require a lawgiver, there is good reason to think that these universal moral laws came from a lawgiver, too.

The word *cosmos*, which is often used as a synonym for the word universe, is actually a Greek word that means an orderly arrangement. Why does our universe exhibit uniform order rather than chaos, so that it can be so beautifully and consistently described by the laws of mathematics?

This low entropy, or highly ordered state of the cosmos causes us to wonder, where did this exquisitely arranged order come from? We have so far discovered no grand theory of everything which dictates that all universes must have the order and fine tuning parameters ours does. Just as Richard Dawkins acknowledged that living things have the appearance of design because of this order, our universe has the appearance of design, too.

But so do moral laws. Since human relationships break down when moral laws are violated, moral laws have the kind of high-order functional design which only comes from intelligences. They are like the safety instructions that come with a new chainsaw. An *intelligence* wrote them, explaining to you how the chainsaw is designed to be used. Those safety rules, which arise from how the chainsaw was intelligently designed, exist whether you believe in them or not. Violate them, and things could go terribly wrong.

But if these moral laws which are a consequence of our design exist whether or not *we* think they do, then to what intelligence do they owe their ultimate origin?

And what is it about this lawgiving intelligence that makes *His* opinion about what constitutes morality *universally* true, when your opinion about morality may not be true?

Richard Dawkins appears to be opposed to this rational line of thought. Because what he calls "otherwise good people" have been driven by their religion to commit acts of terrorism, Dawkins categorically claimed that "religion is evil"![190]

Normally, I am kind and gentle when I point out mistakes that others have made in reasoning. But since Dawkins has been so vociferous in attacking Christianity, I am going to be blunt in critiquing his reasoning. I figure that since Dawkins dishes out blasphemous criticisms of the

---

[190] "Richard Dawkins takes on Islam on Al Jazeera TV - The Selfish Gene: My Interview with Richard Dawkins"
https://www.youtube.com/watch?v=vvcJAl0DDw4 (Last accessed 3/25/2019)

God of Abraham, Isaac and Moses, and God has kindly and patiently reciprocated by not yet striking him by lightning, Dawkins ought to be able to handle valid criticism like a man.

Dawkins' reasoning is wrong on four counts:

1. **It is hypocritical.** Notice that Dawkins is appealing to the concepts of good and evil. Isn't it interesting that even the most avowed and renowned moral relativists will adopt moral absolutes when it suits their purposes?

2. **It is self-righteous.** Hasn't atheism and moral relativism also enabled men such as Hitler, Stalin, Mao, and Pol Pot to justify doing terrible things, which by comparison *dwarf* all religiously motivated crimes against humanity? Following Dawkins' logic, atheism must be an even greater evil! Clearly, it is the *form* of atheism or religion that can result in moral evil.

3. **It is logically incoherent**. The fact that some religions encourage people to do things that are wrong does not mean that all do. If there is only one purely true and good religion or philosophy, and it is the one which completely accords with reality *and* that which is most right - then would not all other religions or forms of atheism be wrong and sometimes even evil to the extent that they stray from it? So certainly, religious practitioners can do evil to the extent that they stray from these transcendent moral laws Dawkins seems to be appealing to. But so can atheists like Richard Dawkins!

4. **Lastly, Dawkins' reasoning is self-contradicting.** If there is no final authority to judge that the 911 attack on the World Trade Center was wrong, or that the atheist Stalin was wrong for killing 34 million people, who is to say that one man's, or one culture's moral opinion is better than another's? Why would Dawkins be appealing to transcendent moral law if it did not actually exist? Denying that there is a God who has given us these universal moral laws logically leads to moral relativism. As many atheists do, Dawkins seems to vacillate between moral relativism and appeals to morality. In an interview, he once said, "What's to prevent us from saying Hitler wasn't

right? I mean, that is a genuinely difficult question." [191]   (That is not to say that all atheists follow this logical implication of their worldview. Many atheists wisely borrow their morality from religion.)

For all four of these reasons, Dawkins' argument is simply wrong.

WHERE DO THE LAWS OF LOGIC COME FROM?

There are also laws of logic. We use these laws in order to abstractly think and reason. Without them, it would be impossible for you to read and contemplate this book. These laws of logic are truly universal, because animals also (without realizing it) use them to think, communicate, and reason in rudimentary ways. Computers utilize them as well.

In fact, when an atheist argues that there is no God, he assumes that the rules of logic always hold true in order to make his argument. His presuppositions could be wrong, but the laws by which he reasons based upon those presuppositions must always hold true. If those laws were inconsistent, he could make no reasonable sounding argument at all.

The question is, *why* do these laws of logic always seem to hold true?

IN CONCLUSION

Where do these universal laws of logic come from? *Where* do these objective, universal moral laws come from? *Where* do the physical laws of the universe come from? *Where* do the laws of the quantum realm come from?

These laws inform us that there is a well thought-out structural order and design to the universe. *Wherever there are well-thought out laws, there must be at least one thinking law giver.* What could be the

---

[191] Larry Taunton, "Richard Dawkins, the Atheist Evangelist." By Faith, Issue number 18, December 1, 2007. https://byfaithonline.com/richard-dawkins-the-atheist-evangelist/ (Last accessed 4/02/2019)

explanation for these laws except a vastly intelligent mind? And hasn't that Mind built the ability to recognize those laws into the *very fabric* of our nature? Are we wise, then, to disregard or ignore these laws?

Descartes said "I think, therefore I am." The most sensible explanation for the bewildering complexities of the cell, the unfathomed wonders of the human brain, the stunningly beautiful order of the universe, the precise tuning of the fundamental forces of nature, and the sensible laws of logic, morality, and physics is a *thinking mind.* A mind which reasons at a level far, far beyond our feeble human capacities, and is therefore divine.

All of these things reveal to us that God thinks, therefore **HE IS.**

15   WHY DO THE INNOCENT SUFFER?

"If I find in myself desires which nothing in this world can satisfy, the only logical explanation is that I was made for another world." — *C.S. Lewis, Mere Christianity*

here is a profound and disturbing question that has long troubled believers and is often raised to challenge the existence of God, and I do not want to neglect consideration of it here, though I will do so only briefly. Much has already been written concerning this, so I only want to add some thoughts to the discussion. For further reading, I highly recommend C.S. Lewis's book, *The Problem of Pain.*

Why would God have created a world like ours, which though originally good, through the sin of Adam and Eve became a place where there is pain, suffering, and death? If God knows all things, He knew that this would become a world in which little children suffer. Why did God not place them in the best of all possible worlds instead?

Perhaps as Leibniz contended, this is the best of all possible worlds in that the necessary evil that would result from man's freewill is at a minimum. If that is the case, one shudders to think of what the *other* possible worlds containing men would have been like! While the suggestion that the evil that could result from man's freewill is minimized in our world is an attractive idea, most of us would agree that this is certainly not the best of all possible worlds. The idea that this is the best of all possible worlds provided Voltaire with much to justifiably poke fun of in his satire, *Candide.*

An idea that makes more sense to me is that God *does* plan to create the best of all possible worlds (or an ideal world), but desires to place in it beings that he can most freely shower his love and blessings on. Among these would be beings who...

... freely choose to love him. If so, it would be necessary to risk creating beings who might choose not to love or serve Him. The existence of moral evil would be a necessary consequence of this.

... have previously demonstrated their love and faithfulness to Him in the midst of trials, suffering, persecution and death.

... do not have delusions of self-sufficiency, but recognize their utter dependence upon Him.

... have had their character tested and purified in the fires of hardship and trials. Some of the kindest, most empathetic people you will ever meet are those who have experienced great suffering. Others have learned some hard life lessons which have taught them to be persons of integrity and character. If these people had been placed in the best of all possible worlds first, they would never have become the persons of beautiful character that they are now, and we would not be blessed with their presence.

... will be able to appreciate His blessings because they have previously experienced suffering and need. Most of us have encountered spoiled children who have had everything they could possibly need and so much more given to them, and yet are selfish, unhappy and ungrateful about all that they have. Is that what would have become of us, if we had been placed in the best of all possible worlds without first experiencing pain, discipline, or hardship?

... have not sold themselves out to do evil. These would need to be separated from those who are placed in the ideal world, or it would no longer be the best of all possible worlds! This means that if heaven is to exist, some people cannot be permitted to enter it. And if someone does not exist not in heaven, then he must be in something somewhat akin to hell. (No one would deny that our world can be a hellish place to live in.) The very nature of heaven, therefore, demands that those who exist outside of it must be in a form of hell, at least to some degree.

... and lastly, perhaps those whom God will be able to, and plans to bless the most in this new world are the innocent who have had to suffer as a consequence of man's sinfulness and injustice, or who have had to suffer the ravages of natural disaster or nature.

Sometimes the justification for abortion is given that a child should not be brought into a world of poverty. And yet, if you were to ask any poor children if they would rather not be here, or if they would like for a pro-abortionist who is using this argument to take them out of this world, nearly all of them will reply that they are glad to be alive and want to continue living. Their lives certainly do not have less meaning simply because they must endure poverty. In fact, since hardship purifies character, their lives probably have *more* meaning, though they may not know it and others may not recognize it.

If you asked people, "Would you rather have freewill and endure suffering as a result of it, or have no freewill but live in a paradise where there is no suffering or death?" Nearly everyone would choose to have freewill. Freewill is part of what makes us human beings, separating us from instinctive animals and robots, no matter how human the robot may appear to be. Most of us would rather endure suffering than be a puppet on a string.

Could it not be that our world, or at least a world like it, is a *necessary prerequisite* to the best of all possible worlds?

How could God place us in such a world after death?

Dr. Jeffry M. Schwartz, a psychiatrist who specializes in treating patients with OCD (obsessive-compulsive disorder), noticed something striking about them. One form of OCD is when a person's brain thinks unwanted thoughts against his will, that he would never act out or want to see happen. Although his patients were thinking undesirable thoughts, they did not want to be thinking them, and were trying very hard not to. This meant, he realized, that there was an aspect of their will or consciousness that seemed to be independent of their malfunctioning brains. He noticed that anxiety about the unwanted thoughts made his patients only more likely to think those thoughts again.

So when His patients would think undesirable thoughts, he instructed them to relax and think, "It's not me. It's my OCD."[192] He went on to write a book entitled, *You Are Not Your Brain*.[193]

What is this hidden aspect of our consciousness, this will, which is independent of our minds, that Dr. Schwartz was observing in action? A materialist would argue that it is merely one part of the brain conflicting with the other. This is probably true to an extent, since we have two brain hemispheres. However, we do not seem to have multiple seats of consciousness, but one. Is there not a part of you that is conscious of what *both* hemispheres of your brain are doing, and seems to tell your brain what to think? The Bible calls this unseen awareness and will your *spirit*. (Your brain does not always obey your spirit however, as we see In the case of bad habits, trying to keep awake to finish a critical task, and unwanted thoughts.)

Your spirit is your inner man, your sober mind, the true you. It is variously called your higher nature, your spiritual nature, your consciousness, your will, or your true self. It is likely the part of you that is still aware and making decisions in the dreamworlds your brain creates while you are asleep.

All that it would take for God to resurrect our true persons rather than a copy of us is to keep our spirits going in an unembodied state after we die, to later raise our bodies, transforming them into immortal ones suitable for the best of all possible worlds, to move our spirits back into the transformed bodies, and then place us in the best of all possible worlds. There would then be continuity of mind, spirit and body between the old world and the new. It would then truly be *us* living in paradise or heaven, rather than a copy of us.

---

[192] Schwartz, Jeffrey M. *Brain Lock: Free Yourself from Obsessive-Compulsive Behavior*, Harper Collins Publishers, 19917

[193] Schwartz, Jeffrey M., *You Are Not Your Brain: The 4-Step. Solution for Changing Bad Habits, Ending Unhealthy Thinking, and Taking Control of Your Life*, Avery Trade, 2012

Revelation 21:4 tells us, "He will wipe every tear from their eyes. There will be no more death or mourning or crying or pain, for the old order of things has passed away."

This is the promise that we all long for. If what we must endure in this mortal life is the pre-requisite for it, how does that weigh in the scales against eternity?

16 GOD'S NEW COMPETITOR: THE ANTHROPIC MULTIVERSE

"In order to avoid believing in just one God we are now asked to believe in an infinite number of universes, all of them unobservable just because they are not part of ours. The principle of inference seems to be not Occam's Razor but Occam's Beard: 'Multiply entities unnecessarily.'" — J. Budziszewski

 he most popular alternative to the hypothesis of a created universe is that of an *anthropic multiverse*. This includes the *anthropic principle*, which is the idea that the nature of a universe must be compatible with any intelligent life that lives within it. As an example of this principle, we should not be surprised that we find ourselves living on earth instead of inhospitable Venus. This idea is often invoked to naturalistically explain the fact that our universe is fine-tuned for life.

However, although a universe must be fine-tuned for the life within it, *this does not at all lower the odds of that universe having been formed by chance.* Those odds are extraordinarily low, as we will discuss shortly. Nor does the anthropic principle demand a natural explanation for a life-containing universe. The principle holds just as true in a theistically created universe. A theist can just as validly say, "Well *of course* we live in a universe capable of supporting human life. If God had not made it like that, He could not have placed us in it. So you should not be surprised that you live in a universe finely tuned for life!"

In short, *the anthropic principle is not evidence for metaphysical naturalism!* Rather, it is a *defense*, intended to keep metaphysical naturalism alive in the face of powerful probabilistic evidence against it.

THE FINE TUNING OF THE UNIVERSE

Let's take a few minutes to consider just *a few* of the fine-tuning pa-rameters of our universe. In his book *Just Six Numbers*, cosmologist Martin Rees lists six fine tuning numbers, without which our universe would be unable to support intelligent life. [194]They are:

- **10^{36}**, which is the strength of the electrical force that holds at-oms together divided by the force of gravity. Rees explains that if this number had only a few less zeroes, the universe would have been too short-lived for life to have formed.
- **0.007**, which is the fraction of rest mass that is converted to energy from the fusion of hydrogen which takes place in stars. Rees points out that if this number were 0.006 or 0.008, "we could not exist."
- **Approximately one,** which is the ratio of the density of the uni-verse to the density it must have to prevent gravitational col-lapse (this is called the critical density). Most of the mass which contributes to this density is thought to come from dark energy. As we discussed in a previous chapter, this value called *Omega*, very closely equals **one** as far as we can tell. And so, this value is finely tuned. Rees compares this to throwing up a stone from the bottom of a well so that it pre-cisely stops at the top of the well.
- **10^{-29} per square centimeter.** There appears to be a very weak antigravity force of this value, since recent observations indi-cate that our universe is expanding at an accelerating rate. If this weak force were much stronger, the galaxies and stars could not have formed. Known as the *cosmological constant* and represented by the Greek letter *Lambda*, this force is thought to be the value of the energy density of the vacuum of space. The idea of a cosmological constant was originally proposed by Einstein. Quantum theory predicts that Lambda should be impossibly large, but observations indicate that it is very small. This is called *the cosmological constant*

---

[194] Martin Rees, *Just Six Numbers*, Basic Books, 2009.

problem. In March 2014, Nemanja Kaloper and Antonio Padilla proposed that Einstein's theory of general relativity be slightly modified to solve this problem. A synopsis of their paper states: "A slight revision of general relativity can avoid an enormously large (and observationally inconsistent) cosmological constant, assuming that our Universe eventually collapses back on itself. "This would mean that the universe is closed and finite in size.[195]

- **10^{-5}** This is the ratio of the gravitational energy which glues galaxies together to their rest-mass energy. This number determines the texture of the universe. If this number were smaller, gas would not have condensed into stars and galaxies; if it were much larger, our universe would be filled with large black holes heavier than entire clusters of galaxies, and in the galaxies that did form, stars would be too closely packed together to create stable planetary systems.

- **Three.** This is the number of dimensions in space. If this were any higher or lower, we could not exist.

Only recently a new fine-tuning number has recently come to light. It is **379 keV** (or 379,000 electron volts). This is the excited state of carbon-12 known as the *Hoyle state.* Carbon-12, from which all life is constructed, could not form in stars if this value were slightly higher. Were it slightly lower, oxygen could not form. Just a small change in light quark mass would cause this value to change. [196]

---

[195] Nemanja Kaloper and Antonio Padilla, "Sequestering the Standard Model Vacuum Energy." Phys. Rev. Lett. 112, 091304 – Published 6 March 2014

DOI: https://doi.org/10.1103/PhysRevLett.112.091304 (Last accessed 3/18/2019)

[196] Evgeny Epelbaum, Hermann Krebs, Timo A. Lähde, et al. "Viability of carbon-based life as a function of the light quark mass." Phys. Rev. Lett. 110, 112502 (2013). DOI: 10.1103/PhysRevLett.110.112502.

This is *by far* not an exhaustive list of fine tuning parameters. Astronomer Hugh Ross has compiled a list of *140 fine tuning parameters!*[197]

So, how are we to account for these finely tuned numbers? Modern cosmologists, Rees says, have been unable to come up with a unifying theory to explain the six he discusses. He therefore attributes them to a huge or infinite multiverse. But this multiverse would have to be *incredibly* vast to explain the chance formation of our own finely-tuned-for-life universe.

Taking some of these fine-tuning parameters of our universe into account, cosmologist and mathematician Roger Penrose calculated the precise "aim" that the Creator would have needed to create a low-entropy (highly ordered) universe such as ours through a big bang. Of course, any time an intelligence takes aim at a target, he chooses only one out of a multitude of other possible targets, so it should not surprise us when an intelligence takes precise aim at only one of many possible targets. But what is amazing, as we mentioned in chapter two, is just how precise that aim would have had to be if God created the universe through a quantum mechanical fluctuation. We must consider, however, that if God created the universe, He could have had any number of methods at his disposal to create it. A "big bang" may not have been His actual choice of "weapons" but rather some other method certain to produce the universe as we observe it.

The number Penrose calculated is useful to our purposes here, however, because it is also reflective of the odds of our particular universe arising by chance in a big bang event. That chance is $1/10^{10^{123}}$. (Just in case you were wondering, the second "10" *does* belong in that number. It is *that* diminutive!) To get an idea of just how low those odds are, if that number were written out, *it would contain vastly more zeros than there are atoms in the known universe!*[198]

---

[197] Hugh Ross, *Why the Universe is the Way it Is*. Appendix C: Fine-Tuning for Life in the Universe, 2008. You may read his list of 140 fine tuning parameters of the universe at https://d4bge0zxg5qba.cloudfront.net/files/compendium/compendium_part1.pdf (Last accessed 3/11/2019)

[198] Penrose, The Emperor's New Mind, Oxford University Press, 2002, p. 445.

The Mystery of the Perfectly Tuned Guitar

You're the lead guitarist in a traveling band and have just purchased a beautiful, expensive new acoustic guitar. You put six new strings on it, but because you have an appointment and do not have time to tune them, you put the guitar back in its case, intending to tune the strings when you return. Yet when you come back later that day and take the guitar out of its case, you discover that all of the strings are perfectly in tune!

"All right, who has been messing around with my new guitar?" you demand of the other guys in the band.

"Not me," they all say.

"I know that someone has been fooling around with it, because it's perfectly in tune, and I did not tune it."

"Look,' the bass guitarist says, "Over the centuries, guitars have been strung millions of times. Don't you think that just once, someone could get the tuning right by sheer chance?"

"*That* is highly unlikely!" You angrily reply.

"Well, I just watched a TV show last night about the Many-Worlds interpretation of quantum mechanics. According to it, there are trillions upon trillions of parallel universes almost just like ours," the rhythm guitarist adds. "Don't you think that in some of them, you would get it right by sheer accident?"

"That's right!" The lead singer continues with a sly smile. "And this could be one of the very universes in which that happened."

"In fact," the drummer adds, "Given an infinite number of universes, I would say it is bound to happen!"

"So true!" the keyboardist eagerly chimes in. "In fact, it's bound to happen an infinite number of times!"

(There are approximately 10^{78} atoms in the known universe.) And all of those zeroes represent incredibly more universes than the number of zeroes!

We have already seen how an incredibly vast or infinite universe is required to explain the chance formation of *life* in our universe without an Intelligent Designer. But we have to suppose much more than that to eliminate God from the picture. We have to explain not only the formation of life by chance, but *also the formation of our highly* ordered universe by chance. Because the odds of a single quantum fluctuation leading to our universe are extremely low, a truly vast or infinite number of universes are also required to explain the formation of our universe forming by chance.

And so we have to suppose two things that we cannot possibly know are true in order to explain our origin by chance: (1) Our universe is incredibly vast or infinite, and (2) that it resides in a multiverse that is incredibly vast or infinite.

Are we wise to accept this hypothetical multiverse as the best explanation for our universe? Please read the story on the previous page entitled, "The Mystery of the Perfectly Tuned Guitar." Would you be gullible to accept this as the explanation for your tuned guitar? Of course. But the question is, *why* is that the case? First of all, we do not know if a multiverse exists. Secondly, although an infinite multiverse may make it probable that something extraordinarily unlikely will happen *somewhere*, it does not make it any more likely that it will happen in *your* particular locality. We called this *The Principle of Insufficient Local Tries.*

Sometimes, an intelligence is simply the most reasonable explanation for something! And so even if there were a multiverse, you still would be perfectly justified in concluding that one of your fellow band members had tuned your new guitar.

Following this sensible principle, you would also be justified believing that life is probably not the product of chance within the observable universe, and that our universe is probably not a product of chance within its metaphysical location.

THE HIGHLY SPECULATIVE NATURE OF MULTIVERSE THEORIES

We have already discussed how, according to the Standard Model, only *4.9 percent* of our universe is thought to consist of ordinary, observable matter. The rest of it is thought to be composed of two mysterious substances known as dark energy (making up 68.3% of the universe) and dark matter (26.8%).[199]

We also have mentioned that we still are not certain what dark matter and dark energy are, although many scientists believe that we are observing their effects. Dark matter is considered to be the "glue" that holds the galaxies in their unique shapes and explains their rotation with its gravitational attraction. And dark energy is the mysterious repulsive force that is causing the universe to expand at an accelerating rate. In response to the question, "What is dark energy?" the NASA Astrophysics website responds:

> "More is unknown than is known. We know how much dark energy there is because we know how it affects the Universe's expansion. Other than that, it is a complete mystery."[200]

Although dark matter and dark energy are necessary to make the Standard Model work, we cannot be certain they actually exist, since some cosmological models that we have already discussed explain the motions of the galaxies and the expansion of the universe without them. Perhaps one of these theories is correct and the Standard Model is wrong. Since so much about the composition of our own universe remains a mystery to us, this means that theories about the formation of our universe and other possible universes are highly speculative.

---

[199] "Dark Energy, Dark Matter." Web article, Nasa Science>Universe>What We Study>Dark Energy, Dark Matter, undated. http://science.nasa.gov/astrophysics/focus-areas/what-is-dark-energy/ (last accessed 3/25/2019)

[200] Ibid.

In addition, the Planck satellite results revealed mysterious anomalies that do not quite fit the standard model. According to the European Space Agency:

> "But hidden in the detail provided by Planck, there was also a hint of something more fundamental beneath the surface: a number of anomalies in the data do not perfectly agree with the predictions of the standard model. Some of these anomalies were found for the first time in the Planck data, while there had been evidence of others in previous experiments. Theoreticians continue to speculate about the implications of these anomalies and to investigate possible ways of extending the standard model."[201]

Not only that, but most cosmologists agree that as we trace the big bang back in time to its beginning, there was a time prior to which the known laws of physics did not apply. What happened prior to that, the time in which the laws of physics did not apply, is known as the *Planck Epoch*. And so naturally, theories regarding what caused the big bang prior to the Planck Epoch are highly speculative and metaphysical in nature, although mathematical calculations can be applied to the assumptions that are made.

Since so much of our *own* universe remains a mystery, theories regarding the existence of other universes are highly speculative. The famous physicist and cosmologist Alan Guth, who developed the idea of cosmic inflation, stated that "such ideas [multiverse cosmologies] are speculation squared." (Though he added that he thought something like them was likely true.)[202]

---

[201] ESA and the Planck Collaboration, "Hemispheric Asymmetry and Coldspot in the Cosmic Microwave Background." sci.esa.int, 21 March 2013. http://sci.esa.int/planck/51559-hemispheric-asymmetry-and-cold-spot-in-the-cosmic-microwave-background/ (Last Accessed 3/25/2018)

[202] Paul Davies, *Superforce: the Search for a Grand Unified Theory of Nature.* Touchstone, New York, New York, P. 200.

THE MULTIVERSE HIERARCHY

With that in mind, let's take a deeper look at these highly speculative multiverse cosmologies. Physicist Max Tegmark has classified multiverse cosmologies into a hierarchy of four levels:[203]

Level I: If our universe is infinite with the same kind of matter and energy that are in our Hubble volume evenly textured throughout, some believe that we could statistically expect that if we travel far enough, the same patterns will repeat themselves. If so, it is often asserted that this means there would be an infinite number of Hubble volumes just like ours, with identical copies of you occurring every $10^{10^{29}}$ meters.

But is this correct? In chapter eight, we mentioned Francisco José Soler Gil and Manuel Alfonseca's paper, *About the Infinite Repetition of Histories in Space.* In it, they point out that the number of possible worlds in an infinite universe is a countable, aleph-null infinity. But the number of possible history lines is much greater, an uncountable infinity. Because the uncountable infinity is infinitely larger than the countable one, the odds of a history line repeating itself would be zero.[204]

Level II: This contains universes resulting from a quantum fluctuation, or as a result of previous quantum fluctuations forming. One form of a level II Multiverse is called *eternal inflation.* After the expansion of our universe occurred, this is thought to have caused other post-expansion "bubbles" producing other universes, with different laws of physics.

Another type of cosmological model which probably falls under this category is called *the big bounce,* and is growing in popularity. In it, a

---

[203] Max Tegmark, "The Multiverse Hierarchy." *In Universe or Multiverse?*, B. Carr ed., Cambridge University Press (2007).
http://arxiv.org/pdf/0905.1283.pdf (Last accessed 3/25/2019)

[204] Francisco José Soler Gil and Manuel Alfonseca, "About the Infinite Repetition of Histories in Space." Theoria, Vol 29, No 3 (2014).
http://www.ehu.eus/ojs/index.php/THEORIA/article/download/9951/11770 (Last accessed 3/25/2019)

big bounce replaces the big bang. Based on quantum mechanics, it is a cyclic universe theory, which holds that the universe rebounds after it collapses due to gravity. Based on quantum mechanics rather than general relativity, big bounce cosmologies have been growing in popularity among cosmologists, and deserve a more detailed look. It is based on a theory called Loop Quantum Gravity (LQG). LQG is an attempt to reconcile quantum mechanics with the geometric concepts of general relativity.

In general relativity, space is considered to be a continuum which is infinitely divisible. That is not the case in LQG. In LQG, space itself is made up of discrete units. These units consist of individual packets, called *quanta*, of intersecting loops of excited gravitational fields. Together these form the network or fabric of space, which is called a *spin network*. When viewed over time, this network is called a *spin foam*.[205],[206]

Bounce cosmology is a form of cyclic universe cosmology (though the cycles need not go on forever). It concerns itself with what happened before the Planck Era, when the laws of general relativity do not apply. The basic idea behind it is that the "Big Bang" is replaced with a "Big Bounce." In bounce cosmology, our universe did not begin at infinite density. Rather, once the crunch of a previous universe reached a certain size (the Planck length), it is believed that a consequence of LQG is that a repulsive force took over and caused the universe to rebound or "bounce back," creating our own universe. Bounce cosmology is a form of multiverse theory, in that multiple successive universes are proposed.

[205] CORDIS, "The Big Bang versus the 'Big Bounce'" phys.org, Home>Physics>Quantum Physics, July 6, 2012. https://phys.org/news/2012-07-big_1.html (Last accessed 3/25/2019)

[206] "Loop. Quanum Gravity" Max Planck Institute for Gravitational Physics, Golm/Potsdam 2015. https://web.archive.org/web/20151031091616/http://www.einstein-online.info/elementary/quantum/loops/ (Last accessed 3/25/2019)

In an interview explaining Big Bounce Cosmology, Big Bounce theorist Ivan Aguillo of Cambridge University explained his idea that entropy is "reset" at each bounce.[207] The new "bounce" will presumably result in a new universe containing some form of low entropy order. This is analogous to erasing a cassette tape which plays random noise and static, so that it becomes a blank tape which plays nothing but silence, and recording fresh music or speech free of static on to it. But some form of *meaningful* music or speech must be recorded onto it for it to be of any use.

If entropy is essentially a state of disorder, and low entropy a state of order, then we have to ask ourselves, "What *specific* order or information state are we talking about?" *There are many conceivable simple low entropy universes that would not produce life.* In fact, most of them would not. In our universe, our particular low entropy state includes the physical laws of our universe and their fine-tuning parameters. So a simple "reset" of entropy as Aguillo was speaking of would hardly explain the odds of our particular low entropy state of order arising. We would need a lot of bounces. But it seems hard to reconcile this idea with our current universe, in which for all we can tell omega equals one. If omega equals one, our universe will never collapse due to gravity. So it would have to have always been slightly less than one for multiple bounces to have taken place. Since time is directional, like a vector ray, there could not have been an infinity past of bounces, either.

Most Level II universes will have different physical laws than our own. Because of this, the odds of getting a life-generating universe and history line out of them would be even lower than in a Level I universe.

Level III: This is also called the "Many Worlds" interpretation of quantum mechanics. The idea here is kind of like a movie with alternative storylines at various points that you can select with your Blu-ray

---

[207] See https://www.youtube.com/watch?v=IFcQuEw0oY8 for an informative interview documentary explaining Big Bounce Cosmology entitled "Before the Big Bang 1 - Loop. Quantum Cosmology Explained."

remote. If some of the hypothetical ideas of quantum physics are true, then every possible thing that could happen does, with parallel universes expressing every possibility constantly branching off. This would mean that there is a parallel universe in which Michelle Obama said "No" when Barak asked her to marry him, and others in which he lost the election to Mitt Romney. However, the specific quantum mechanical theories upon which Level III universes are based are highly speculative and controversial.

Level IV: What if some or all of the exotic mathematical structures that mathematicians have come up with correspond to some reality? For instance, just as you can fit an infinite number of lines in a plane, and an infinite number of planes in a cube, you could conceivably fit an infinite number of 3D Universes or "branes" in a 4 dimensional space. Level IV universes are those that are would exist if exotic hypothetical mathematical structures such as this correspond to reality. Computerized virtual universes would fall under this category.

BEFORE YOU JUMP ON THE MULTIVERSE BANDWAGON, CONSIDER THE FOLLOWING...

There's No Conclusive Observational Evidence of a Multiverse

Analysis of the data from the European Space Agency's Planck satellite revealed no evidence of the hoped for "dark flow" – a stream of galaxies moving in the same direction due to the influence of other universes.[208]

The Planck satellite seemed to have turned up *possible* evidence of other universes, however, by finding anomalies in the cosmic microwave background radiation (CMB). These anomalies are *anisotropies* (exceptions to a smooth, homogenous isotropic sky) that are bigger

---

[208] Maggie McKee, "Blow for 'dark flow' in Planck's new view of the cosmos." New Scientist, Space column, 3 April 2013. http://www.newscientist.com/article/dn23340-blow-for-dark-flow-in-plancks-new-view-of-the-cosmos.html#.U2_B3YFdV8E (Last accessed 3/25/2019)

than can be explained by the standard model. Laura Mersini-Houghton, a theoretical physicist at the University of North Carolina was almost certain that these were evidence of other universes: "These anomalies were caused by other universes pulling on our universe as it formed during the Big Bang," she said.[209]

However, other scientists were more cautious. George Efstathiou, professor of physics at Cambridge, who co-authored documents describing the Planck findings, considered Mersini-Houghton's idea to be speculative but "very interesting."[210]

Some cosmologists alternatively proposed that these anomalies indicate that the universe is saddle shaped (hyperbolic, or negatively curved.)[211]

Further study of these anomalies has resulted in *most* of them being explained, confirming *nearly* all of the predictions of the standard model. But not all of them have been explained (as of March 2019). Three stubbornly remain. The Planck Website described these in 2013, and they have not yet been explained (as of March 2019):

> While the observations on small and intermediate angular scales agree extremely well with the model predictions, the fluctuations detected on large angular scales on the sky – between 90 and six

---

[209] Rosie Taylor, "Is our universe merely one of billions? Evidence of the existence of 'multiverse' revealed for the first time by cosmic map." Daily Mail, May 2013. https://www.dailymail.co.uk/sciencetech/article-2326869/Is-universe-merely-billions-Evidence-existence-multiverse-revealed-time-cosmic-map.html (Last accessed 3/25/2019)

[210] William W., "Our Universe Could be One Of Billions, Paper Explains." Space Industry News, September 22, 2013. https://web.archive.org/web/20140702024316/http://spaceindustrynews.com/our-universe-could-be-one-of-billions-paper-explains/ (Last accessed 3/25/2018)

[211] Charles Q. Choi, "Weird findings suggest that we live in a saddle-shaped universe." NBC News, Space Column, Sep. 12, 2013. http://www.nbcnews.com/science/space/weird-findings-suggest-we-live-saddle-shaped-universe-f8C11133381

degrees – are about 10 per cent weaker than the best fit of the standard model to Planck data would like them to be. Another, perhaps related, anomalous signal appears as a substantial asymmetry in the CMB signal observed in the two opposite hemispheres of the sky: one of the two hemispheres appears to have a significantly stronger signal on average. An additional peculiar element in the data is the presence of a so-called 'cold spot': one of the low-temperature spots in the CMB extends over a patch of the sky that is much larger than expected.[212]

In a paper entitled "Preferred Axis in Cosmology," Web Zhao and Larissa Santos write:

> The foundation of modern cosmology relies on the so-called cosmological principle which states an homogeneous and isotropic distribution of matter in the universe on large scales. However, recent observations, such as **the temperature anisotropy of the cosmic microwave background (CMB) radiation**, the motion of galaxies in the universe, the polarization of quasars and the acceleration of the cosmic expansion, indicate preferred directions in the sky. If these directions have a cosmological origin, the cosmological principle would be violated, and modern cosmology should be reconsidered.[213]

Some of the cosmologies built upon the Biblical account of creation and interpretations of it may explain the mysterious alignment of the plane of the earth's orbit about the sun (and that of the other planets) with these preferred directions. These were discussed in chapter eleven. It is also possible, however, that there is something about our solar system that is affecting CMB measurements. This alignment

---

[212] "Simple But Challenging: The Universe According to Planck." http://sci.esa.int, 21 March 2013. http://sci.esa.int/planck/51551-simple-but-challenging-the-universe-according-to-planck/ (Last accessed 3/25/2018)

[213] Wen Zhao and Larissa Santos, "Preferred axis in cosmology." arXiv:1604.05484v3 [astro-ph.CO] 5 May 2016. https://arxiv.org/pdf/1604.05484.pdf (Last accessed March 25, 22019)

appears to be a direct violation of the Copernican principle (the idea that there is nothing special about the earth in the cosmic scheme).

Here's an image of the cosmic hemispherical asymmetry identified by the Planck satellite, which aligns with the plane of our solar system:

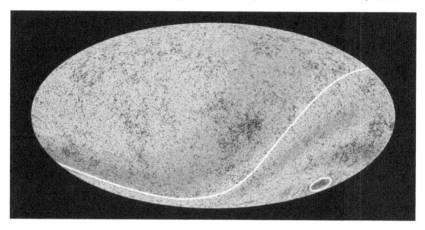

CMB Anomalies: Two of the three unresolved anomalies in Planck's map of the Cosmic Microwave Background can be seen here: The hemispheric temperature asymmetry (known as "the axis of evil" because it aligns with the plane of the earth's orbit around the sun), and the cold spot. Credit: ESA and the Planck Collaboration.

Some have offered the exotic explanation that the cold spot is a "bruise" from another universe bumping into our own. [214] But again, there is no conclusive evidence of this.

Why Would a Quantum Fluctuation Produce a Universe?

Can a simple quiver in a vacuum *really* create a highly complex, structured universe such as ours that follows orderly laws? *Or is this simply a modern creation myth?* How do we know that a quantum fluctuation would create universes? Why not some other structure? Doesn't something less complex, like two simple positive and negative particles

[214] Ivan Baldry, "Could Cold Spot in the Sky Be a Bruise from a Collision with a Parallel Universe?" ScientificAmerican.com, The Conversation US on June 2, 2017. https://www.scientificamerican.com/article/could-cold-spot-in-the-sky-be-a-bruise-from-a-collision-with-a-parallel-universe/ (Last accessed 3/25/2018)

seem much more likely? Why would a quantum fluctuation create universes and then randomly dial the fine-tuning parameters of each one, analogous to creating an infinite number of slot machines and pulling each one's lever?

Can a simple fluctuation *really* create a universe that always follows orderly laws rather than exhibiting chaos? Do we have any reason to believe that a quantum fluctuation could produce such complex, ordered behavior? According to Jeff Miller:

> Writing in the *Skeptical Inquirer* in 1994, Ralph Estling voiced strong disapproval of the idea that the Universe could create itself out of nothing. He wrote:
>
>> "I do not think that what these cosmologists, these quantum theorists, these universe-makers, are doing is science. I can't help feeling that universes are notoriously disinclined to spring into being, ready-made, out of nothing, even if Edward Tryon (ah, a name at last!) has written that 'our universe is simply one of those things which happen from time to time....' Perhaps, although we have the word of many famous scientists for it, our universe is not simply one of those things that happen from time to time."
>
> Estling's comments initiated a wave of controversy and letters to the Skeptical Inquirer, eliciting a response by Estling to his critics. Among other observations, he said,
>
>> "All things begin with speculation, science not excluded. But if no empirical evidence is eventually forthcoming, or can be forthcoming, all speculation is barren.... There is no evidence, so far, that the entire universe, observable and unobservable, emerged from a state of absolute nothingness" (1995, 19[1]:69-70).[215]

---

[215] Jeff Miller, "Can Quantum Mechanics Produce a Universe from Nothing?" Reason and Revelation Volume 33 #2 February 2013. http://apologetics-press.org/pub_rar/33_2/1302.pdf (Last accessed March 25, 2019)

The Possibility of a Created Multiverse

If a multiverse does exist, are universes constantly popping into existence in it? Perhaps not. The Bible makes room for a possible *created* multiverse when it speaks of the "heavens and the heavens that are above the heavens." The Christian apologist CS Lewis envisioned the possibility of other created universes long before the idea of a multiverse became popular, in his *Chronicles of Narnia* series. If other universes exist, they too may have been specially created by God, as Lewis imagined it.

A Multiverse Leaves the Question of the First Cause Unresolved

Causality must exist in the quantum realm of Level II and IV multiverses, in order for vacuum fluctuations to be initiated and universes to spring from them. And so that merely pushes back the problem of the first cause - it does not answer it. These questions remain:

- Where did the quantum mechanical laws that produced the fluctuations come from?
- From where did the vacuum field originate?
- From where did it's energy originate?
- What causes the fluctuations?

Let's ponder these things. As we discussed previously, it is conceivable that causality can exist in a timeless realm. In time, all events do not happen at once. Outside of time, all events happen at once. This means that outside of time, all causal chains have infinite velocity. Time is therefore the succession of events at a finite velocity. Since infinite time can never be achieved at a finite velocity, all time-bound realms must have had a beginning. Therefore, if the quantum realm of a multiverse is subject to some form of time, that multiverse must have had a beginning. And if it had a beginning, then something or someone must have caused it.

Even if a quantum multiverse has no time, cause and effect must exist within it for fluctuations to occur and for universes to spring into existence from them. Since an infinite causal chain has no end, any events within it must lie *on* that chain, not at its end. There could therefore not have been an infinite succession of causes prior to any event. All causal chains therefore must have had a beginning, including any quantum multiverse which is subject to cause and effect. Therefore if we lie within a timeless quantum multiverse, it is subject to cause and effect, and must have had a cause.

The very first cause must have of necessity been causeless. It therefore must have been pre-existent. It is *not* "turtles all the way down"!

Since time by its very nature must have had a beginning, the first cause must have been timeless. And this timeless first cause *must* have had the agency to produce time, time-bound causation, our finely-tuned-for-life universe, its orderly laws, and the complex and highly ordered life within it. Just think of how unlikely it is that a single simple vacuum fluctuation could actually *do* all of that! Isn't an intelligence a more sensible explanation? A causeless, timeless and transcendent first cause which is also an intelligent agent aligns precisely with the Judeo-Christian concept of God!

Is the Multiverse Simply an Attempt to Deny Mounting Evidence that there is a God?

Consider just how much metaphysical naturalism has had to retreat as new data about the complexity of life and the nature of the universe has poured in. First the idea of spontaneous generation was dashed. Then, when it became evident that the universe had a beginning, the idea of a steady-state universe lost credibility. Next, the idea of abiogenesis gave way to the concept of biopoesis. When it became evident that biopoesis was also unlikely, and that our finely-tuned-for-life universe was unlikely, the hypothesis of a vast naturalistic multiverse (along with the accompanying anthropic principle) became much more attractive. One wonders, just *how far* will naturalists retreat to invent new hypotheses to deny the evidence, which continues to mount, that there is a God?

God Would Be Bound to Exist

Cantor associated his concept of the *Absolute Infinite*, a set that transcends all transfinite sets, with God.[216] If all of the remarkable mathematical possibilities of Level IV Multiverses exist, the probability that a Transcendent Creator God exists is therefore assured, since the Absolute Infinite is a mathematical possibility. Or to state it another way:

If we live in a level IV multiverse, every mathematically possible thing that can exist will exist. Therefore, the greatest and most perfect of all immortal beings mathematically conceivable must exist. The greatest and most perfect of all immortal beings mathematically conceivable transcends all other things, including all other universes and transfinite sets, and is by definition God. Therefore, if we live within a Level IV multiverse, God must exist.

Because of this, to deny the existence of a God who could have created us, an avowed metaphysical naturalist would find the idea of a multiverse that is vast but *finite* preferable.

Paul Davies: "gods" Would Be Bound to Exist, Too!

In his NY Times Opinion piece *A Brief History of the Multiverse*, cosmologist Paul Davies writes,

> "Taking the multiverse theory at face value, therefore, means accepting that virtual worlds are more numerous than 'real' ones. There is no reason to expect our world -- the one in which you are reading this right now -- to be real as opposed to a simulation. And the simulated inhabitants of a virtual world stand in the same relationship to the simulating system as human beings stand in relation to the traditional Creator.
>
> Far from doing away with a transcendent Creator, the multiverse theory actually injects that very concept at almost every level of its

---

[216] Jané, I. Erkenntnis "The role of the absolute infinite in Cantor's conception of set." (1995) 42: 375. https://doi.org/10.1007/BF01129011

logical structure. Gods and worlds, creators and creatures, lie embedded in each other, forming an infinite regress in unbounded space."[217]

Applying Ockham's Razor to the Multiverse Hypothesis

As we have already discussed, Ockham's razor is useful when choosing between alternative hypotheses, as long as the evidence can support either idea. Even if theism and the multiverse had equal explanatory power (and they do not), a popular and sensible saying that is derived from Ockham's Razor is "Don't multiply entities beyond necessity." Although our analysis leads us to believe *one* single transcendent God is necessary to explain our universe and life, the many creator entities of multiverse theory are not.

Philosopher Richard Swinburne wrote,

> "To postulate a trillion trillion other universes, rather than one God in order to explain the orderliness of our universe, seems the height of irrationality."[218]

Swinburne elegantly makes the point. In fact, one must postulate *much* more than a trillion trillion universes to explain our own!

Cellular Automata Models Indicate That the Multiverse Hypothesis Lacks Explanatory Power

In a recent paper, Francisco José Soler Gil and Manuel Alfonseca used model computerized "universes" containing cellular automata (the 2-D self-replicators described in chapter five) to see if the multiverse hypothesis could explain the finely-tuned-for-life parameters of our universe.

---

[217] Paul Davies, "A Brief History of the Multiverse." The New York Times, April 12, 2003. https://www.nytimes.com/2003/04/12/opinion/a-brief-history-of-the-multiverse.html (Last accessed 3/25/2019)

[218] Swinburne, Richard. Is There a God? Oxford, Oxford University Press, 1995, p. 68

They found that in a mathematical multiverse, our universe would not be a *typical* life-containing universe because it attains a high degree of complexity with laws and physical constants that are uniquely simple. Since there would be infinitely more *typical* life-containing universes, "the probability of our existence in a world such as ours would be mathematically equal to zero."

Here's why: Since any number divided by zero equals infinity, any number divided by a number infinitely larger than it equals zero.

$$\text{Since } {}^N\!/_0 = \infty, \ {}^N\!/_\infty = 0$$

They concluded, "All the multiverses which have been proposed, except the mathematical multiverse, are too small, so that they merely shift the problem of fine tuning up one level. But the mathematical multiverse is too large, in the sense that, in its context, the simplicity of our world becomes inexplicable."[219]

Multiverse Cosmologies Are Metaphysical in Nature

Even if we did discover conclusive evidence for other universes, we probably could not be certain that any more universes exist that those that were near enough to have influenced our own. And so the proposals of a vast multiverse remain, and probably will remain, *unproven hypotheses* that require faith to believe in. Not only that, but as Francisco José Soler Gil and Manuel Alfonseca have made clear, they do not explain the improbability of our existence.

Although some multiverse theories make some predictions that are falsifiable, some creationist cosmologies do, too. But like the creationist cosmologies, these multiverse cosmologies also include metaphysical elements that are not scientifically falsifiable. If these multiverse cosmologies should be accepted as valid scientific hypotheses because

---

[219] Francisco José Soler Gil and Manuel Alfonseca, "Is the multiverse hypothesis capable of explaining the fine tuning of nature laws and constants? the case of cellular automata." March 2013, DOI: 10.1007/s10838-013-9215-7. http://arxiv.org/ftp/arxiv/papers/1105/1105.4278.pdf (Last accessed 3/25/2019)

they are partly falsifiable, so should creationist theories that are partly falsifiable.

Since multiverse cosmologies are not completely scientifically testable and involve speculations about existence outside of the observable universe, they cross over the line from science into the philosophical category known as metaphysics. Given the metaphysical aspects of multiverse hypotheses, they should not be regarded as fully testable hypotheses that can be conclusively confirmed by observation. Since it would probably be impossible for information to travel between universes, we may *never* be able to confirm that these other universes exist.

In the Oxford Journals publication *News and Views in Astronomy and Geophysics*, George Ellis pointed out:

> "Even though multiverse proposals are good empirically based *philosophical* proposals for the nature of what exists, they are not strictly within the domain of science. There is nothing wrong with empirically based *philosophical* explanation — indeed it is of great value provided it is labelled for what it is — but I suggest that cosmologists should be very careful not to make methodological proposals that erode the essential nature of science in their enthusiasm to support specific theories." [220] [Italics mine.]

In the previously mentioned *A Brief History of the Multiverse*, cosmologist Paul Davies also wrote,

> "Extreme multiverse explanations are therefore reminiscent of theological discussions. Indeed, invoking an infinity of unseen universes to explain the unusual features of the one we do see is just as ad hoc as invoking an unseen Creator. The multiverse theory may be dressed up in scientific language, *but in essence it requires the same leap of faith.* At the same time, the multiverse theory also

---

[220] George Ellis, "Opposing the Multiverse," Astronomy & Geophysics, Volume 49, Issue 2, pp. 2.33-2.35. (http://astrogeo.oxfordjournals.org/content/49/2/2.33.full)

explains too much. Appealing to everything in general to explain something in particular is really no explanation at all."[221] [Italics mine.]

---

[221] Paul Davies, "A Brief History of the Multiverse."

17 Why Metaphysical Naturalism Is Theism's Stepsister

"The people in the popular group say there is no peer pressure because they are at the top of the food chain. Really what they are doing is just eating away at everybody else." — *Lauren Greenfield*

"Your Grace? Your Grace, please, wait. May I try it on?" — *Cinderella*

 hy is strict naturalism considered to be a metaphysical philosophy, and not science? Lee Strobel's book *The Case for a Creator* is one of the best books I have ever read. In it, he pointed out what for me was a true eye-opener. When we strip metaphysical naturalism naked, down to its basic presuppositions, it consists of six basic premises. To quote Strobel:

- Nothing produces everything
- Non-life produces life
- Randomness produces fine tuning
- Chaos produces information
- Unconsciousness produces consciousness
- Non-reason produces reason [222]

Take a little while to reflect upon each of these presuppositions in light of the nature of our universe. How rational, logical, and intuitive do they seem to you? How *probable* do they seem to you?

These are essentially beliefs or tenets without any conclusive observational evidence. In fact, they go *against* our everyday empirical observations! So does it not seem hypocritical for atheists to be so loudly proclaiming that empirical science is on their side?

---

[222] Lee Strobel, *The Case for a Creator,* Zondervan, Grand Rapids, Michigan, p. 277.

While many atheists might deny that metaphysical naturalism is a religious belief system, *it is in precisely the same metaphysical category.* These tenets require faith to believe in, and belief in them could profoundly affect how a person lives his or her life. So then the most fitting way to categorize metaphysical naturalism would be to call it an *atheistic religion.*

Although naturalistic beliefs like this are in the same philosophical category as religious beliefs, they enjoy privileged status in modern science. Why? Because unlike theistic hypotheses, they do not violate the reigning philosophy of science known as *methodological naturalism.* As mentioned in the first chapter, this is not to be confused with the scientific method. Nor is it quite the same thing as metaphysical naturalism. Methodological naturalism is the philosophy that for purposes of science, we should act as though God does not exist - whether He does or not. Methodological naturalism can indeed prove useful when investigating the causes of most natural phenomena. Obviously, we should not hastily presume "God must have done it!" every time we do not understand how something happened.

But an alternative theistic philosophy of science, that God created the universe to follow orderly laws which He usually does not interrupt, works *just as well* for conducting science. The great theistic scientists of the past followed this philosophy and conducted exceptionally good science. If they could conduct science so well without holding to methodological naturalism, then *the claim that science cannot function without methodological naturalism simply isn't true.*

A third alternative, and agnostic approach, would also work. While not assuming that God exists, it would at least be open to the possibility that He does, and that He might occasionally act upon the universe. It would permit an examination of the evidence for this.

If MN is so critical to science, one cannot help but wonder, just *how* did science manage until the articulation of this concept in the 1980s?

These last two philosophical approaches to science have an advantage over methodological naturalism, for when natural explanations seem virtually impossible (as the chance formation of life in our observable universe does), they provide us with the freedom to follow the evidence to the most likely and logical explanation.

And so, when investigating the origin of life and our universe, it does not make sense to restrict science to methodological naturalism. In a matter so critical and important, what possible good could come from a philosophical bias that prevents science from following the evidence wherever it may lead?

If the true nature of methodological naturalism, as well as these alternative philosophical approaches to science were properly understood by our courts, I believe that a neutral, agnostic philosophical approach which assumes that the universe normally follows natural laws, but that it *might* occasionally be influenced from things or intelligences external to it, is the only one that would meet the test of constitutionality for US government sponsored science.

In the comedy movie *Nacho Libre*, Nacho encouraged his friend Stephen to "pray to the Lord for strength" when faced with a formidable opponent in the wrestling ring. Suddenly realizing that He had no place to turn for help, Steven replied to Nacho with a look of fear in his eyes, "I don't believe in God. I believe in science." [223]

Stephen thought that God and science were not compatible. In his mind, you could not believe in both. Since most people do not know that methodological naturalism is the reigning philosophy of science, like Stephen, many of them have jumped to the erroneous conclusion that naturalistic presuppositions are "scientifically based" and therefore must be more intelligent. As a result, they conclude that science and theism are mutually exclusive. *This includes many atheistic scientists who sadly have had very little or no training in the philosophy of science.* Some use this misunderstanding as a basis to promote atheism as intellectually superior to theism. When they ignorantly do this

---

[223] *Nacho Libre.* Directed by Jared Hess. Performances by Jack Black and Héctor Jiménez. Paramount Pictures, 2006. A clip. of this scene is available at https://www.youtube.com/watch?v=T Héctor Jiménez V_S5QNWaSl (Last accessed 3/25/2019)

however, what they are adhering to is of course not unbiased science, but what has come to be known as *scientism.*

In this neo-religion of scientism, prominent scientists who zealously promote atheism are the new high priests, and scientific jargon and complex math are the Latin scriptures the poor lesser-educated masses cannot understand well enough to evaluate on their own and must have explained to them by the clergy class. The scientific method is the source of revelation, and it indeed would be a useful source of information, but they assert that it must be filtered through the lenses of methodological naturalism, with the convenient result that no other religion can compete with atheism in science.

Many, perhaps most of these high priests of scientism do not *ever* want any hypotheses that could harmonize with theism to be allowed in science, and they are quite outspoken about it. Theists who dare to include any hint of God in science are considered dangerous "heretics" who must be ostracized, ridiculed and punished to protect and bolster the power structure.

Just like any other cultic religious belief system, scientism feeds and grows on ignorance. Because of this ignorance of the philosophy of science, just as poor Cinderella was usurped by her stepsisters, metaphysical naturalism has displaced anything remotely resembling theism in science, including ID (Intelligent Design hypotheses). But if these zealots of metaphysical naturalism continue to get their way, and succeed at keeping theism locked away in an attic room and out of sight in science, how will science *ever* know if theism can wear the glass slipper in the matter of origins?

A common but misguided criticism of ID is that "It is only thinly disguised religion." Most ID proponents only want to identify the distinguishing characteristics of intelligent design, and see if those characteristics are recognizable in nature, similar to the marks of intelligence that the scientists at SETI look for when examining extraterrestrial radio emissions. What is wrong with that? ID proponents, sticking to methodological naturalism, leave the question of *who* the intelligent designer is unanswered.

"Well, we all know who they *hope* you will conclude the Intelligent Designer is," opponents of ID counter. But what difference does that make? The motives of those who suggest a hypothesis have *no bearing at all* on whether or not that hypothesis is true.

For instance, suppose that I am a homicide detective who intensely dislikes a man suspected of murdering his wife and thinks that he is guilty, so I dig really hard to find evidence against him. And in fact, I do find conclusive evidence that he is guilty. Let's further suppose that I have very good reasons for disliking the suspect, because I learned that he often beat his wife. Should the evidence I uncovered be discounted in a court of law simply because of my motive – an intense dislike of the man - for uncovering it? Of course not. Otherwise, a murderer might walk free!

What *counts* is whether or not the evidence confirms or denies the hypothesis that this man is the murderer, not my motives for coming up with that hypothesis. To reject a scientific hypothesis or a proposed method of scientific investigation, not on the basis of facts and evidence, but on the basis of the suspected motives of the person who proposed it, is not conducting true science at all. Rather, it is corrupting science for the sake of a favored metaphysical ideology. Are we to exclude hypotheses because the people who propose them think that they think are probably true?

Shouldn't science be free to follow the evidence where it leads, rather than restrained by a naturalistic metaphysical bias? Otherwise, how could modern science possibly be making an open and honest inquiry into origins?

THE MULTIVERSE OF THE GAPS

Lastly, aren't zealous adherents of methodological naturalism who want to exclude theistic hypotheses from consideration in theoretical science, but then turn right around and promote highly speculative atheistic metaphysical hypotheses being hypocritical? If theistic metaphysical speculations and theories should be excluded from science, shouldn't atheistic metaphysical speculations and theories be too?

When faced with the mysterious complexity of life and the fine tuning of our universe, saying "The multiverse did it!" is an appeal that is just as metaphysical in nature as saying "God did it!"

18 REASONS TO BELIEVE GOD EXISTS

ir Francis Bacon, who is known as *the father of empiri-cism,* wrote, "It is true, that a little philosophy inclineth man's mind to atheism, but depth in philosophy bringeth men's minds about to religion; for while the mind of man looketh upon second causes scattered, it may sometimes rest in them, and go no further; but when it beholdeth the chain of them confeder-ate, and linked together, it must needs fly to Providence and Deity."[224]

Following Bacon's advice, let's trace the chain of causes and effects backwards and not stop partway, but attempt to logically go all of the way back, to the beginning. Here is a summary of the philosophical reasoning we have been following which leads us, like Bacon, to the conclusion that there is a God. This reasoning is presented in the form of simple logical syllogisms consisting of a reasonable major premise, a factual minor premise, and a logical conclusion.

OUR UNIVERSE HAD A BEGINNING

If our universe did not have a beginning, then it could not have been created. These three syllogisms explain why our universe must have had a beginning.

Why Our Universe Must Have Begun to Exist

(*Entropy* is a state of disorder and also a state in which less energy is available to do work. Since order is less probable than disorder, like a battery discharging or a sandcastle eroding, on average all things in our universe are moving from order to disorder, and to a state in which energy is no longer available to do work.)

---

[224] Francis Bacon, "Of Atheism" (1561–1626). *Essays, Civil and Moral, XVI,* The Harvard Classics. 1909–14. http://www.bartleby.com/3/1/16.html (Last accessed 3/25/2019)

- Our universe began in an improbable, low entropy state of order, and is moving towards a more probable state of disorder.
- If there were an infinite past, our universe would now be at a state of maximum entropy, but it is not.

∴ (Therefore) our universe is of a finite age and had a beginning.

Why Our Universe Must Have Had a Cause

This is known as the *Kalam Cosmological Argument,* and has been popularized by philosopher William Lane Craig.

- Everything that begins to exist has a cause.

- Our universe began to exist.

∴ (Therefore) our universe has a cause.

Why Time As We Know It Must Have Had a Beginning

(Something that is *finite* is of limited quantity. Something that is *infinite* has no limit.)

- Since everything does not happen at once, time as we know it advances at a finite rate of speed.
- You can't reach an infinite sum by successive addition of finite units (such as seconds) at a finite rate of speed.

∴ (Therefore) there could not have been an infinite past, and time as we know it must have had a beginning.

WHY THERE MUST HAVE BEEN A FIRST CAUSE

Many atheists appeal to the possibility of an infinite regression of events. This is because if there is an infinite regression, there is no need for a Creator. The following two syllogisms show why there could not have been an infinite regression.

The Argument From the Radiation of Causality

- All effects radiate from causes.
- Every kind of radiation has a source, such as light.

∴ (Therefore) everything that is caused has an ultimate first cause, which is its source.

The Argument From the Endless Nature of Infinity

- Since all causes radiate from a source, an infinite magnitude of causes and effects can result only from cause and effect *without end*.

- The events leading up to our universe *ended* when the universe began.

∴ (Therefore) the number of events leading up to our universe could not have been infinite, so there must have been a beginning to the events that led up to the formation of our universe.

WHAT WAS THE NATURE OF THE FIRST CAUSE?

Just as we can discern things about an author by examining his writing, or a painter from her paintings, we can discern things about the cause of our universe by examining the nature of our universe.

The First Cause Was Timeless

This is an extension of the *Kalam Cosmological Argument,* popularized by philosopher William Lane Craig.

- Everything that begins has a cause.
- Time began.

∴ (Therefore) time must have ultimately had a timeless cause.

The First Cause Was Someone or Something Preexistent

- The First Cause could have had no cause, or it would not have been first.
- Nothing comes from absolutely nothing. (This philosophical principle is called *ex nihil, nihil fit.*)

∴ (Therefore) the first cause was someone or something preexistent that required no cause.

The First Cause Was Immaterial

- All material things are contingent, meaning that they have a cause.
- Our universe is material.

∴ (Therefore) our universe has an ultimate immaterial cause.

The First Cause Was Powerful

- Only an extremely powerful cause could create a vast universe containing immense energy and mass.
- We live in a vast universe containing immense energy and mass.

∴ (Therefore) the cause of our universe was extremely powerful.

WHY THE CAUSE OF OUR UNIVERSE WAS INTELLIGENT

There are many reasons to believe that the first cause was not something, but someone extremely intelligent.

The Information Origin Argument

(You may read a further explanation of this argument in chapter six.)

- Once information content becomes improbable, then when only eight additional bits of information are added, the probability of chance formation begins running next to zero, and the probability of intelligent origin grows exponentially more certain with every additional bit.

- The fundamental components of our universe and even the simplest form of life have so much functional order that they contain *far* more than eight bits of information beyond improbability.

∴ (Therefore) it is almost certain that life and our universe were created by an intelligence.

The Argument From the Existence of Moral Laws

- All laws are the products of thinking minds.
- There are transcendent moral laws (moral laws that hold true even if humans do not agree with them, such as "It is always wrong to be needlessly cruel.")

∴ (Therefore) moral laws are the product of a Transcendent Mind.

The Argument From the DNA Code

- Languages are invented only by intelligent minds.
- The DNA Code is a language for storing and transmitting instructions for the synthesis of complex proteins.

∴ (Therefore) the DNA Code owes its origin to an intelligent mind.

The Argument from Genomes

- Long strings of meaningful or functional information originate only from intelligent minds.
- The genomes of living creatures contain long strings of functional and meaningful information (how to assemble a complex functioning organism).

∴ (Therefore) the genomes of living creatures owe their origin to an intelligent mind.

The Argument From the Order of the Universe

- The naturalistic formation of complex functional order is improbable.
- The fundamental components of our universe have complex functional order.

∴ (Therefore) the naturalistic formation of our universe is improbable.

The Fine Tuning Argument

- An intelligence is the most probable explanation for multiple things being finely tuned (such as the accurately tuned strings of a concert harp).
- Our universe has at least 140 finely tuned parameters, without which life could not exist.

∴ (Therefore) an intelligence is the most likely explanation for the fine tuning of our universe.

The Argument From Complexity

- Only very intelligent beings can create highly complex functioning systems.
- All forms of life are highly complex functioning systems.

∴ (Therefore) the Creator of life was an extremely intelligent being.

WHY THEISM IS TO BE PREFERRED TO THE ANTHROPIC MULTIVERSE

The defense to some of the above arguments is that perhaps there is an infinite anthropic multiverse. The following arguments are in reply to that defense. (An infinite multiverse is a hypothetical realm containing an infinite number of universes. The anthropic principle is the idea that in any universe in which life exists, that universe must be suitable to support that life, no matter how improbable the formation of that universe may be. Combining these two ideas together, we get the concept of an "infinite anthropic multiverse."

The Argument From Local Improbability

- The formation of a universe capable of supporting life as we know it is highly improbable in any single given instance of a universe.
- We live in a single given instance of a universe.

∴ (Therefore) the naturalistic formation of life as we know it in our given location in an infinite multiverse is highly improbable.

The Argument From Metaphysicality

- All other things being equal, a naturalistic argument that cannot be confirmed by observation or measurement has no advantage over a theistic argument that cannot be confirmed by observation or measurement.
- An infinite universe or multiverse cannot be confirmed by observation or measurement.

∴ (Therefore) the concept of an infinite universe or multiverse has no advantage over theism.

The Argument From Ockham's Razor

- The principle of Ockham's Razor holds that all other things being equal, a single entity is to be preferred over multiple ones as an explanation, because a single entity is a simpler explanation.
- A pre-existent creator-God of one unitary essence is a simpler explanation than an infinite multiverse, which would contain innumerable embedded creators, with one creator creating another who creates another.

∴ (Therefore) Ockham's razor prefers creation by God.

The Argument From Pandora's Box

- All other things being equal, the explanation that results in the smoothest functioning of civilization and society, and the greatest happiness to the most human lives is to be preferred.
- Metaphysical naturalism opens up a Pandora's box of moral relativism which can lead to moral violations, bringing with it increased human suffering and injustice.

∴ (Therefore) creation by God is the preferred explanation.

The Argument From Hope

I first heard this argument expressed informally by William Lane Craig in debate. Here it is expressed as a formal syllogism.

- All other things being equal, an explanation that results in hope rather than despair is to be preferred.
- Belief in creation by God brings with it more hope than metaphysical naturalism, which can lead to depression and nihilism.

∴ (Therefore) creation by God is the preferred explanation.

Why the Anthropic Principle Is Not Evidence for Naturalism

- A principle that is applicable to both theism and naturalism is not evidence for either.
- The anthropic principle can apply to both theism and naturalism: "Well of course God (or chance) created our highly improbable life-bearing universe! If God (or chance) had not, we would not be here to observe it!"

∴ (Therefore) the anthropic principle is not evidence for naturalism.

The Argument From Avoiding Further Explanations

- All other things being equal, an explanation that requires no further explanation is to be preferred to one that requires further explanation.

- Creation of our universe by a pre-existent, necessary Being re-quires no further explanation, but a multiverse does, merely pushing back the question of the origin of our universe. (This is because we must then ask, "Where did the multiverse come from?")

∴ (Therefore) creation by a pre-existent, necessary being is to be preferred over a multiverse as an explanation for our universe.

The Argument From the Prescriptive Nature of Laws

- Our material universe and the quantum realm could not exist without the laws that govern them, and they obey those laws, so those laws are prescriptive.
- Only a thinking mind can prescribe laws and design methods of implementing them.

∴ (Therefore) the laws of our universe and the quantum realm owe their origin to an immaterial thinking mind.

Why The Anthropic Multiverse Hypothesis Is Not Evidence for Naturalism

- An hypothesis is not evidence if another reasonable explana-tion is available, and especially if a more reasonable explana-tion is available.
- For all of the reasons given above, creation by God is a more reasonable explanation for the universe than the anthropic multiverse.

∴ (Therefore) the anthropic multiverse is not evidence for natu-ralism.

More Reasons to Reject the Anthropic Multiverse

We only *know* of one universe that exists, and at the most have *possible* (but highly doubtful) evidence of only a *few* other universes that might exist. If we base our reasoning only upon what we *know* exists, then our universe was clearly designed and created by an Intelligence, and not formed by chance. Even if we were to discover incontrovertible evidence of a few other universes because they have influenced our own, we still would have to come to this conclusion if we based our reasoning only upon *what we were certain existed.*

Even if there were a vast or infinite number of other universes (something we could never know), the odds of a universe like ours forming by chance is still zero, according to the research conducted by Francisco José Soler Gil and Manuel Alfonseca using cellular automata as model universes (see page 261).

What We may Conclude About the Creator of Our Universe

For all of the reasons we have stated above, the cause of our universe, and indeed of all things, must have been an immaterial self-aware consciousness (a spiritual intelligence).

Computer game universes and the imaginary universes of the human mind illustrate that it would be possible for an unembodied mind to create a universe that is distinct from it important ways (clearly, though a computer game depends on the computer to exist, it is *not* the computer). The detail of that universe would depend upon the characteristics of that mind. This may not be the way that God created the universe (we discussed other ways in this book), but it is one conceivable way.

Given the immensity of our Universe, its orderly laws, and its fine-tuning parameters, the Creator of our universe must have been able and willing to create, manipulate and control the most fundamental particles of our universe. That Intelligence therefore must have been exceedingly powerful and capable in relation to our universe.

Given the staggering complexity of life, that Intelligence must also have been exceedingly wise.

Such unfathomable power, capability and wisdom are attributes of divinity. Therefore, the preexistent Spiritual Intelligence that created our universe was divine.

Because there are transcendent moral laws that hold true no matter what the opinion of man is concerning them, this transcendent law-giver must be ethical and moral (holy).

Life is too improbable to have formed by chance in our observable universe. Therefore that divinity must not have merely set the universe in motion, but also personally designed and created the life within it. He is therefore a theistic God who cares about His creation, not a deistic one.

Knowing these things, what should you do? That's what the next chapter is all about.

"God is a Spirit: and they that worship him must worship him in spirit and in truth." - John 4:24

"For since the creation of the world God's invisible qualities--his eternal power and divine nature--have been clearly seen, being understood from what has been made, so that people are without excuse." – Romans 1:20

---

19 WHAT THIS MEANS FOR YOU...

"To believe in a God means to see that the facts of the world are not the end of the matter." - from Ludwig Wittgenstein's *Journal.*

"For the scientist who has lived by his faith in the power of reason, the story ends like a bad dream. He has scaled the mountains of ignorance; he is about to conquer the highest peak; as he pulls himself over the final rock, he is greeted by a band of theologians who have been sitting there for centuries." - Robert Jastrow, *God and the Astronomers*

PASCAL'S WAGER

 n light of these things, should you place your faith in chance, or in God?

What would you think of a detective who said, "I do not see or hear a murderer at this scene, so there must not be one," and ignored fingerprints, blood and skin under the deceased's fingernails, and dirty footprints on the floor?

If you were to say, "I cannot detect God with my physical senses, so He must not exist," and ignored the complexity of even the simplest cell, the information in the genome, the marvel of the human brain, the information transmitted by a ray of light, the fine-tuning of the universe, the delights of music and art (which are not necessary for survival), the earth's privileged place and composition, and the stunningly beautiful order of the cosmos, then would you not be just like that detective?

Even if for some reason, you think that the evidence is not completely conclusive, consider this. In his posthumously published *Pensées* or *Thoughts*, the French philosopher, mathematician and physicist Blaise Pascal proposed what became known as *Pascal's Wager*. He argued that if we are not certain whether or not God exists, the safest thing to do is to believe in him.

> "Let us weigh the gain and the loss in wagering that God is," Pascal wrote. "Let us estimate these two chances. If you gain, you gain all; if you lose, you lose nothing. Wager, then, without hesitation that He is."[225]

In other words, if God exists and you serve Him, you gain everything. But if he does not, you lose nothing except some temporal pleasures, which in the long run, amount to nothing. In light of the evidence, the probability calculations we can now make, and reason, Pascal's wager seems like a more sensible bet now than it ever did.

As William Paley pointed out, if you came upon a watch in the forest, and someone tried to convince you that it had not been made, but had formed naturalistically, would you believe him? [226]No, because common sense tells you that the odds of the watch's chance formation are extremely low. For the very same reason, creation by God is the most sensible, common-sense explanation for the origin of our universe and the complex life within it.

(There is a widely circulated myth that the philosopher David Hume refuted Paley's arguments. However, Hume died in 1776, but Paley's *Natural Theology* was not published until 1802. Paley had in fact read Hume and even mentions him in *Natural Theology*. You may read refutations of the myths circulating regarding Paley, Hume and Darwin in Dr. Vincent Torley's article, *Paley's argument from design: did Hume refute it, and is it an argument from analogy?*) [227]

---

[225] Blaise Pascal, *Pensees*. Section III, #233. http://www.classicallibrary.org/pascal/pensees/pensees03.htm (Last accessed 3/25/2019)

[226] William Paley, *Natural Theology, or Evidences of the Existence and Attributes of the Deity,* Oxford, 1836. https://archive.org/stream/naturaltheologyo02pale#p./n5/mode/2up. (Last accessed 3/25/2019)

[227] VJ Torley, "Paley's Argument From Design: Did Hume Refute It, And Is It An Argument From Analogy?" Uncommon Descent, December 30, 2012. https://uncommondescent.com/intelligent-design/paleys-argument-from-design-did-hume-refute-it-and-is-it-an-argument-from-analogy/ (Last Accessed 3/25/2019)

At one time, the once popular arguments of Pascal and Paley seemed obscured by scientific theories *that have since been demonstrated to be untrue*. Time has granted renewed credibility to their arguments. They are more relevant now than ever.

You wouldn't invest your entire life's savings in a company that had only one chance in a million of succeeding, would you? Then why bet your *very soul* that God does not exist, when the odds of that appear next to impossible?

However, you are not limited to evaluating the existence of God based on probability and reason. If God exists, it may be possible to communicate with Him, and even to enter into a friendship with Him.

For Montezuma, the king of the Aztec empire, to pragmatically acknowledge to the conquistador Cortez that the more powerful King of Spain existed was one thing. But placing his trust in this king and agreeing to serve him was quite another. Likewise, concluding God exists is merely a first step. It is a very important step, but it is only a first one.

> You believe that there is one God. Good! Even the demons believe that--and shudder. - James 2:19

In my lifetime, I have met people who are persuaded that there is a God, but have no desire to serve him. Other things are more important to them. Clearly, believing that God exists alone is not enough. Saving faith goes deeper than mere intellectual assent. It is a trust and reliance on God. One important sign of faith is obedience. If you are an investor and you really trust your investment counselor, you will not just verbally agree with his advice. You will put your money on the line by following it. Likewise, if you really trust God, it will make a difference in how you live your life. This will not be just because of you. The Bible teaches us that when a person comes to saving faith in Christ, God transforms him into a new creation, and comes to live inside him (or her). This is what is known as being *born again.*

Pascal's wager makes sense, but even if you decide to take the next step of trusting in God and serving Him, that should be motivated by more than just playing it safe. Otherwise, it would be like marrying a citizen of another country just so that you could escape living under an oppressive regime. Wouldn't your new spouse deserve to have your heart also, if he or she was a good person who truly loved and cared for you? Doesn't a God who is perfectly good (holy), merciful, just and loving also deserve to have your heart? Though a human spouse might not realize that your motive wasn't true love until after the marriage, God would of course know this from the start, so you cannot really come to Him in faith without also giving Him your heart.

WHY NOT CONDUCT YOUR OWN PERSONAL "SETI" PROJECT?

If there is a God, He can, if He chooses, reveal himself to you. If He does, then probability calculations and logical reasoning will pale in importance, because then you will *know* that He exists. If God reveals himself to you, you can then honestly testify to others that you know He exists. On the other hand, no atheist can honestly testify that He *knows* there is no God.

As G.K. Chesterson wrote, "Atheism is indeed the most daring of all dogmas... for it is the assertion of a universal negative."

It seems that theists and deists have an upper hand over atheists in that regard! Likewise, the multiverse, if it exists, cannot intelligently communicate with you. But God can if He exists. That is very good reason to seek for Him to communicate with you.

A computer game programmer exists independently of the computer game world he has created. Likewise, if God created the universe, He must exist independently of it. A character in a computer game universe cannot "find you" unless you reveal yourself to her. Neither can you find God unless He chooses to reveal Himself to you. According to Jeremiah 29:13, there is way to persuade God to reveal Himself to you:

"You will seek Me and find Me when you search for Me with all your heart."
Jeremiah 29:13

In light of those words, why not conduct your own personal "SETI" project, not in search of alien life residing on other planets, but in search of a much greater extraterrestrial intelligence - *God?*

According to this verse in the book of Jeremiah, the way to move God to reveal Himself is to *search for Him with all of your heart.* A half-hearted, insincere, pessimistically distrusting, or short-lived attempt may not be enough.

You should be encouraged by the fact that not just a few people, but *millions* have reported success after engaging in this endeavor. Those are a lot of witnesses who testify to the existence of God! If God does not exist, then they must suffer from a *mass delusion* (as Richard Dawkins asserts). But arguing against that idea is the fact that among them are very many honest, sane, intelligent and educated people whose conscience cannot bear telling a lie. These are the kind of people who are least likely to suffer from a delusion. Clearly, they *honestly* believe that God exists and that they have entered into a close relationship with Him. I encourage you not to dismiss the testimony of that many good and honest people lightly. At the very least, their testimony should prompt you to earnestly try to find out for yourself if there is a God.

Should you decide to search for God with all of your heart, you should not dictate to Him how He must reveal himself to you. If you insist on a physical voice, a miraculous sign, or a bolt of thunder, God may not cooperate. Since God, if He exists, is all-knowing, in His wisdom He may choose to act in ways that make perfect sense to Him but are mystifying to you. God, by definition, is not a cosmic genie that you can order around.

Do you remember the movie *The Matrix*, in which Neo learned martial arts by having the information downloaded into his mind? Whole concepts and ideas were being communicated at once. It was much better than verbal instruction. Likewise, God may prefer to communicate with you in some other way - perhaps superior to anything you have ever experienced. And, those who testify that God has revealed himself to them, sometimes say that God chose a meaningful way in which to communicate, or a special time or place in which to do it.

Please keep in mind that God does not always in reveal Himself in dramatic ways. Sometimes it is simply through looking at nature and realizing that it must have had a Creator, or sensing the love of God in another person. It could happen while you are observing the stars at night. It might happen while you are beholding the beauty of a sunset, or as a caring person is speaking to you. It might even be happening now, as you are reading this. However it happens, you move from unbelief in God to not only believing He exists, but *trusting* Him. You "cross through the river" so to speak, from unbelief to the peaceful assurance of faith. It is God Himself who gives you this faith, All that you must do is receive it as a gift.

This happened to me when I was very young, at the age of nine. My family had moved to a new neighborhood, where I fell under the influence of some other children who did things that were wrong. I began to imitate them, indulging in vandalism and dirty jokes. I also began imitating them by cursing. My new behavior was in such contrast with my former behavior, that I became intensely stricken with guilt. This

> *"For God so loved the world, that He gave His only begotten son, so that whosoever believes in Him will not perish but have everlasting life."*
>
> *John 3:16*

lasted for months, until a kind person read the words of John 3:16 in the New Testament to me:

After I placed my faith in Christ, I felt cleansed of the sin and evil that had been clinging to me. My behavior changed for the better without me even giving much conscious thought to it.

After coming to Christ as a child, without any adult coercing me to do it, I began to read the Bible. Strange behavior for a kid, I know, but I genuinely *wanted* to read it. The only version of the Bible that we had then was the old King James English version, but somehow, despite the archaic language, and the fact that I was so young, God seemed to be enabling me to understand much of what I was reading. As a result of that, something funny happened. In school I wrote a poem using King James English that began with the line, "I seek a fountain that lies in yonder mountain." My school teacher, thinking that I had plagiarized the poem, asked to meet with my parents. After they confirmed to her that I had truly written it, she wanted to move me up to another grade level, but my parents wisely declined.

That was the beginning of a lifelong friendship with God. Since then, there have been many times in which God has communicated with me in special ways of His own choosing, reconfirming His existence to me. I am nothing special at all, however. *Millions* past and present also testify of similar experiences.

THE GREATEST MORAL TEACHER THE WORLD HAS EVER KNOWN

Many years have passed since that important day when I was young, enough time to compare the teachings of the founders of the major world religions. I compared their teachings with those of Christ, because I wanted to make sure that I had not erred. After all, I was very young when I came to Christ, and being of a skeptical and inquisitive mind, as I grew older, my intellect desired to confirm what I seemed to be spiritually experiencing.

This began when I spent the last of my teenage years as an American living in Iran. Muslim clerics teach that the Old and New Testaments are inspired of God, but that where the Quran differs from the Bible, it is because Christians and Jews have made changes to the Bible. While living in Iran, I purchased a copy of the Quran and began to compare it with the Bible.

My comparison of the content of the Bible and the Quran led me to believe that where they differ, it was the Bible that was reliable. I discovered that in the Quran, it is taught that Jesus is not God's son (Surah 112:3). Later I learned it teaches that He was not crucified, because Allah provided a substitute to die in his place (Surah 4:157). And yet these two things are very important themes that run *throughout* the New Testament, and are *much* too pervasive for them to have been added to it later. Had that been done, it would quickly have been recognized and stopped by the rapidly growing Christian community, which was enthusiastically copying and sharing the scriptures with each other.

Later I went on to study many of the other world religions and the cults. Though I have certainly found good (and bad) in what the founders of the other world religions had to say, my studies of other religions did not weaken my faith. Instead, my studies *strengthened* my persuasion that the Christian faith is genuine.

One reason for this is because the New Testament teaches us that God is love. That idea is very attractive. It is so easy to place your trust in a God who is love! But how could God have been love before anything had been created, without an object to love? If God is Triune as we Christians believe– one being composed of three persons, with the Son and the Spirit generated by the Father before time began - then each person in the Trinity loved one another before anything else had been created. This would explain why Jesus said, "Before Abraham existed, I AM." It would also explain why in the book of Genesis, the Hebrew word for God, (Elohim), is plural in form but used as though it is singular, and also why God said "Let us make man in our image."

Another reason that I have remained a Christian is because the teachings and life of Jesus still resonate within me the most. Why is that?

There are many, many reasons, but among the most important is because moral teaching reached its apex with Jesus.

First of all, Jesus taught us that the two commandments from Moses *to love* God and others summarized all of the Law and Prophets:

> One of the teachers of the law came and heard them debating. Noticing that Jesus had given them a good answer, he asked him, "Of all the commandments, which is the most important?"
>
> "The most important one," answered Jesus, "is this: 'Hear, O Israel: The Lord our God, the Lord is one. Love the Lord your God with all your heart and with all your soul and with all your mind and with all your strength.' The second is this: 'Love your neighbor as youself.' There is no commandment greater than these." – *Mark 12:26-31*

But then Jesus went on to give us a new commandment, which was to love one another with an even greater love than that with which we love ourselves. He commanded us to love each another *sacrificially,* just as He loved us:

> A new commandment I give to you, that you love one another: just as I have loved you, you also are to love one another. –*John 13:34, ESV*

He even called us to love our enemies:

> But to you who are listening I say: Love your enemies, do good to those who hate you, bless those who curse you, pray for those who mistreat you. – *Luke 6:27*

Lastly, the many teachings of Jesus in regard helping the poor, the oppressed and the needy resonated strongly within my spirit as just, true and right. Among these is the parable of the sheep and the goats.

> Then the king will say to those at his right hand, "Come, you that are blessed by my Father, inherit the kingdom prepared for you from the foundation of the world; for I was hungry and you gave

me food, I was thirsty and you gave me something to drink, I was a stranger and you welcomed me, I was naked and you gave me clothing, I was sick and you took care of me, I was in prison and you visited me." - Matthew 25:34-36

There are many verses such as this, but they are all summed up in one particular commandment that Jesus gave. Confucius gave us the *Silver Rule*:

"Don't treat anyone in a way you would not want to be treated."

But the *Golden Rule* Jesus taught us is so much better:

"Do to others as you would have them do to you."– *Luke 6:31* [228]

KEYS TO HEAL OUR BROKEN WORLD

Take just a moment to think of how these wonderful commands of Jesus, to the extent that we have obeyed them, *have improved the condition of humanity.* If only all men fully obeyed these teachings of Christ, think of how it would transform the world:

- There would be *no more war* and the horrible suffering it produces.
- There would be *no children starving from hunger* due to uncaring hearts and selfish materialism.
- There would be *no more slavery.*
- There would be *no more worker exploitation* such as child labor, hazardous working conditions, long hours and poverty wages.
- There would be *no more injustice* at the hands of oppressive political and military rulers.
- There would be no more child abuse.

---

[228] As we should expect with a universal principle of human conduct, Jesus was not the first to teach the Golden Rule, but only a few ancients expressed it as well and with the emphasis on positive *action* that He did, and none made it as popular as He did. Most, like Confucius, merely taught the Silver Rule.

- There would be no more spousal abuse.
- There would be no more *environmental pollution* resulting from corporate greed.
- There would be no more *children living in poverty* because of fathers who do not love them enough to take responsibility for them.
- There would be *marital and family happiness* due to family members putting each other first
- People would know *the joy and fulfillment* that comes from living a life of love.
- And most importantly, people would *know, love, and walk with God.*

Truly, the moral teachings of Jesus *are* part of the prescription to heal our broken world! If God really did send His Son into the world to save us from our misery, aren't these just the kind of *transformative* teachings we would expect to hear from such a person?

This brings us to some other very important things that Jesus taught, which we cannot ignore. Jesus said the following things:

> "I am the way and the truth and the life. No one comes to the Father except through me."- John 14:6

> "How can you say to the one whom the Father has consecrated and sent into the world, 'You're blaspheming,' because I said, 'I'm the Son of God'?" – John 10:36

> "Very truly I tell you," Jesus answered, "before Abraham was born, I am!" – John 8:58

Of all of the world's religions, Jesus declared that He is the only one of those paths that leads to the Father. He also claimed to be divine – the only begotten son of God. Was He wrong about these things? Would the greatest moral teacher the world has ever known have *deliberately* lied? Probably not. But could a man of such acute moral perception and understanding have been *deluded* about these two things? There seems to be a moral failure that comes with that sort of delusion – an ultimate moral failure, in fact. The teachings of Jesus do not equate with a man of that kind of moral insensitivity and dullness. In short, both of these ideas seem inconsistent with what we know about the man. By contrast, the idea that He understood the truth, and spoke it, seems more compatible with the evidence. Lastly, this was in keeping with the Old Testament prophecies which said that the Messiah would be God's Son and therefore divine:

> Kiss **His Son**, or he will be angry and your way will lead to your destruction, for his wrath can flare up in a moment. Blessed are all who take refuge in him. – *Psalm 2:12*

> Who but God goes up to heaven and comes back down? Who holds the wind in his fists? Who wraps up the oceans in his cloak? Who has created the whole wide world? What is his name—**and his son's name**? Tell me if you know! – Proverbs 30:4

> For to us a child is born, to us a son is given, and the government will be on his shoulders. And he will be called Wonderful Counselor, **Mighty God**, Everlasting Father, Prince of Peace. – *Isaiah 9:6*

> But you, Bethlehem Ephrathah, though you are small among the clans of Judah, out of you will come for me one who will be ruler over Israel, **whose origins are from of old, from ancient times.** – *Micah 5:2*

> "The days are coming," declares the Lord, "when I will raise up for David a righteous Branch, a King who will reign wisely and do what is just and right in the land. In his days Judah will be saved and Israel will live in safety. This is the name by which he will be called: **The Lord Our Righteous Savior.**" – *Jeremiah 23:5-6*

> Your throne, **O God**, endures forever and ever. You rule with a scepter of justice. You love justice and hate evil. Therefore **God, your God**, has anointed you, pouring out the oil of joy on you more than on anyone else. - *Psalm 45:6-7*

THE FULFILLED PROPHECIES

Another reason why I chose to remain a Christian, despite having a skeptical mind, are the Old Testament prophecies that were fulfilled by Jesus. At one time, I began to wonder, "If Jesus really is the Messiah, then why have most of the Jewish people rejected Him?"

This prompted me to begin an intense study of the Old Testament prophecies concerning the Messiah. Although there are many such prophecies, I will mention only the two that struck me as the most profound. One is found in the book of Daniel, and the other in the book of Isaiah. No competent biblical scholar questions the fact that these two books were written prior to the birth of Christ.

Daniel 9 is contained in the Septuagint, the Greek version of the Old Testament that was completed hundreds of years before Christ, between 200 – 300 BC.[229] When the events recorded in Daniel chapter 9 took place, Jerusalem lay in ruins. And yet in this chapter the Jewish people were told that Jerusalem would be rebuilt, given the date that the Messiah would come, informed that He would be put to death, and that Jerusalem would then be destroyed yet again:

> "Know and understand this: From the time the word goes out to restore and rebuild Jerusalem until the Anointed One, the ruler, comes, there will be seven 'sevens,' and sixty-two 'sevens.' It will be rebuilt with streets and a trench, but in times of trouble. After the sixty-two 'sevens,' the Anointed One will be put to death and will have nothing. The people of the ruler who will come will destroy the city and the sanctuary. The end will come like a flood: War will continue until the end, and desolations have been decreed. *-Daniel 9:25-26*

Here is how this prophecy was fulfilled:

---

[229] See http://www.septuagint.net for more information regarding the Septuagint. (Last accessed 3/25/2019)

- Each of the 'sevens' is a group of seven years. The years were not solar years, but Jewish prophetic years of 360 days each.[230] This happens to be the average of a lunar and solar year, rounded up to the nearest day. Isaac Newton wrote,

  "All nations, before the just length of the solar year was known, reckoned months by the course of the moon, and years by the return of winter and summer, spring and autumn; and in making calendars for their festivals, they reckoned thirty days to a lunar month, and twelve lunar months to a year, taking the nearest round numbers, whence came the division of the ecliptic into 360 degrees."[231]

- In 444 BC, King Artaxerxes decreed that Jerusalem should be rebuilt by Nehemiah. (This decree is recorded in Nehemiah 2:1-8.)
- Seven 'sevens' or 49 years later, the rebuilding of Jerusalem was complete, and the last book of the Old Testament, Malachi, was written.
- Sixty-two 'seven's or 483 years later, in Nisan 10 of AD 33, Jesus rode on a donkey into Jerusalem, in fulfillment of this prophecy and in fulfillment of Zechariah 9:9: "Rejoice greatly, O daughter of Zion! Shout in triumph, O daughter of Jerusalem! Behold, your king is coming to you; He is just and endowed with salvation, Humble, and mounted on a donkey, Even on a colt, the foal of a donkey."
- Jesus was crucified shortly afterwards.
- In 70 AD, Jerusalem was destroyed by the Romans.

And so this prophecy was *precisely* fulfilled by Jesus!

---

[230] See http://jewishroots.net/library/prophecy/daniel/daniel-9-24-27/360-day-prophetic-year.html for additional information concerning the 360-day prophetic year. (Last accessed 3/25/2019)

[231] Anderson, Robert. *The Coming Prince*. London: Hodder & Stroughton, 1894.

The other prophecy which profoundly affected me was Isaiah 53. This chapter in Isaiah was preserved in its entirety in the Great Isaiah Scroll, found among the Dead Sea Scrolls.[232] Carbon 14, paleographic, and scribal dating techniques have ascribed an age of 100 to 335 BC to the Great Isaiah Scroll, long before the birth of Christ.[233] I am quoting from the public domain 1917 Jewish Publication Societies' English translation of the Jewish Bible known as the Tanach. Read it yourself, and see if it does not sound like Jesus to you.

> Who would have believed our report? And to whom hath the arm of the Lord been revealed? For he shot up right forth as a sapling, and as a root out of a dry ground; he had no form nor comeliness, that we should look upon him, nor beauty that we should delight in him.

> He was despised, and forsaken of men, a man of pains, and acquainted with disease, and as one from whom men hide their face: he was despised, and we esteemed him not.

> Surely our diseases he did bear, and our pains he carried; whereas we did esteem him stricken, smitten of God, and afflicted.

> But he was wounded because of our transgressions, he was crushed because of our iniquities: the chastisement of our welfare was upon him, and with his stripes we were healed.

> All we like sheep did go astray, we turned everyone to his own way; and the Lord hath made to light on him the iniquity of us all.

---

[232] Fred P. Miler, "The Translation of the Great Isaiah Scroll." 2001. See http://www.ao.net/~fmoeller/qa-tran.htm for a translation of chapter 53 in the great Isaiah Scroll. (Last Accessed 3/25/2019)

[233] "Dead Sea Scrolls." AllAboutArchaeology.org, 2018. http://www.al-laboutarchaeology.org/dead-sea-scrolls-2.htm (Last accessed 3/25/2019)

He was oppressed, though he humbled himself and opened not his mouth; as a lamb that is led to the slaughter, and as a sheep that before her shearers is dumb; yea, he opened not his mouth.

By oppression and judgment he was taken away, and with his generation who did reason? for he was cut off out of the land of the living, for the transgression of my people to whom the stroke was due.

And they made his grave with the wicked, and with the rich his tomb; although he had done no violence, neither was any deceit in his mouth.'

Yet it pleased the Lord to crush him by disease; to see if his soul would offer itself in restitution, that he might see his seed, prolong his days, and that the purpose of the Lord might prosper by his hand:

Of the travail of his soul he shall see to the full, even My servant, who by his knowledge did justify the Righteous One to the many, and their iniquities he did bear.

Therefore will I divide him a portion among the great, and he shall divide the spoil with the mighty; because he bared his soul unto death, and was numbered with the transgressors; yet he bore the sin of many, and made intercession for the transgressors. – *Isaiah 53, Jewish Publication Society, 1917*

Later, I read the words of a Jewish man who wrote that he was having doubts that ran in the other direction! "If Jesus is not the Messiah" he wondered, "then why have most of the Gentiles accepted him?"

This reason for this is because it is in fulfillment of the words of Isaiah the prophet, who foretold that the Messiah would be a light to the nations, but despised and abhorred by the Jewish nation:

"And now says the LORD, who formed Me from the womb to be His Servant, To bring Jacob back to Him, so that Israel might be gathered to Him (For I am honored in the sight of the LORD, And My God is My strength), He says, 'It is too small a thing that You should be My Servant to raise up the tribes of Jacob and to restore the preserved ones of Israel; I will also make You a light of the nations so that My salvation may reach to the end of the earth.' Thus says the LORD, the Redeemer of Israel and its Holy One, To the despised One, to the One abhorred by the nation, to the Servant of rulers, 'Kings will see and arise, Princes will also bow down, Because of the LORD who is faithful, the Holy One of Israel who has chosen You.'" – *Isaiah 49:5-7 NIV*

And yet, Zechariah also foretold that there will eventually be a time in which the Jewish people will recognize Jesus to be the Messiah:

"And I will pour out on the house of David and the inhabitants of Jerusalem a spirit of grace and supplication. They will look on me, the one they have pierced, and they will mourn for him as one mourns for an only child, and grieve bitterly for him as one grieves for a firstborn son. On that day the weeping in Jerusalem will be as great as the weeping of Hadad Rimmon in the plain of Megiddo. The land will mourn, each clan by itself, with their wives by themselves: the clan of the house of David and their wives, the clan of the house of Nathan and their wives, the clan of the house of Levi and their wives, the clan of Shimei and their wives, and all the rest of the clans and their wives." - *Zechariah 12: 10-13*

My study led me, just as it has countless others, to the conclusion that *Jesus is the only historical person who matches all of the OT prophecies concerning the Messiah.* Sadly however, most of the modern Jewish people that I know have not taken the time to read and research the Old Testament prophecies concerning the Messiah.

As further evidence for the Christian faith, don't the four Gospels which record the life of Jesus (Matthew, Mark, Luke and John), the miracles Jesus worked, the wonderful things he taught, the sacrificial life of love that He lived, and the more than *500 witnesses* who saw him after he was raised from the dead,[234] all also testify that He was speaking the truth?

Lastly, don't the multitudes of people who have found God through Him (including yours truly) also testify to the truth of what he was saying?

Given the fact that the moral teachings of Jesus could transform our world, and lift us out of our terrible misery, why does mankind not fully embrace them? *Because of the condition of our hearts.* But Jesus offered us a solution for that, too.

THE CURE FOR HEARTS SICK WITH SIN

The very best doctors attack illness with a two-fold approach. They treat not only the symptoms, but also the root cause. Jesus is no different. The worse symptoms of our illness is a severed relationship with God, and unjust and unkind actions towards our fellow man. The root cause of our illness is the state of our hearts and minds that causes us to sin and reject God for the sake of pleasure, popularity, comfort, and materialistic desires. Here is Jesus' two-fold approach to heal us:

---

[234] In I Corinthians 15:3-11, the Apostle Paul wrote: "For what I received I passed on to you as of first importance: that Christ died for our sins according to the Scriptures, that he was buried, that he was raised on the third day according to the Scriptures, and that he appeared to Cephas [Peter], and then to the Twelve [the Twelve Apostles]. After that, he appeared to more than five hundred of the brothers and sisters at the same time, most of whom are still living, though some have fallen asleep. Then he appeared to James, then to all the apostles, and last of all he appeared to me [Paul] also, as to one abnormally born. For I am the least of the apostles and do not even deserve to be called an apostle, because I persecuted the church of God. But by the grace of God I am what I am, and his grace to me was not without effect. No, I worked harder than all of them—yet not I, but the grace of God that was with me. Whether, then, it is I or they, this is what we preach, and this is what you believed."

Firstly, Jesus Offers Us Forgiveness and Restoration to God.

All of us have done things that are wrong, and justice demands that the damage we have done be rectified. All of the other religions of the world promise that through our own futile self-efforts, we can make up for this damage we have done. But try as we might, can we restore a broken glass vase to its former condition? Not only that, but our efforts to live the ideal moral life, though they may be noble, always fail in some way, don't they? No matter how resolutely we make up our minds that we will never sin again, all of us end up doing it again.

Clearly, we are not strong enough to rescue ourselves from sin. We are therefore its slaves. We are like drowning men from a sunken ship, who are too weak to swim to a faraway shore. Unless someone rescues us from our sin and its tragic consequences, we are doomed. This is how I felt before I came to faith in Christ.

And that is precisely why God sent His Son Jesus to save us. "For while we were still helpless," the Bible tells us, "at the right time Christ died for the ungodly." Like Sydney Carton, the kind man in *A Tale of Two Cities* who exchanged clothes with a condemned prisoner to die in his place, Jesus suffered the punishment for our sins when He died on the cross.

Secondly, Jesus Offers Us Transformed Hearts and Minds.

> "I tell you the truth, no one can see the kingdom of God unless he is born again." – Jesus

> "Therefore, if anyone is in Christ, he is a new creation; the old has gone, the new has come!" – The Apostle Paul

Our hearts need to be changed so that we will stop living in sin. Since we cannot change our hearts ourselves, Jesus offers to transform them for us. That is what happened to me when I placed my faith in Christ. This is what Jesus was speaking of when He said, "I tell you the truth, no one can see the kingdom of God unless he is born again."

Now, because of what Jesus did on the cross, God also offers for-giveness to you. And through the mighty power of His Spirit, He offers to transform your heart. He offers these two things to you, not as something you must earn, but as a free gift. But like all gifts, to obtain it, you must accept it. If you reject it saying, "No thank you. I do not need your help, Jesus. I think I can achieve moral perfection on my own," then you are rejecting the only means God has offered for you to be saved. It is like a drowning man proudly telling a lifeguard who swam out to save him, "Leave me alone! I don't need help. I will make it to shore on my own."

I hope that will not be your response if you sense God communicating with you. Perhaps you sense that He is doing that even now, as you are reading this. This may be the first time you have ever acutely rec-ognized His presence. Or it may have already happened to you many times, but you ignored the message. If so, I would not throw away the opportunity this time. *It may never come again.* The important thing is to recognize it when it happens, to listen to the message that is being spoken to your inner being, to accept the wonderful forgiveness God offers through Jesus, and then, to let Him transform you into a new person, the kind of person He wants you to be.

Like a filthy person washed clean. Like a dying patient cured. Like a slave set free. Like a caterpillar changed into a butterfly. It's a new birth, a *spiritual* birth into eternal life! The birth of a new child of God. That's what happened to me when I placed my faith in Christ, and I want you to know this wonderful experience too.

If this transformation has not yet happened to you, then *do not rest content.* You know that you could die at any time, so when it comes to this very important matter, *time really is of the essence.* As Pascal wisely advised, and as probability indicates, I urge you to wager that God exists, and search for Him with all of your heart.

If you truly and earnestly do so, I fully expect that you too will find God, as I did, through Jesus, God's only begotten Son. When I came to be-lieve in Jesus and placed my trust in Him and the One who sent Him, my thirst for eternal spiritual life was finally quenched. As Jesus said in John 5:24,

> "Truly, truly, I say to you, whoever hears my word and believes Him who sent me has eternal life. He does not come into judgment, but has passed from death to life."

Through Jesus, your hunger and thirst to know the living God can also be fulfilled. You too can drink from the spring of eternal spiritual life. And what could possibly compare to a personal friendship - *with God?*

There are many things you could seek to achieve in life, but of them all, is there any goal more worthy of pursuing first?

ABOUT THE AUTHOR

Rusty Entrekin has a B.A. in theology from Louisiana College, which has been furthered by a lifetime love of apologetics, reading, popular science, and contemplation. He is a Christian author, Biblical counselor and IT consultant.

He lives in Kennesaw, Georgia with his wife Julie and their three youngest children, where he enjoys hiking, creating music with his guitar, and writing apologetics, theological and Biblical counseling articles for his three websites, ThingsToCome.org, BeNotConformed.org, and Peace-Brooke.org.

Made in the USA
Monee, IL
10 February 2023

27358128R00177